GOOD FOR BUSINESS

ALSO BY THE AUTHORS

The Future of Men (2005)

Buzz: Harness the Power of Influence and Create Demand (2003)

Next: Trends for the Near Future (1999)

GOOD FOR
BUSINESS

The Rise of the Conscious Corporation

ANDREW BENETT
CAVAS GOBHAI
ANN O'REILLY
GREG WELCH

palgrave
macmillan

GOOD FOR BUSINESS
Copyright © Andrew Benett, Cavas Gobhai, Ann O'Reilly, and
Greg Welch, 2009.

All rights reserved.

First published in hardcover in 2009 by
PALGRAVE MACMILLAN®
in the US—a division of St. Martin's Press LLC,
175 Fifth Avenue, New York, NY 10010.

Where this book is distributed in the UK, Europe and the rest of the world,
this is by Palgrave Macmillan, a division of Macmillan Publishers Limited,
registered in England, company number 785998, of Houndmills,
Basingstoke, Hampshire RG21 6XS.

Palgrave Macmillan is the global academic imprint of the above companies
and has companies and repressentatives throughout the world.

Palgrave® and Macmillan® are registered trademarks in the United States,
the United Kingdom, Europe and other countries.

ISBN: 978–0–230–10345–0

Library of Congress Cataloging-in-Publication Data

Good for business : the rise of the conscious corporation / Andrew
Benett ... [et al.].
    p. cm.
Includes bibliographical references and index.
ISBN 978–0–230–61687–5
(paperback ISBN 978–0–230–10345–0)
1. Social responsibility of business. 2. Corporations—Social aspects.
3. Branding (Marketing) I. Benett, Andrew.

HD60.G662 2009
338.7'4—dc22   2009011860

A catalogue record of the book is available from the British Library.

Design by Newgen Imaging Systems (P) Ltd., Chennai, India.

First PALGRAVE MACMILLAN paperback edition: December 2010

10 9 8 7 6 5 4 3 2 1

Printed in the United States of America.

CONTENTS

ACKNOWLEDGMENTS

Good for Business was initially conceived within the strategy department at Euro RSCG Worldwide. It has its origins in The Future of the Corporate Brand, a global study the agency conducted in late 2007 and early 2008 to understand how evolving consumer expectations and demands are driving change within corporations. To achieve a more holistic view of how the corporate landscape is changing, Andrew Benett and Ann O'Reilly sought out the expertise of Cavas Gobhai and Greg Welch, whose experiences—in corporate strategic collaboration and executive search and consulting—were vital to providing the broad perspective a work of this nature requires. This book reflects the learning and insights of all four authors and their respective teams. The result, we hope, stands as testament to the value of collaboration, an essential tenet of the Conscious Corporation.

Many people besides the named authors contributed to this book, but no one more than Alexa Knight, director of network strategy at Euro RSCG's New York headquarters. From our first authors' meeting through to the final stages, Alexa helped to shape this project by taming unruly chapter outlines, managing logistics, and contributing both primary research and chapter content. Also essential to this effort was Roxane Marini, researcher and fact-checker extraordinaire, who devoted months to providing us with vital information—and then making sure no facts were harmed in the making of the book. We are also deeply grateful for the contributions of Stuart Harris, writer and CEO of the U.K.–based strategic consultancy Meaning Business. In addition to contributing content for three of the chapters, Stuart shared with us valuable insights and a global perspective that has informed our work.

This book would not have been possible without the support of David Jones, global CEO of Havas Worldwide and Euro RSCG Worldwide. We are also grateful for the contributions of Euro RSCG New York, in particular from Mary Perhach, global chief communications officer, who found a home for the book at Palgrave Macmillan and was instrumental in getting the project off the ground. Our thanks also to Richard Notarianni, executive creative director for media, for all his input and especially his perspective on the humanization of the corporate brand; Conway Williamson, chief creative officer, who conceived and designed our compelling book jacket; Philip Buehler, chief marketing strategist, whose keen analysis was critical to each of the agency studies cited in this book; Mariya Kutmanova, for coming in at the eleventh hour to create our appendix and help us finalize the manuscript; Michelle Deamer, for her logistical support throughout the process; and also Kelly Wright, Angelique Moreno, Harrison Schultz, and Jesse Lawson for their assistance. We also are grateful to Laurent Habib, CEO of Euro RSCG C&O, Euro RSCG Worldwide PR, and Euro RSCG Event France for sharing with us his thinking on the future of corporate brands. And we thank Schuyler Brown, formerly of Euro RSCG New York, for her insights into the evolution of business leaders.

Also critical to this book were the efforts and support of Spencer Stuart. Special thanks go to Greg's mentor and friend, Spencer Stuart chairman Kevin Connelly, and to David Daniel, Joe Kopsick, Tom Snyder, Rich Kurkowski, and Dave Rasmussen. Thanks also to Ben Machtiger for his thoughtful contributions to content, to Jim Citrin for his wisdom in becoming an author and inspiring Greg to do the same, and to Beth Harvey, Nancy Arenberg, Tim McNary, and Amy Haffling for their always amazing and ongoing support.

Cavas would like to express his thanks to those real-life Leaders of Tomorrow who have generously shared insights with him through the years, for their commitment to conscious leadership and to creating alignment through Useful Statements of Direction: Jose Alvarez, a member of the faculty of Harvard Business School; Fred Joseph, former CEO of Drexel Burnham Lambert and currently a founder at Morgan Joseph, who has always demonstrated a humanistic brand of leadership while promoting the cultural values of creativity and collaboration; Charlie Frenette, a valued client and mentor in his roles at both The Coca-Cola Company and SABMiller; Lance Friedmann of Kraft, who has been an inspiring example for his seamless integration of our four cornerstones into his domestic and global leadership positions; Peter Klein, former strategic leader at Gillette and a trusted consultant to CEOs across a varied spectrum of industries; and John Pepper of Boloco, who has demonstrated that integrating the cornerstones of the Conscious Corporation is not an activity suited only to the Fortune 500, but can also help to drive a forward-thinking startup.

A special thank-you from all of us to those who sat through interviews and helped to shape the book's message and content: Jack Krol and Jim Kilts for their leadership and for the example they have set for many of us over the years, Robert "Bob" Redford and Tom Jolley from the Sundance Group, Beth Comstock from GE, John Replogle from Burt's Bees, Mike Minasi from Safeway, John Wallis and Brigitta Witt from Global Hyatt Corporation, Aaron Magness from Zappos.com, Alex Castellanos and Bruce Haynes from National Media Inc., Steve Knox from Procter & Gamble's Tremor, David Wilkie from M50, Margaret Carlson from Bloomberg News and *The Week*, Dave Reibstein from The Wharton School of Business, Nick Utton from E*trade, Peter Sieyes from Diageo, Mark-Hans Richer from Harley-Davidson USA, Patrick Doyle from Domino's Pizza, Jake Siewert from Alcoa, C. J. Fraleigh from Sara Lee, Elizabeth Spiers from Dealbreaker.com, author Polly LaBarre, and Lee Applbaum from Radio Shack.

We would also like to extend our gratitude to the wonderful team at Palgrave Macmillan, who helped shepherd this book from its infancy through to the final product. Our editor, Laurie Harting, helped shape both the concept and content of *Good for Business*. Her patience and encouragement have meant a great deal throughout the process. Editorial assistant Laura Lancaster was a tremendous help in answering our questions and taking care of all the details that can so easily bog down a project of this nature. Many thanks to you both!

Finally, we would like to thank all those people who have played a role, big or small, in pushing business toward a more conscious future. It is our great hope that this book will serve as a blueprint for those who would seek to grow their companies in a way that creates value for shareholders and society alike.

—*Andrew, Cavas, Ann, and Greg*

PREFACE: VISUALIZING A NEW WAY FORWARD

> Should corporations continue to have the rights of an individual
> when they have "no soul to save and no body to incarcerate"?
> —Question posed on ProCon.org (quoting Baron
> Thurlow, Lord Chancellor of Great Britain)[1]

A t the World Economic Forum in Davos, Switzerland, a decade
ago, a call went out for corporations to adopt a more "human
face." There is an irony in this desire for businesses to be more
humanized, for the rampant growth of corporate power over the past
century and a half can be traced back to the notion that corporations
are human—or at least are to be considered "persons" under the law.

It might come as a surprise to some that corporations were originally formed not to line their own coffers but to benefit the greater
good. In the United States, up to the last quarter of the nineteenth
century, corporations existed at the pleasure of government and could
have their charters revoked at the first sign their interests conflicted
with those of the public.[2] The power lay with the people.

That balance of power shifted in 1886, thanks to the actions of a
lone court reporter. Working on the headnotes of the Supreme Court
case of *Santa Clara County v. Southern Pacific Railroad*, J. C. Bancroft
Davis jotted down a comment made by Chief Justice Morrison Waite at
the start of the trial. Waite had indicated that, for the purposes of that
case, corporations were to be considered as *natural persons* and, as such,
should be accorded the equal protection of the law.[3] Although not part
of the formal opinion, this notation ultimately served to free corporations from most of the constraints that had bound them. As "persons,"

corporate entities now had legal standing and were entitled to such rights as due process, privacy, and free speech (including the right to influence government in their own interests—and thus lobbying was born).[4]

Had corporations shown a "human face" in ensuing decades, the world would look very different today. Instead, many companies accepted all the rights and privileges of being "human" without adopting most of the positive traits that arguably constitute such, including empathy, respect, fairness, and generosity. Once freed from the charters that had bound them, these businesses sought to maximize profit and growth at any cost. By the first quarter of the twentieth century, corporations' power was such that New York City Mayor John Hylan referred to them as "the invisible government which like a giant octopus sprawls its slimy length over city, state, and nation."[5] By 1997, the top 500 corporations controlled 42 percent of the world's wealth, and more than half of the world's 100 largest economies were corporations, not countries.[6] What had been conceived by government for the good of the people had become more powerful than the people—and even more powerful than most of the world's governing bodies.

So, what sort of "person" has the modern corporation shaped up to be? In his 2004 documentary *The Corporation*, University of British Columbia legal scholar Joel Bakan likened today's corporation to "an institutional psychopath" who exhibits the traits of "antisocial personality disorder."[7] Not exactly someone with whom one would want to spend time. And that, for corporations, is suddenly a real problem— and an opportunity. For spending time with brand partners is precisely what the new consumer wants to do, and that is creating a new path for forward-thinking corporations to follow into the future.

CORPORATE BRANDING: A NEW PATH TO PROFITS

> Business is about problem-solving, but it does not always have to be about maximizing profit....You can also have social objectives. Ask yourself these questions: Who are you? What kind of world do you want?
>
> —Muhammad Yunus, founder, Grameen Bank and winner, Nobel Peace Prize, 2006[8]

Until now, there was a compelling reason for public companies to avoid making business decisions with an eye to the greater good.

Their fiduciary duty was clear: They were in business to maximize profits for shareholders. Period. So, while it was permissible to make charitable contributions—after all, they bring with them tax deductions and good PR—anything beyond ran the risk of being perceived as a breach of duty.

Today, the notion that corporate "do-gooding" is antithetical to profits has been turned on its head. As we will discuss in this book, study after study has shown that reputation and a more ethical approach to business reap riches. That is why as many as nine in ten Fortune 500 companies now have dedicated initiatives focused on corporate social responsibility. And it is why risk to a company's reputation is now seen as more important to guard against than any other risk, including regulatory, credit, and market risks.[9]

The fact is, corporate reputation matters more today because *brand* matters more. Over the past half century, we have moved beyond markets dominated by commodity goods to a world in which it is virtually impossible to buy anything that doesn't have some form of logo or other identity mark stamped on it. And consumers are increasingly identifying themselves with and through the brands they buy. A self-avowed "Mac person," for example, does not simply buy Apple computers because he or she prefers a particular operating system; Mac fanatics are also drawn to the brand story of creativity, nonconformity, and fun. They value the associations their purchases provide, and that allows the products to command not just consumer loyalty, but also a higher price. However advanced the technology or appealing the design of an iPod, MacBook, or iPhone, the product's value is exponentially increased by the fact that it carries the imprint of the Apple corporate icon.

This book was conceived by four authors working in three different fields of business who nevertheless share a vision of how the most successful corporations will operate in the future—a future dominated not by individual product brands, but by *corporate brands*. In their role as advertising executives and strategic planners with communications group Euro RSCG Worldwide, Andrew Benett and Ann O'Reilly regularly counsel clients on how best to turn the radical shifts they are seeing in the relationship between consumer and corporation into a competitive advantage. Over the past decade (most markedly since the corporate scandals of 2001 and the bailouts of 2008 and beyond), consumers have begun to pay a lot more attention to the companies with which they do business—and even to companies with which they have no direct affiliation. Throughout this book, Andrew and Ann share their vision of what changes companies must make in order to grow and thrive in this new century. They talk about some of the inspirational brands and individuals that are leading the charge, and they explore how companies can turn new pressures into more robust profits and growth.

In his work with global executive search firm Spencer Stuart, Greg Welch helps corporations bolster their brands, not through marketing and communications, but through people. By making smart choices about whom they hire and how they train and equip their workforces to respond to the needs of multiple stakeholders, companies can reap the benefits that come from operating according to a consistent strategic alignment. With a background in brand management for global companies, Greg is uniquely positioned to advise corporate clients on how to strengthen reputation and brand value through talent management. Laced throughout this book are Greg's insights into the new pressures facing corporations, and on the current and past business leaders who best exemplify the mindsets and skill sets most likely to meet with success in the future.

Over a career spanning more than three decades, Cavas Gobhai has worked to infuse a culture of strategy-centered creativity and collaboration into organizations, including some of the world's largest companies, entire towns, educational institutions, and international NGOs (nongovernmental organizations). He brings to this discussion the viewpoint that a corporate brand can only be as strong as the group processes that underlie it. Here, he shares insights into the benefits of creating and sustaining systemwide strategic alignment in the current business environment. Cavas also offers practical advice on how companies can build stronger brands by integrating a future-focused statement of direction into both day-to-day activities and long-term planning.

The authors draw on their own personal and business experiences, as well as on an array of proprietary tools and resources available through their businesses. These resources include a series of global quantitative studies fielded by Euro RSCG Worldwide on the future of the corporate brand and the new consumer, Euro RSCG's Brand Momentum and Decipher analytical tools, the Spencer Stuart CMO Survey, and the Spencer Stuart Board Index.

Together, the authors aim to provide a clear point of view and comprehensive approach to the most important challenge facing business today: the need to actively engage multiple stakeholders—including employees, customers, shareholders, and the broader public—in the future of the brand. Because going forward, the corporate brand truly will *be* the business.

Part I

THE CONSUMER AND THE COMPANY OF THE FUTURE

Chapter One

RETHINKING THE ROLE OF THE CORPORATION

I hope we shall...crush in its birth the aristocracy of our moneyed corporations which dare already to challenge our government to trial and bid defiance to the laws of our country.

—Thomas Jefferson[1]

W hat might Thomas Jefferson make of the modern-day corporation? In 1776, the year he penned the Declaration of Independence, the U.S. population stood at 2,527,450.[2] That is just half a million more people than are currently employed by Wal-Mart alone. Far from "daring" to challenge government to a trial of strength, corporations have grown so big that fifty-one of the world's one hundred largest economies are now businesses, not countries.[3] Moreover, corporate power has become so concentrated that, at the start of this decade, sales of the two hundred largest corporations represented more than a quarter of total world economic activity.[4]

Jefferson and his peers had a clear understanding that greater size more often than not translates into greater power—a power likely to be of detriment to the common man. It is a concern that has only deepened in modern times, as corporations have too often stepped outside the boundaries of acceptable—even lawful—behavior. In this decade alone, we have borne witness to a string of scandals that has rocked financial markets, toppled once-mighty companies, and given the public more reason than ever to regard Big Business through a prism of suspicion and fear. Enron may have emerged as the poster child for early-twenty-first-century corporate excess and greed, but it has had plenty of company. Even domestic diva Martha Stewart had to put aside her muffin tins for a stint behind bars for insider trading—an offense that seems almost quaint now that we have seen the likes of Bernie "King of the Ponzi Scheme" Madoff.

In the current environment, it is virtually impossible to tune out negative news of the business world. Our fears of the deepening recession and mortgage foreclosures are interrupted by massive recalls of contaminated pet food and children's toys. Gas prices fall, but then banks begin to fail. We can't even escape by putting in a DVD: Tales of corporate scandal and immorality have been fed to us through a steady slate of films exposing the dark sides of industries ranging from pharmaceuticals (*The Constant Gardener*) to health care (*Sicko*), from weapons dealing (*Lord of War*) to the diamond trade (*Blood Diamond*), and from Big Oil (*Syriana*) to corporate law (*Michael Clayton*).

Is it any wonder our faith in business is shaken? In 2007 consumer confidence in large corporations, as measured by the Gallup Poll, hit its lowest point in history. At that time, only 18 percent of Americans claimed to have a "great deal" or "quite a lot" of confidence in Big Business; that was down from 30 percent in 1999.[5] Two years on, in the midst of an even worse economic crisis, the media are full of stories of board-level greed alongside relentless reports of layoffs, government bailouts, and a "stimulus" package that at least initially produced far more fear than hope. By early 2009, Edelman's Trust Barometer had found steep falls in consumer trust in business in major developed countries. In the United States, 77 percent of consumers had less trust in corporations compared with the year prior; internationally, that figure was 62 percent. Harris Interactive's 2009 Reputation Quotient survey results were just as bleak: 88 percent of respondents rated the reputation of corporate America as "not good" or "terrible."[6] As the *Financial Times* reported after the 2009 World Economic Forum in Davos, business leaders are stunned by the extent to which the public has lost faith in business.[7]

Yet, something interesting is happening. Even in the face of the global economic meltdown, people have not entirely given up on business. To the contrary, they have begun to look to corporations to play an expanded role in society—to step in where governments have failed and craft solutions to our greatest global challenges. For as much as the public is cognizant of the damage corporations can wreak when left unchecked, they have also gotten a glimpse of the potential of corporations to drive meaningful change. Once content to let Big Business exist on a separate plane and carry out its work in secrecy, the public is now demanding that corporations become full-fledged global citizens. Rather than simply assume the rights of "natural persons" under the legal systems in which they operate, corporations now also are expected to accept the responsibilities that come with being part of the human family.

However bleak the current economic situation, we believe it is actually creating a unique window of opportunity for today's business leaders. The desire to "believe in something" is deeply ingrained in human nature—whether one is talking about how a child wishes to view a parent or the faith one might put in a newly elected official during a particularly difficult time. Such a dynamic provides a powerful platform for business leaders who are capable of taking bold steps in addressing both consumers and the marketplace at large.

MORE POWER, MORE RESPONSIBILITY

How is it that people who have grown more wary of corporations have also come to want and expect more from them? The most important reasons are these:

- Government has historically fallen short.
- Consumers live closer to business.
- The empowered public demands payback.

Government has historically fallen short: First, we are looking to corporations for help because they may be our last, best hope—even in a time of government bailouts. The safety nets provided by governments around the world have grown increasingly tattered, and many people feel our largest global problems are simply beyond the capacity of governments to solve—even when working together. Such organizations as the United Nations, World Trade Organization, and European Union are widely regarded as too cumbersome and bureaucracy bound to act sufficiently, quickly, or decisively, and their level of commitment and motivation is often questioned, especially regarding issues concentrated in less developed countries.

In contrast, over the past decade, we have seen some familiar corporate faces actively tackle such issues as disease eradication, hunger, and global warming. In 2008, the Bill & Melinda Gates Foundation dispersed $2.8 billion in grant payments under its health and development programs.[8] To put that in perspective, the entire annual budget of the UN's World Health Organization is $4 billion.[9] As a private entity, the foundation is able to avoid a lot of the procedural steps that bog down government agencies, so the funds can go further. Virgin Group founder and chairman Sir Richard Branson has taken on global warming as his pet project. Through the Virgin Earth Challenge, he is offering a $25 million prize to the first person or organization to come up with a viable way to remove greenhouse gases from the atmosphere. Nortel and Sun Microsystems have each taken leading roles in pushing low-cost and free technology and online learning materials into Third World classrooms.

The extent to which the public now counts on business leaders to act in difficult times has been made abundantly clear over the course of the last decade, especially as governments have struggled to coordinate their own responses. In what has been termed "the first step in the globalization of corporate philanthropy,"[10] Fortune 500 companies contributed more than a quarter of a billion dollars to relief efforts in the immediate aftermath of 2004's Asian tsunami. The following August, while the U.S. federal, state, and local governments were so famously bungling their response to Hurricane Katrina in Louisiana, Mississippi, and other southern states, the private sector stepped in with $1.2 billion in relief funds.[11] While the Federal Emergency Management Agency (FEMA) was adrift in red tape, miscommunication, and mismanagement, companies such as The Home Depot and Wal-Mart were on the ground, providing not just funds, but also tools, other materials, and guidance to local organizations. It makes sense, then, that as Hurricane Rita bore down on Texas one month later, 87 percent of Americans polled by Cone, Inc. said they expected corporations to play a major role in rebuilding affected areas from that storm, and nearly two-thirds (62 percent) agreed companies are better able than government agencies to respond effectively to disasters.[12]

This notion that Big Business should play a leading role in disaster response has been bolstered by the concerted efforts of corporations to do just that. Frustrated by their inability to effectively coordinate their efforts with those of the federal government in the wake of the

September 11, 2001 terrorist attacks on the United States, some of the nation's top business leaders devised a plan to create a disaster-response task force, to be called on as needed. The task force is now a permanent arm of the Business Roundtable, an association of chief executive officers of leading U.S. companies. Comprising nearly a third of the total value of the U.S. stock market and employing in excess of ten million workers, member companies have both the resources and the clout to get things done quickly. Among other initiatives, the task force has created an around-the-clock phone link to the Department of Homeland Security and maintains "swat teams" capable of flying into any disaster site within twenty-four hours, assessing what's needed, and then reporting back to both the government and corporate leaders.[13]

Consumers live closer to business: The public also expects more of Big Business because we feel more connected than ever before to the companies that have a presence in our daily lives. We consider them part of human society and, as such, expect them to share our burdens.

There was a time when businesses lived apart from everyone but employees and shareholders. They were figuratively—and sometimes literally—housed behind tall iron gates that denied admittance to all those not central to the organization's operations. Ordinary citizens had precious few avenues through which to influence corporate decisions—and, in most cases, had little opportunity even to learn what policies and practices existed. Moreover, most of the products consumed were commodity items. People didn't go to a supermarket to buy Perdue chicken and Dole broccoli; they went to the butcher for meat and poultry and to the green grocer for produce. No brand names, no logos, no marketing messages...and no emotional relationship between producer and buyer.

That is no longer the case. Today, brands matter a lot, and the companies with which we do business matter. We all know Mac people and PC people. People who swear by Pepsi and others who insist on Coke. Drivers who wax eloquent about their Toyotas or Jaguars and others who intend to go to their graves without buying any car other than a Ford. The brands we own—and especially the brands we love—tell a story about us that goes far beyond the contents of our home offices, refrigerators, or garages. They speak to the sort of people we are, to the values we hold dear and the way we both perceive ourselves and wish to be perceived.

As part of its benchmark Prosumer Pulse® Study,[14] communications agency Euro RSCG Worldwide asked consumers in ten markets about the role brands play in their lives. A majority in most markets—including 69 percent in the United States—claimed to be very aware of brand names. Nearly four in ten U.S. respondents agreed the brands they own say something about who they are—higher than expected, given that Americans typically are loath to admit they are influenced by marketing. Even greater percentages of respondents in some developing countries agreed the brands they use say something about who they are: 47 percent in China and 65 percent in India.

It has been interesting to watch brand logos become part of people's identities over the years. Logos matter, and not just as a brand identifier. Having a brand name or symbol emblazoned on one's chest, handbag, or wristwatch gives one a sense of connection to the company; and that, in turn, tends to make one feel more invested in how that brand acts and is perceived. A woman who totes around a bag with the Whole Foods logo on it is broadcasting a few things about herself: She cares about the environment and the foods she puts in her body, and she can afford to shop at a higher-priced store. The sense of satisfaction she derives from carrying that bag may well fluctuate with good or bad news about the company. Would you have worn a JetBlue-branded baseball cap in the week following the airline's public relations fiasco in early 2007? As you may recall, a Valentine's Day ice storm left more than 1,000 passengers trapped for hours on the tarmac of New York's John F. Kennedy International airport. One day, the brand logo is worn proudly as a symbol of a hip and trailblazing company; the next day, it is associated with overflowing toilets, food-deprived infants, and apoplectic passengers.

Importantly, as we will discuss in greater detail in Chapter Two, the recollections many of us have of the ordeal JetBlue's travelers went through that day came directly from the trapped passengers themselves. In this age of Internet communication and democratized media, those passengers had all sorts of ways to voice their displeasure, both directly to JetBlue's corporate headquarters and to the world at large. An incident that in an earlier age might have been swept under the rug was replayed again and again online in all its gory detail. JetBlue, in turn, responded in a way that reflects a new approach to crisis communications. CEO David Neeleman did not simply address those customers who had been aboard the affected planes that ill-fated day; he appeared on numerous television shows, including the morning programs and "Late Show with David Letterman," and also posted a direct response on YouTube, in which he pledged that the company would do better, outlined changes being made to ensure such a disaster never recurs, and introduced a new JetBlue Customer Bill of Rights.[15]

David Neeleman's post-crisis response speaks clearly to a new relationship between company and consumer. Corporations are far more vulnerable to consumers today, which means they have no choice but to hold themselves more accountable. They can no longer operate outside the bounds of public scrutiny, and that means they have far more reason to engage with consumers and take actions that bolster their public standing.

The empowered public demands payback: The third reason consumers have heightened expectations of what corporations can and should do is in keeping with the biblical admonition: "For of those to whom much is given, much is required."[16] We are at a tipping point, a time when consumers have become acutely aware of the disconnect between how much corporations are raking in, in terms of profits and power, and how much they are giving back to the greater community in return.

At the tail end of 2007, Euro RSCG surveyed nearly 2,000 consumers in the United States, United Kingdom, and France as part of its Future of the Corporate Brand study (see Appendix for additional findings). The consensus from the three markets is that corporations have benefited enormously from their business dealings in recent years but have yet to return the favor to the consumers and communities that have supported their growth. Nearly eight in ten respondents (79 percent) agreed corporations had become more profitable over the five years prior, but only one in four (24 percent) think businesses have become more philanthropic during that time. That's a gap of fifty-five points! Moreover, only a minority believe corporations have raised their standards or become more accountable.[17] (See Graph 1.1.)

So, what exactly is it people want and expect from corporations? The answer is both simple and revolutionary: They want their brand partners to internalize a set of humanized values that directs everything they do. They want Big Business to take a stand on key issues and put the weight of their wealth and influence behind activities that will benefit the greater good. And, on a larger scale, they want companies to be more involved in propelling communities, countries, and the world forward. Nearly six in ten people surveyed in the three markets (59 percent)

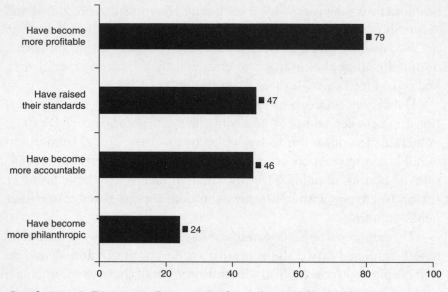

Graph 1.1 A Disconnect Between Profits and Principles: Public Perceptions of How Corporations Have Changed, 2003–2008

Note: The data reflect the percentage of respondents who agreed with the statement, "Over the past five years, corporations have become XXX."

Source: The Future of the Corporate Brand, Euro RSCG Worldwide, 2008 (*n* = 1,851).

believe corporations have become better positioned over the past five years to create positive social change. Yet few, if any, companies are seen as doing all they can in that regard. And that is important at a time when a large majority of those surveyed (74 percent) believe businesses bear as much responsibility as governments for driving positive social change. *What once was the view of a leftist fringe is now mainstream thinking.*

AN OPPORTUNITY: REIMAGINING THE CORPORATION OF THE FUTURE

The idea that business is just a numbers affair has always struck me as preposterous. For one thing, I've never been particularly good at numbers, but I think I've done a reasonable job with feelings. And I'm convinced that it is feelings—and feelings alone—that account for the success of the Virgin brand in all of its myriad forms.

—Richard Branson[18]

Devising a new blueprint for the successful corporation of the future is not just about corporate responsibility or paying attention to the triple bottom line of "people, planet, and profit." Nor is it simply about finding new ways to engage consumers and become a more integral part of their lives. It is about all those things—and a lot more.

We believe the most successful corporate brands of the future will have a larger presence in both the consumer's private life and in the public sphere. They will assume a bigger cultural role and will behave in a way that is decidedly human, using the best connotations of that word. And they will make these changes not merely out of a sense of altruism or fear of regulation or other consequences, but because this new way of envisioning and conducting business is in the best long-term interests of the company, its stakeholders, and its corporate brand.

Later in this book, we will talk more about the value of reputation and how smart companies are infusing reputation management into their business practices. Although many of the front runners in this race are brands that do business directly with consumers, we believe such practices will prove to be equally relevant for business-to-business companies, whether it be Intel, DuPont, Cisco, or any other. For now, suffice it to say that, as we make our way into the second decade of the new millennium, businesses of all types have a "second chance"—an opportunity for retrenchment and redemption that will enable them to continue to accrue wealth and power without inciting the resentment and retribution that so often comes with "excess success." By reinventing themselves in a way that grows profits and drives loyalty among customers *and* shareholders, while also addressing the most compelling issues of the day, corporations will have a new purpose: a broader social role that has the capacity to energize them and help them achieve optimal growth.

So, how does this corporation of the future think and behave?

The Corporation of the Future Is Imbued with Human Values

> Well, you know, I was a human being before I became a businessman.
>
> —George Soros, billionaire financier, philanthropist, and political activist[19]

Up to this point in history, the largest corporations have been accorded many of the rights and privileges of human beings without necessarily adopting a humanlike conscience or human mores. The perceived amorality of business has a rich history within Western culture, from Charles Dickens's characterization of Ebenezer Scrooge in *A Christmas Carol* ("Squeezing, wrenching, grasping, scraping, clutching, covetous, old sinner"[20]) through to Gordon "Greed Is Good" Gekko in Oliver Stone's *Wall Street*. Perhaps no one has encapsulated the antisocial aspects of business better than the character of C. Montgomery Burns, owner of the Springfield Nuclear Power Plant on "The Simpsons." In his words: "I'll keep it short and sweet: Family. Religion. Friendship. These are the three demons you must slay if you wish to succeed in business."[21]

What if this were to change, if corporations were to begin to think and behave more like mindful, caring people? What if, rather than maintaining a single-minded focus on rational profit, they began to adopt a more holistic view that takes into account every consequence of every action—and inaction? What if corporations were to measure their success based on how well they satisfy the needs of everyone whose lives they touch, not just the people who hold shares in the business? All, of course, without losing sight of the necessity of sustained profit and growth.

This all may sound like nothing more than high-minded (and utterly unrealistic) claptrap, but, in our view, this next phase of business evolution—*the humanization of corporate culture*—has already begun. More and more business leaders are coming to see the correlation between doing good and doing well. And they are learning that good things happen when they take into account the points of view and concerns of the broader community.

John Mackey, founder of Whole Foods, articulates this new approach to business as follows: "At Whole Foods, we measure our success by how much value we can create for all six of our most important stakeholders: customers, team members (employees), investors, vendors, communities, and the environment.... It is the function of company leadership to develop solutions that continually work for the common good."[22]

Greed will always be present. It is a basic human emotion and will always serve as a motivator in business—as in life. But, increasingly, values-based competitiveness is proving itself a worthy alternative to outright avarice. As we will discuss in Chapter Three, competitive advantage has already begun to accrue to those businesses that demonstrate moral and ethical leadership, and that help their own employees operate in a way that is not antithetical to their own values and priorities as human beings.

History tells us that when corporations existed on the outskirts of culture, it did not matter quite so much if decisions were made solely on the basis of self-interest. But in the twenty-first century, no company is an island. And no public-company CEO is sufficiently powerful to withstand the pressures brought to bear on corporations considered to be acting against the public interest. To be successful, the corporation of the future will need to interact with the general public and various stakeholders in a more human way, encouraging multiple channels of communication and ceding some of the prerogatives taken for granted in previous eras.

Corporations are now citizens, with all the civic responsibilities that entails. Those that wish to succeed will have no choice but to augment their business skills with vital social skills, including the ability to listen, communicate, and empathize.

The Corporation of the Future Builds Emotional Connections

> People don't ask for facts in making up their minds. They would rather have one good, soul-satisfying emotion than a dozen facts.
>
> —Author Robert Keith Leavitt[23]

When business was based on the trade of tangible commodity goods, it did not matter quite so much how a buyer felt deep down about the items he or she purchased. A pair of shoes was judged on style, durability, and comfort—not on the name or symbol sewn onto the side. But now we are living in the "intangible economy," a world in which corporate value often has less to do with what is owned and produced than with how those products are valued by individuals and how the company is perceived by the consuming public. It has been estimated that intangibles—including brand equity, human capital, and intellectual property—now make up some 60 to 80 percent of the market capitalization of public companies.[24]

Under these circumstances, the *idea* of the product becomes at least as important as its physical nature, and the financial value of a product directly correlates with the level of emotion it elicits in the consumer. Place the same gold wedding band in a box from Kay Jewelers and a box from Tiffany, and one will be worth markedly more.

There are plenty of ways for a brand to connect with consumers on an emotional level, but none more powerful than connecting through shared values. Look at the greatest brand success stories of today and you will find that each one communicates on an emotional level: Google talks about not being "evil." Nike extols the incredible potential of the human body—and the human spirit. Harley-Davidson has built its brand not just on the size and power of its machines, but also on the sense of community it works so tirelessly to build among its customers. Similarly, Apple has developed an intensely loyal following by emphasizing its role as an icon of creativity and free-spiritedness rather than as a producer of technology. The fact that the logos of all four companies have been seen tattooed on the bodies of some of their devotees provides ample proof of the extent of the emotional connections they have managed to forge.

The corporations best positioned to dominate their markets in the future will be those most able to build meaningful, emotions-based relationships with their customers and the wider world. At present, too many companies attempt to accomplish this with one-off promotions and overt marketing tactics. Far more valuable is the creation of a genuine brand personality that draws the consumer in—that makes him or her want to engage with *the company*.

Some of the most powerful brand personalities can be traced directly back to their company founders. The irreverence and adventurous spirit that defines the various entities within the Virgin Group can be plainly seen in the person of Sir Richard Branson, just as the kinetic energy, intelligence, and creative enthusiasm of Steve Jobs is imbued in the Apple brand. Other successful companies have found they can best connect with consumers' emotions by creating a brand persona from scratch, as Britain's Innocent Drinks has done with the childlike drawings on its labels; its grass-covered or cow-themed vans; and its quirky approach to communications.

In Chapters Three and Four, we will showcase some of the brand personalities that exemplify how the more-conscious corporations of tomorrow will think about themselves, express their unique personalities, and communicate in an emotionally engaging way.

The Corporation of the Future Inspires Trust

With "hard" competitive advantages becoming ever scarcer...the real economic value of a corporation increasingly comes not from the assets that it owns, or the employees that it supervises, but from the domain of trust that it has established with its customers.

—*The Economist*[25]

"Whom can I trust?" Conscious or not, that simple question underlies all our interactions, whether with individuals or with organizations. At the individual level, trust means knowing the other person will be honest and responsible and will live up to his or her promises. On the organizational level, trust means knowing the company or other entity will operate fairly and competently, and with equal regard for all its constituents.

There is a reason, in his poem *Inferno*, Dante reserved the lowest *bolgia* of hell for those who betray trust. In its absence, a mutually beneficial relationship of any significant depth cannot develop. Yet in today's environment, trustworthiness can no longer be assumed. Ever.

We are living in an age in which the traditional pillars of trust have proved unreliable. No one knows what financial crisis, terrorist attack, health threat, or violent outbreak (at an international level or in the halls of the local elementary school) will greet us tomorrow. Change is taking place so rapidly around the world that we no longer have faith in our ability to predict even the most immediate future. Our star athletes are doping up, our government officials are taking kickbacks, our religious leaders are embroiled in all manner of sinful acts, and celebrities we once admired turn out to be nothing like the people we believed them to be. Is it any wonder we have grown skeptical?

As consumers, we can no longer count on the fact that our investment advisors are acting in our best interests or that our insurance companies will pay out on our policies as agreed; we cannot assume our homes and workplaces are structurally sound or that the person behind the wheel of a bus or controls of an airplane is not under the influence of alcohol or drugs; we cannot assume the stores we frequent will treat us equitably or that government regulators will not deliberately mislead or manipulate us. We cannot even assume the food on our plates is safe.

In this environment, the most powerful brands will be those that inspire our faith—and earn our trust—over time. These companies and brands will consistently fulfill their obligations and meet their promises. They will be predictable in how they handle crises and correct their own failings. And they will subscribe to a higher, longer-term value than immediate self-interest.

The benefits these brands reap will be enormous in this age of free-floating fear and anxiety, for the ability to count on a brand's trustworthiness and reliability is more important to consumers than ever before. In 2005–2006 (the most recent study available), the Ipsos MORI Captains of Industry survey asked various groups of people in the United Kingdom which were the most important factors they took into account when making a judgment about a company. For captains of industry, financial performance was paramount, while investors focused most on quality of management. For NGOs, corporate responsibility and business ethics were of primary importance. And the general public? Their number-one priority was honesty and integrity. That trumped every other factor, including product quality and customer service—a clear indication that today's consumers are hungry for brand partners on which they can rely. We expect this is even more the case today in light of the increased economic turmoil.

IMPLICATIONS FOR THE CORPORATE BRAND

In this opening chapter, we have touched on many of the themes we will be addressing throughout this book and have outlined a number of imperatives for companies and the brands that represent them. In so doing, we have built a case for one imperative that arguably is more important than any other: the need to establish a powerful corporate brand. For the demands that will be placed on the corporation of the future are such that no portfolio brand—and certainly no product or service brand—can hope to meet them.

There are plenty of reasons to place the corporate brand front and center. Some are enormously practical: A strong, highly recognizable corporate brand can allow a company to reduce media costs and cut through brand clutter by concentrating the bulk of its marketing activities on a single brand name. Done right, that brand name will instantly communicate an overarching brand essence, thereby allowing the company to move into new areas more easily and less expensively. Think of FedEx's seamless acquisition of the Kinko's retail properties or the ease with which Dunkin Donuts launched its branded coffee into the grocery store channel.

A strong corporate brand is also an excellent way to bring together far-flung employees (in terms of both function and geography) under a single banner and with a shared sense of purpose. Under the careful leadership of CEO George David, United Technologies has managed to create a corporate brand identity sufficiently powerful to unify several very strong divisional brands in disparate industries (including Sikorsky, Pratt & Whitney, Otis, Carrier, Hamilton Sundstrand, Chubb, and Kidde).

Also of importance, a strong corporate brand can provide a highly visible platform through which to demonstrate and communicate corporate social responsibility, making it easier to get credit for good works. It is a powerful platform from which to remind—or inform—potential investors of all the worthy brands in a portfolio. (We know many CEOs who could use some "good news" material to share on investor calls these days.) And it is the only type of brand sufficiently powerful and loud to serve as an engine of genuine social change.

In this fast-moving world rife with uncertainty, consumers are looking to their brand partners—and to business leaders in general—as sources of not just stability and security, but also progress. This presents an enormous opportunity for corporations to create value by putting into place new business models better suited to the needs of this new century.

Today, business too often serves as an obstruction to progress. It is all too common for change to be mandated by government regulators or pushed into existence by watchdogs and NGOs, rather than being driven by the corporate leaders themselves.

Tomorrow, there is opportunity for corporations to create new standards, to build more ethical management practices, and to work with consumers, government, NGOs, and others to drive meaningful change, both within and outside the corporation. Where once the interests of companies and the public were thought to be antithetical, we can now see more clearly the symbiotic relationship that exists. As the next several chapters will demonstrate, far from eating away at corporate profits, doing right by *all* stakeholders—including the public—will yield tremendous advantages in terms of competitive differentiation, brand image, and customer loyalty.

Our aim with this book is to show how to best move from today to tomorrow.

Chapter Two

WELCOME TO THE CONSUMER REPUBLIC

The increasingly tenuous relationship between producer and consumer is manifesting in multiple ways across cyberspace. Aided by a host of information and communication technology tools, consumers have found that it is now both quick and relatively easy to kick-start personal tirades against business giants, find like-minded allies and rally support for their cause, all without ever having to leave their homes....Welcome to the new era of the empowered consumer.

—Lilei Chow, writing in *New Straits Times* (Malaysia)[1]

When politicians and NGOs address the need to rein in corporate power, they speak about such things as regulation and lobbying reform. In their view, corporate behavior can be self-regulated, imposed by government dictate, or encouraged by government incentives. The role of the consumer in corporate governance is largely ignored.

That is a mistake.

Today's business leaders would be foolhardy not to recognize, and respect, the extent to which consumers have gained power in recent decades. Leadership within the Conscious Corporation—men and women the authors have come to think of as the "Leaders of Tomorrow" (LOTs)—will factor public preferences and attitudes into virtually every major business decision. For, more than shareholders, government, or the media, consumers are the stakeholders that increasingly will determine whether a company lives or dies. Clearly, this influence will be more strongly felt within consumer-based businesses, but we believe even nonconsumer companies will feel increased pressure from the public as a consequence of their own societal impacts.

In this chapter, we will explore the most significant ways in which consumers have changed and grown more powerful, and will look at what this means for their relationships with brand partners going forward. The most successful companies of the future will be those that put forming and nurturing these "partnerships" atop their lists of priorities. For in the new environment, consumers increasingly are calling the shots.

THE NEW CONSUMER IS SAVVIER AND BETTER INFORMED

It would be difficult to overstate the impact of the Internet on consumer behavior and empowerment. In the mid-1990s, the early days of Internet adoption, businesses talked about the potential for some portion of commerce to move from traditional brick-and-mortar stores into "cyberspace." What many analysts failed to consider was the much farther reaching impact of the Internet on shopping in general. For even those people who choose not to make purchases online now have access to a world of new consumer tools and information—and this is changing the balance of power between companies and the people who buy their goods and services.

In 2008, Euro RSCG Worldwide conducted The Future of Shopping, an online survey of 2,800 consumers in the United States, France, the United Kingdom, and China. As is illustrated in Graph 2.1, a large majority of people around the world have embraced the Internet as an integral part of their shopping process. Comparing the U.S. data with an earlier study[2] the agency conducted, we see a sharp drop in the percentage of people who claim the Internet has had little to no impact on their shopping, down from 20 percent in 2004 to just 9 percent in 2008 (not shown in graph).

Before we all got wired (and now wireless), our limited choices contained the game. If we wanted to buy a product, we went to a local store or called a mail-order company. If we wanted to contact a business, we placed a call during regular business hours or contacted them via post. This manner of conducting business applied not only to individual

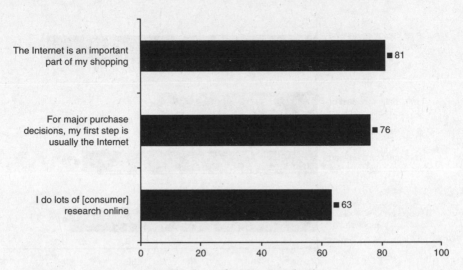

Graph 2.1 The Internet Is Changing the Way People Shop

Note: The data reflect the percentage of respondents who agreed with each statement.

Source: The Future of Shopping, Euro RSCG Worldwide, 2008. Fielded in the United States, the United Kingdom, France, and China (*n* = 2,800).

consumers but also to transactions between companies. Regardless of the channel used, we, as purchasers, were forced to play by the rules the producer or seller imposed. What other choice did we have?

Today, if we want to make a purchase (regardless of category), we browse the Web to find the best deal. We read peer reviews and ratings, and consider recommended alternatives. In some cases, we will visit corporate websites to get more information about the product and the people behind it. Once we settle on a particular item and vendor (online or not), we do a quick scan to see if we can find a coupon or promotional code that will drive the price down further. We might even find we can get a better deal by making the purchase through an auction site or by buying it from an individual seller on Amazon Marketplace or a similar venue.

In Graph 2.2, also from The Future of Shopping, we see just how proactive consumers have become given their new online capabilities. A majority of respondents not only read customer reviews when making a purchase decision, they also write them. And those reviews can have a real impact on a company's bottom line: A study by Compete, Inc. found, for instance, that more than $10 billion a year in online travel purchases is influenced by consumer-generated content,[3] including reviews, ratings, and blog entries.

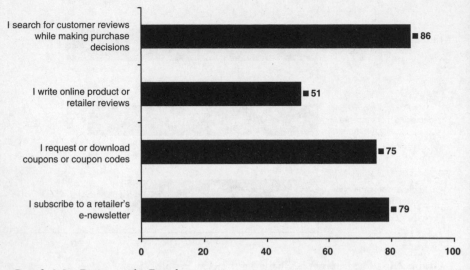

Graph 2.2   Power to the People

Note: The data reflect the percentage of respondents who agreed with each statement.

Source: The Future of Shopping, Euro RSCG Worldwide, 2008. Fielded in the United States, the United Kingdom, France, and China (*n* = 2,800).

Consumers have also discovered the strength that can come from banding together. Before the economic bubble burst in 2001, startups such as LetsBuyIt.com and Mobshop were introducing e-shoppers to the concept of group purchasing power, enabling retail customers to bargain for wholesale prices. Those particular sites eventually failed, largely due to unsustainable business models. Now, group buying has been reborn, this time in China, and looks set to have a second coming in the West. Known as *tuangou*, group buying is being reinvented by such sites as Liba.com and TeamBuy.com.cn. The key difference from the earlier incarnation is that consumers join forces online, but then actually meet at a brick-and-mortar store to make their purchases. At the designated time, leaders chosen by the shoppers negotiate the best group deal they can. The stores are given a heads-up about the buying event, so they are sure to have adequate stock on hand. Typical discounts range from 10 to 30 percent off the retail price.[4]

A survey conducted by TNS Retail Forward in eight countries in 2008 found that 77 percent of nearly 5,000 primary household shoppers polled expect group buying online to be widespread in their countries by 2015.[5] It is yet another indication of consumers' growing awareness of new tools at their disposal.

Advantage: Customer

We can see the radical change taking place in the corporate-consumer relationship in a series of television commercials by two financial services companies: Capital One and LendingTree. The ads from Capital One depict the old balance of power in which companies unilaterally dictated the terms. In one commercial, two fat-cat bankers sit in an office eating lunch ("Ah, the fruits of big banking!"). One of them complains about the wobbly table, at which point a miniature man pops out from behind a water glass and begins to ask for a loan. "I have a better idea," sneers one banker, as he traps the would-be borrower in the glass and then uses him as a shim under the table leg. "He's good for something after all," the banker laughs.[6] The depiction may be over-the-top, but this ad nicely encapsulates the lopsided relationship that prevailed for so long between companies and consumers.

In a campaign from LendingTree, we see the modern-day flip side of that balance of power. In one commercial, as detailed by Barry Silverstein on brandchannel.com, "a customer walks into a bank and is greeted by his banker. The customer tells the banker he is using LendingTree to get competitive bids on a mortgage. The banker appears hurt, but the customer assures him that the bank is included in the bidding process because it participates in LendingTree. The customer pats the banker on the arm, smiles knowingly, and says, 'And I want you to know, I'm pulling for you.'"[7] Silverstein describes the ad as "a wonderful role reversal, vaulting the consumer into the position of power normally reserved for the banker."[8]

What It Means for the Corporate Brand of Tomorrow

> There has been a power shift. The consumer has his finger on the "no thanks" button and can reject your message in an instant. And for good, if we're not careful; an opt out can be a one-way ticket.
>
> —Martin Nieri, managing director,
> Clark McKay & Walpole[9]

Consumers are not "smarter" today because the human population has seen a sudden spike in intelligence; they are smarter because they have better and easier access to information and better and easier ways to communicate between and collaborate among themselves (and with businesses). This positions them to make smarter choices.

If companies could control information available online in the same way they controlled information prior to the Internet, their traditional ways of doing business might well suffice. Marketers could continue to cast out information about how amazing and indispensable their products are and hope to attract a lot of bites. In this model, any negative reviews would be limited to individual conversations, the average consumer having no way to broadcast his or her thoughts and experiences beyond immediate circles of family, friends, and acquaintances.

Today, that scenario has been turned on its head. Word of mouth has gone from a couple of people talking on the street or on the phone to potentially thousands spreading a viral video or scathing piece of hate mail about a product or company. Complete strangers from halfway around the world are now influencing the purchase decisions of others.

Why do the opinions of often-anonymous reviewers influence us? Peer reviews matter more today because the public's trust in business and institutions is so low. Unlike corporate communicators or even expert reviewers, "ordinary" people are not seen as having a financial stake in whether a product flies off the shelf or gathers dust. Their reviews are more trusted because they are considered more honest and typically communicate in a highly relatable way. A survey by public-relations firm Edelman confirms this point: 2,000 people identified as opinion leaders agreed the most credible source of information about a company is not the CEO, but "a person like me." Tellingly, trust in "a person like me" increased a whopping 48 percent in just three years, from 20 percent in 2003 to 68 percent in 2006.[10]

In today's marketing-savvy (read: skeptical) society, it is easy to understand why a person might trust the opinion of a fellow shopper/homemaker/techie/DIYer/traveler over the published review of a paid professional. Plus, there is the added benefit of having multiple people weigh in on any topic rather than being forced to rely on a single source of opinion, however expert. As we write this, nearly 3,000 individuals have posted user reviews on Amazon.com about the Garmin nüvi 350 portable GPS navigator, awarding it a cumulative four-and-a-half stars (out of a possible five). Meanwhile, three people have cumulatively given the Magellan Maestro 3250 portable GPS navigator the same number of stars. Each is a favorably reviewed product, but which one would you be more confident in buying? The wisdom—and experience—of crowds matters.

As Web 1.0 gives way to Web 2.0, bloggers and amateur reviewers will continue to see their influence grow. Not only is online product research a firmly entrenched habit, it is also becoming more reliable and pervasive, thanks to the advent of camera phones, text messaging, and other tools that make it easier for people to communicate in compelling ways. It is one thing to read about substandard hotel accommodations and quite another to be presented with a photograph of a hair-clogged drain in all its megapixeled magnificence.

Today's proactive consumers and entrepreneurs are also coming up with innovative ways to weigh opinions, thereby making them more valuable to the individual shopper. Trustedopinion.com is a site that invites networks of friends to rate movies, restaurants, and nightclubs. The site gives most weight to the opinions of one's friends, followed by one's friends' friends, and so on down the chain. The premise is that a friend's recommendation is more meaningful and reliable than that of a stranger. Netflix.com lets users see how closely a reviewer's movie ratings resemble their own, making it easy to dismiss the opinions of people with dissimilar tastes.

In an era in which consumers have so many product and service choices, smart marketers will take full advantage of consumer content—and influence—online. That means making improvements based on user reviews, rather than wasting time trying to muzzle critics or rig results. It also means operating in a way that is both transparent and collaborative. This is important whether one is trying to boost short-term sales or bolster corporate reputation over the long term. With approximately 1.4 new blogs being created every second (roughly 120,000 daily), ordinary people are finding new ways to communicate more powerfully.[11] It is absolutely critical that brands (product and corporate) be involved in consumer conversations in a positive way. And that applies not only to manufacturers, but also to organizations in such industries as real estate, medicine, and law. The days when product and service providers could ride roughshod over the "little guy" are coming to a close.

THE NEW CONSUMER IS MORE
CONSCIOUS AND CONSCIENTIOUS

Consumers' wants and needs are constantly evolving, mutating in response to new product offerings, attitudes, pressures, and technologies. Over the course of the past century, we have seen the United States (among other countries) move from a culture of thrift to one marked by a sort of hyperconsumerism that has added to our vocabulary such terms as *retail therapy, compulsive shopping,* and *spending addiction.*

Now the authors of this book are seeing consumers move in a new direction. Through our work in the United States and around the world, we have seen a clear shift toward *conscious consumption*—a movement that is quickly gaining ground not just in the United States, but also in Canada and Western Europe, among other places. A growing number of people are looking at the products on offer with a more critical eye, rejecting excess in favor of simplicity. At the same time, they are seeking brand partners that offer a sense of human values and authenticity. For these more mindful consumers, shopping is not just about the merchandise; it is also about the people who produce and sell the goods, and the impact purchases have on the broader world. As we will address later in this book, this shift has important implications for business leaders.

The move toward mindful consumption is increasingly reflected in corporate advertising. When Toyota asked in an ad campaign, "Can you have an impact by making none at all? Why not?" it was more than just a tagline. The advertisement focused on the company's efforts to reduce emissions and waste, but also served as recognition of people's increased awareness of the consequences of their consumption choices. In the developed world, consumers are under increasing pressure, both societal and self-imposed, to limit the damage they cause.

Why the sudden concern? After all, mindless consumption has run rampant for decades—and has certainly been encouraged by advertisers. For many people, concern over global warming has been the single most important impetus for change, prompting them to take a closer look not just at what they buy, but also at how they live. Unlike most other eco-threats (e.g., rainforest destruction, endangered species), global warming offers plenty of opportunity for individual accountability and action. Numerous websites offer calculators that measure and track one's carbon footprint, and there is a growing market of products geared toward responsible living.

In the United States, a good measure of credit for this increased awareness can rightly go to Al Gore's *An Inconvenient Truth,* the fourth-highest-grossing documentary film ever. The movie clearly reached a receptive audience: A companion book authored by Gore spent thirty-eight weeks on the *New York Times* best-seller list, including four weeks at number one.

Minding Our Collateral Damage

The Future of Shopping uncovered a sizeable percentage of shoppers who are now factoring ecological concerns into their purchase decisions. Nearly eight in ten consumers surveyed in the United States, France, and the United Kingdom purchase environmentally friendly products and buy energy-efficient light bulbs, and seven in ten bring reusable bags to the grocery store. Importantly, most expect to increase their "green" purchases in the future.[12] Mintel International confirms that consumers are not only buying more eco-friendly products, but that they are also willing to pay more for them. In a 2009 study, 43 percent of Americans polled indicated they are willing to pay as much as 10 percent more for green products.[13] To the surprise of some analysts, sales of green products showed no signs of slowing in the first quarter of 2009, despite the recession.

Conscientious consumption is not limited to concern for the environment. Consumers are also looking to vote with their pocketbooks, supporting those companies that share their values and refusing to do business with those that do not. Nearly six in ten respondents to The Future of Shopping (see Graph 2.3) said they avoid doing business with stores that treat their employees unfairly. And half of those surveyed are making purchase decisions based on a company's expressed values or sociopolitical activities. A near majority avoid buying products from a particular country or region. Clearly, the core retail values of convenience, quality, and price are being augmented by higher-minded concerns.[14]

Longing for Less

It might be tempting to dismiss conscientious consumption as a short-term fad fueled by the trendy appeal of "eco chic." And there is certainly room to argue that many people buying green today won't ever make the changes necessary to radically alter the impact of their consumption. However, there is underlying evidence of an emerging mindset that speaks to a fundamental longing for a new approach to consumerism. Euro RSCG saw telltale signs of this back in 2004 in its

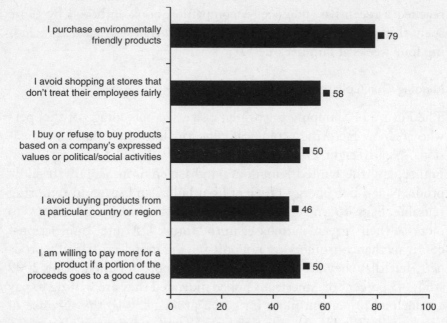

Graph 2.3 A Move Toward Conscientious Consumption

Note: The data reflect the percentage of respondents who agreed with each statement.

Source: The Future of Shopping, Euro RSCG Worldwide, 2008. Fielded in the United States, the United Kingdom, France, and China (*n* = 2,800).

Prosumer Pulse® benchmark study: More than four in ten American, British, and Japanese consumers surveyed agreed with the statement, "I have too much stuff—less would be better." That sentiment was even apparent in the emerging market of India, where more than one-third of respondents expressed a desire to cut back on their consumption.

A study the agency conducted at the beginning of 2009 (Euro RSCG Value Study) found that three in ten U.S. consumers believe their lives would be better if they "owned fewer things," and slightly more than half reported deriving a sense of satisfaction from reducing their purchases during the economic downturn. Nearly half said they do not intend to go back to their old shopping patterns even when the economy rebounds.[15]

At its most basic, the desire to "declutter" is just that: People want to clear their homes of a lot of the physical junk that has accumulated due to excess consumption. Embracing the concept on a deeper level are those who also want to get rid of psychic and emotional "junk." These people are rethinking the very nature of their consumption and are taking the time to question whether their values and priorities have become skewed—and whether that is damaging their quality of life. A common question that has emerged is: "Do I own all this stuff, or does it own me?"

Evidence of a fundamental desire to break away from consumerism can be seen in the growing number of adherents to the "voluntary simplicity" movement, advanced by such organizations as the Simple Living Network and the Center for a New American Dream. Search for *simplicity* under book listings on Amazon.com, and you will find hundreds of volumes, including Janet Luhrs' *The Simple Living Guide* and Tim Kasser's *The High Price of Materialism*. A growing number of grassroots campaigns around the world are speaking to this trend, including National Downshifting Week in the United Kingdom and Canada's Buy Nothing Christmas. And then there are the more hardcore adherents who have cast off all but their most vital possessions and are now homesteading or living "off the grid," with no source of energy other than what they can produce themselves.

After decades of "trading up," many consumers are finding a great deal more satisfaction in trading down—whether that means replacing a gas guzzler with a hybrid car; moving into a small, more sustainable home; or maintaining a vegetable garden in the backyard. It is not just about saving money, it is also about feeling good; excess consumption has finally worn out a lot of people, and they are sick of playing the accumulation game.

Two studies from Yankelovich (now The Futures Company) back up our perceptions: A 2008 survey found that 62 percent of Americans agreed with the notion that "people today consume far more of everything than they really need"—up from just 49 percent a year earlier.[16] Far more surprising, a majority of consumers surveyed in 2008 agreed that "If Americans turn out to be less well-off in the future than they have been in the past, they may actually be happier for it."[17] That is a pretty astonishing shift for a nation that has for so long equated financial success and material possessions with happiness. In the span of a decade, we have somehow moved from bumper stickers that proclaim "He who dies with the most toys wins" to stickers that read "Insatiable is not sustainable."[18]

What It Means for the Corporate Brand of Tomorrow

Now that consumers are becoming more mindful of what they buy, they expect companies to act in an equally enlightened way, which

includes behaving in a manner that is not detrimental to the environment or people. In other words, they expect corporations to behave as
concerned citizens. Too often, the reality disappoints.

Euro RSCG's Future of the Corporate Brand study asked respondents how well corporations in general are delivering on a set of issues.
Only 12 percent said companies are exceeding expectations with regard
to making environmental impact a core factor in their decision making; in contrast, half the sample said corporations are falling short in
this regard (see Graph 2.4). Similarly, nearly half the respondent base
said corporations are failing to pay fair value for their use of natural
resources, while just one in ten said companies are exceeding their
expectations on this issue. In terms of treatment of employees, half the
sample said corporations are failing to hit the mark, and only 14 percent said they are doing more than expected.[19]

This notion of companies not living up to public expectations is of
considerable import, given that more than three-quarters of respondents in each market are less likely to trust a company with a poor

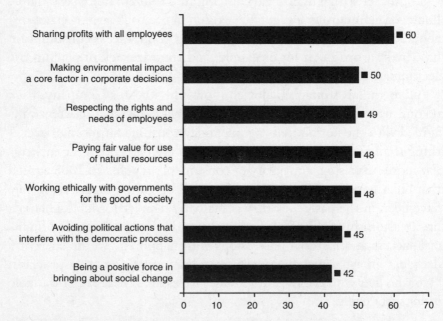

Graph 2.4   Areas in Which Corporations Are Failing to Meet Expectations

Note: The data reflect the percentage of respondents who said companies are delivering below
expectations or significantly below expectations in each area.

Source: The Future of the Corporate Brand, Euro RSCG Worldwide, 2008 (*n* = 1,851).

reputation for environmental and/or social responsibility.[20] As we will discuss in more detail in Chapter Four, companies that are out of sync with consumer expectations and attitudes will lose out on the considerable competitive advantage a better-than-average reputation brings.

The corporate brands that own the future will understand it is no longer enough to provide products and services and operate within what used to pass for acceptable standards of behavior. Today's consumers demand more: They want to continue to enjoy the pleasure of consumption, while also knowing their purchases are contributing to the greater good, or at least not detracting from it. And they want to feel they are playing a part, however small, in contributing to positive change. The most successful corporate brands will be those that address these twin pulls of selfishness and altruism, and help consumers feel that what is good for them is also good for the world.

THE NEW CONSUMER IS MORE POWERFUL

When we talk about the newly empowered consumer, we are referring, in part, to consumers' greater access to information and tools as detailed earlier in this chapter. However, consumers have also grown more powerful in another, arguably even more significant way—one that will play an important role in shaping the corporate brand of the future.

There was a time not so long ago when the average person had no role within a corporation other than as a past, present, or potentially future customer. For the most part, the only impact a consumer could have was at the checkout counter. To be truly "heard" by a company required substantial stock holdings, media credentials, or a company identification card. That slowly changed as companies discovered the value to be gained from focus groups, consumer panels, and the like, but that level of consumer influence was nothing compared with the empowerment now afforded by the Internet. Today, anyone with a dial-up connection or broadband access can voice his or her gripes and criticisms about a company to a potential audience of millions, and can rally others to join him or her in a common cause.

There are all sorts of examples of consumers' increasing ability to impact the behaviors of corporations, but perhaps none as compelling as a 2006 case involving Texas power company TXU. As reported by columnist Thomas L. Friedman in the *New York Times*, when TXU announced plans to build nearly a dozen coal-fired power plants in the United States, environmental activists rallied the eco-troops to fight back.[21] A generation ago, that would have involved sending out mass mailings to members of environmental groups, circulating petitions door-to-door and in supermarket parking lots, and similar analog tactics. This time was different for two reasons: First, two national environmental groups, Environmental Defense (ED) and Natural Resources Defense Council (NRDC), went straight to the Internet, creating a dedicated website (Stoptxu.com) and building a national constituency opposed to the plan. Second, TXU was the intended buyout target of two large firms, Kohlberg Kravis Roberts & Company (KKR) and Texas Pacific Group, neither of which had any intention of striking a $45 billion deal (the biggest leveraged buyout in history) if TXU was mired in battle with consumers and environmental activists. The firms essentially announced they would only go forward with the deal if they had the blessing of environmentalists.[22]

TXU was still attempting to operate within the old context of corporate hegemony, while KKR and Texas Pacific recognized the existence of an entirely new world order. As far as the energy company was concerned, according to Thomas Friedman, having the governor of Texas on its side was all that was needed to push those power plants through. The CEO refused to even meet with the leaders of ED and NRDC. The buyout firms, in contrast, understood environmental concerns had moved out of the fringe and into the mainstream, and that the transparency of the Internet would make it impossible to cut any sort of backroom deal. Whatever decisions were made, the public would be aware of them and vocal in their criticism.

In the end, TXU and the buyout firms agreed to reduce the number of new coal plants from eleven to three, to support a U.S. cap on greenhouse gas emissions, and to invest $400 million in energy-efficiency programs, including doubling the purchase of wind power; in return, the environmentalists blessed the deal.[23]

In the words of Thomas Friedman:

> TXU not only didn't understand that the world was getting green; it didn't understand that the world was getting flat.... So, what TXU had hoped would be just a local skirmish was instead watched on computer screens in every global market.... TXU could not manage its reputation by just hiring a P.R. firm and issuing a statement—because, thanks to the Internet, too many little

people could talk back or shape TXU's image on a global basis through the Web, for free.[24]

Whether politically motivated activists or simply run-of-the-mill disgruntled customers, the public now has far more powerful weapons in its fight against corporate powers. And ordinary people are increasingly considering corporate oversight not just a possibility, but also a responsibility.

The Tables Have Turned

"Big Brother is watching you."

This phrase, taken from George Orwell's prophetic novel *1984*, has been in frequent use over the past half-century and stands as a testament to the traditional balance of power. Whether referring to the government or Big Business, the words suggest ongoing surveillance—and control—of the general population by all-powerful and intrusive authority figures. Today, Orwell would likely be surprised by the extent to which the tables have turned on corporations. For all the fears of Big Business tracking consumer movements with digital cookies and RFID (radio frequency identification) tags, the truth is that consumers are keeping equally close, if not closer, tabs on corporations. Anyone with Internet access can easily look up an annual report, track corporate movements, and contribute to conversations about what a particular company, industry, or brand is doing right or wrong.

In Chapter One, we touched briefly on the public-relations fiasco JetBlue faced in the aftermath of the Valentine's Day 2007 incident, in which more than 1,000 passengers were stranded on an iced-in tarmac for as long as sixteen hours (reports vary). This is a great example of how easily an aggrieved customer—especially an aggrieved customer armed with a video-enabled phone—can spread the word about corporate transgressions or errors in judgment. While still stuck inside the airplanes, reportedly with virtually no food or water or usable bathroom facilities, passengers used their cell phones and PDAs to send out messages and photos chronicling their ordeal. Some contacted newspapers and television news bureaus directly, and at least one passenger filmed a confrontation with a pilot and posted it on YouTube later that day. Other passengers contributed to blogs, providing their own details of what came to be known online as the JetBlue "hostage crisis." One former "hostage" even set up a website and an online community at Jetbluehostage.com. The site serves as an archive of passengers' experiences on that day and also contains news articles, blog posts, press releases, and e-mails from JetBlue's corporate headquarters. More than two years later, the brand has managed to regain some measure of public trust and goodwill (thanks in part to JetBlue's quickly penned and released Customer Bill of Rights), but all the unpalatable details of the passengers' experiences will reside in cyberspace in perpetuity. To this day, disgruntled customers continue to post to the site with negative thoughts and details of more recent customer-service experiences involving the airline.

Major corporations are used to dealing with crisis communications, but they now need to update their playbooks. Today's proactive consumers are not simply responding in crisis periods; they are keeping watch on corporations year-round. Having witnessed the damage Big Business can cause when left unchecked, a growing number of citizen-consumers feel they have a right to monitor corporate actions and take companies to task whenever they step out of line. To a certain extent, this shift can be attributed to the fact that people have more familiarity with corporations today. As discussed earlier, the physical and emotional distance that used to separate large companies from the "unwashed masses" has all but disappeared. Respondents to the Future of the Corporate Brand survey were asked whether they feel corporations have become a more important part of their respective cultures. In each of the three markets, a majority said yes.[25]

Now that consumers "live closer" to their brand partners and have higher expectations of them, they feel they have more of a stake in knowing what corporations are up to. Nearly six in ten respondents to Euro RSCG's study said they had become more interested in corporations' conduct and brand images over the past few years. In addition, more than four in ten had actively sought out information regarding the reputation or ethics of a company in the few months prior to the survey. In a sign of their increased interest, a majority of consumers surveyed indicated they would like to join an online community centered on sharing opinions and information about companies and brands.[26]

Consumers are not monitoring corporations and engaging in brand conversations online as a hobby; they are using the information they uncover to make decisions regarding immediate purchases and long-term brand partnerships. Corporations and brands are being rated, in part, on issues pertaining to quality, reliability, and customer service. Beyond that, they are also being judged with regard to how in tune they are with mindful consumption. Are they minimizing their impact on the planet? Are they treating people fairly? Are they taking a leadership role in solving societal problems? Companies unable to answer those questions in the affirmative will increasingly find they are being held accountable for those perceived failings.

For many consumers, purchases now carry a moral dimension. Three-quarters of respondents to The Future of the Corporate Brand believe they, as consumers, have a responsibility to censure unethical companies by avoiding their products. And they are walking that talk: Nearly two-thirds claim to have already made a purchase decision based on a company's conduct.[27] (See Graph 2.5.)

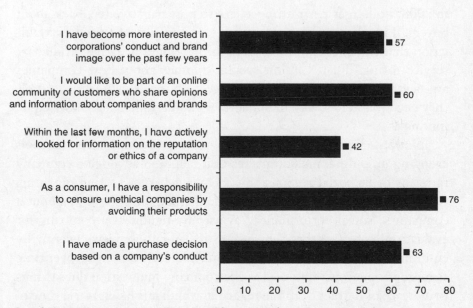

Graph 2.5 Consumers Are Keeping Closer Watch on Corporate Behavior
Note: The data reflect the percentage of respondents who agreed with each statement.
Source: The Future of the Corporate Brand, Euro RSCG Worldwide, 2008 (*n* = 1,851).

Consumer-to-Consumer Empowerment

Cognitive scientist Steven Pinker observes that human beings are constantly weighing trustworthiness, ready to detect any twitch or inconsistency that might mean someone is trying to deceive them. The best way to spot hypocrisy, he says, is by comparing notes with others.[28] Offline, this process is often dismissed as "gossip." Online, such conversations have become more systemized, with new mechanisms in place to allow people to more easily share their views and experiences—thereby empowering others in their own purchase decisions and brand interactions. Amazon and eBay were leaders in this area, understanding ahead of most other e-tailers that shoppers yearn for the assistance and affirmation of others like them. CEO and founder Jeff Bezos defines Amazon's community as "neighbors helping neighbors make purchase decisions."[29]

eBay facilitated user-to-user communication from the start, not just through ratings and feedback, but also through dedicated blogs, discussion boards, and chat rooms. After more than a decade in business, the auction site made a significant change to its feedback policy in 2008, no longer permitting sellers to post negative feedback about buyers. The change was made to prevent the sort of tit-for-tat retaliation that let sellers punish buyers for posting a negative product or service rating. That decision speaks volumes about how companies are beginning to recognize the value of giving consumers the tools they need to interact with manufacturers and retailers on a more equal footing.

Now, we are seeing even more consumer-empowerment tools cropping up online, including sites that help people judge a company in terms of its social responsibility. One such site, Dotherightthing. com, allows visitors to post the good, the bad, and the ugly about a company's "social performance." A user first submits a company for evaluation; other visitors then weigh in, and their views eventually culminate in a social performance score. That score changes over time as more people contribute and as the company in question does things to increase or detract from the regard in which it is held. At the time of writing, specific companies were being taken to task for such purported transgressions as incorrectly labeling products as "organic," violating privacy rights, and using "dirty tactics" to hijack computer browsers. On the flip side, other companies were being praised for such things as charitable contributions, sustainable practices, and transparency.

Oftentimes, increased scrutiny leads to action, whether that takes the form of a decision to buy or not to buy, a feedback rating, or a full-blown anti-brand campaign. Consumer pressure has been credited with all manner of corporate policy changes, from companies banning the use of bisphenol A (BPA) or trans fats in their products to Apple compensating first-wave iPhone purchasers after what some considered a too-rapid discounting of the initial purchase price. Whatever their intent, ordinary people now have the wherewithal to force corporations to respond to their complaints and demands.

What It Means for the Corporate Brand of Tomorrow

In ways that would have been all but unthinkable half a century ago, ordinary individuals have wrested a large measure of control from companies, big and small. We can see the evidence in every industry. Take pharmaceuticals, where drug companies are making end runs around the medical profession to whisper in the ears of consumers—who are then expected to influence the prescription and treatment choices of their own doctors. Yet even Big Pharma cannot control the messages consumers hear or what they do with them. People are gathering their own medical information online, investigating potential treatments, blogging about unpleasant or even dangerous side effects, and sharing tips and tactics for dealing with the medical industry at large. In acknowledgement of consumers' increasingly proactive behavior, the Federal Drug Administration now issues safety- and product-related alerts and podcasts directly to the public—no more filtering information through doctors, hospitals, and insurers.

Smart companies are not waiting to be taken to task by these newly empowered consumers. Instead, they are factoring consumer attitudes and preferences into their strategic planning. And they are actively engaging consumer stakeholders in an ongoing dialogue, online and off-.

In the next chapter, we will explore what future-focused companies are already doing to build strong and enduring relationships with the more powerful and proactive consumers of today and tomorrow.

Chapter Three

FOUR CORNERSTONES OF THE CONSCIOUS CORPORATION

Many business leaders are asking fundamental questions about what business they're in, why they are doing it and how it can be used as a means of healing human and natural communities.

—Amory Lovins, environmentalist and author of *Natural Capitalism*[1]

I n business, as in nature, natural selection has a way of getting rid of the weakest links. Unlike in the animal world, however, what constitutes strength and weakness in business is in a state of greater-than-normal flux. Where size used to triumph, now agility may be more prized. Where tradition was once a key asset, now innovation reaps greater rewards. Profit still sits at center, but it is no longer the only priority. For, natural selection has begun to favor those companies that have adopted a more humanized approach to commerce—an approach that takes into account the motivations and demands of the new consumer and the radically changed rules of the marketplace.

Not so long ago, integrating high ethical standards and community consciousness into a company's policies and practices would have been dismissed as unnecessary "do-goodism." It might have been seen as a way to reap minor reputation benefits, perhaps, but not as something capable of driving profits, strategy, or growth. Now we are seeing a shift in mindset in which the Leaders of Tomorrow are beginning to grasp the benefits of enlightened self-interest. Reputation has emerged as a key component of corporate success and doing "good" has proved to be a smart business practice in an environment in which consumers and other outside stakeholders hold real power. As Polly LaBarre, former senior editor of the business magazine *Fast Company* and coauthor of *Mavericks at Work*, put it, "If you want to compete, if you want to win, if you want to genuinely excite the imagination of the broader marketplace, you have to offer up a distinctive point of view about the future—and a compelling alternative to the worst practices of your industry."[2]

This chapter explores what some of today's most forward-thinking companies are doing to strengthen their positions within these new business realities. We will detail what we have come to regard as the four essential cornerstones of the most successful companies of tomorrow: a purpose beyond profit, a people-centered culture, a sustainable approach to business, and respect for consumers' power. Each one of these cornerstones has at its core the simple recognition that corporations are now a part of human culture—and are expected to behave as such.

THE CORPORATION OF THE FUTURE HAS A PURPOSE BEYOND PROFIT

Customers must recognize that you stand for something.

— Howard Schultz, CEO of Starbucks[3]

Think about the leading companies of today—the ones that get the most positive media attention, have the most solid reputations and arguably the most loyal customer bases; companies that are pushing their categories toward an optimal future. Among those likely to spring to mind are Google, Nike, and Whole Foods. Different industries, different leadership styles, different processes, but they all have one important element in common: a compelling set of beliefs that is clearly articulated and genuinely embedded in the organization and the brand.

In the space of a decade, Google went from a college research project to a publicly traded company with a brand value estimated at more than $86 billion, all while seeking to live by its credos of "Don't be evil" and "Work should be challenging, and the challenge should be fun."[4] By 2007, Google had managed to knock Microsoft off the top perch of the Harris Interactive Reputation Quotient. And as of January 2009, Google led the search market by a more than comfortable length, capturing 63 percent of searches, compared with just 21 percent for once-mighty Yahoo! and 8.5 percent for Microsoft, according to comScore.[5]

Nike grew to become the world's leading supplier of athletic shoes and apparel by centering its brand on a message of personal empowerment and unlimited human potential. With three simple words, the footwear maker became an empowerment brand, giving it room to stretch and grow. In the words of Scott Bedbury, the marketing executive behind the company's best-known campaign:

> "Just Do It" was a watershed moment for Nike. It established a broad communication platform from which we could talk to just about anyone. It wasn't only about world-class athletics; it was about fundamental human values shared by triathletes and mall walkers alike. It wasn't a product statement either. It was a brand ethos. Nike had found a way to respect its past while embracing its future. "Just Do It" was a much-needed re-expression of timeless Nike values.[6]

From its marketing communications to its corporate social responsibility (CSR) activities and high-profile endorsement deals, Nike continues to celebrate the human spirit and the limitlessness of human potential. In 2008, despite the global downturn, the company's net income soared 26 percent, to $1.9 billion, while earnings per share for the year grew 28 percent.[7] Its closest competitor, adidas, earned 60 percent of the $56.1 billion Nike earned in fiscal years 2003–2007.[8] We would argue one factor in that disparity is adidas's lack of clearly expressed values beyond soccer and athletic prowess.

Our third example, Whole Foods Market, has built its brand on a simple philosophy of "whole foods, whole people, whole planet"—and, in doing so, has managed to become one of the world's fastest-growing retailers. Between its health-conscious product offerings, its empowering retail atmosphere, and its corporate good works, Whole Foods makes its customers feel as if they are contributing to their own health and the health of their communities and the planet simply by shopping there. The company's influence can be seen across its category: Three in four conventional grocery stores in the United States now carry organic foods, according to the Food Marketing Institute.[9] Sales of natural and organic food and beverages have burgeoned to just under $33 billion in 2008,[10] up from $3.6 billion in 1997, according to the Organic Trade Association.[11]

The success of Google, Nike, Whole Foods, and other values-based brands is both cause and consequence of the public's growing expectations of Big Business. People see a major company taking on a social role or cause, and they question why others are not following suit. At the same time, corporate executives see the very real financial value to be derived from socially responsible activities (see Chapter Four), and they reconsider the place of CSR within their overall business strategies.

The notion that businesses should be about more than profits may be antithetical to the beliefs of such twentieth-century theorists as Milton Friedman, but it is deeply ingrained within twenty-first-century society—and is rapidly gaining credence within the C-suite,[12] as well. When Euro RSCG surveyed nearly 2,000 adults in the United States, France, and the United Kingdom for its Future of the Corporate Brand study, more than *eight in ten* respondents indicated it is important for a company to stand for something other than profitability. Moreover, only around one-third of respondents believed the most important responsibility of the chief executive should be to generate shareholder profits.

Whether for reasons of idealism or enlightened self-interest, a growing number of corporate leaders are accepting the challenge to adopt a broader purpose. From their examples, we can glean valuable lessons about how to ensure a company's purpose beyond profits benefits not just the cause, but also the corporate brand.

Shout It Out

It is not enough simply to stand for something. The most benefit accrues to those companies that take a bold stance and publicly declare their values and clearly defined objectives. It would be difficult to miss ice-cream maker Ben & Jerry's social mission; after all, it is plastered right on the wall of each and every store: "To operate the company in a way that actively recognizes the central role that business plays in society by initiating innovative ways to improve the quality of life locally, nationally, and internationally."[13] In its stores, handmade cosmetics company Lush posts a list of brand beliefs ranging from no testing on animals to "making our mums proud." Similarly, some Whole Foods locations feature walls festooned with the company's six core values, including "satisfying and delighting customers" and "supporting team member happiness."

Brewing a better world

The best way to "shout out" one's values is by communicating them at every possible touch point. Vermont's Green Mountain Coffee Roasters (GMCR) has grown its business from a single café in 1981 to more than 7,000 customer accounts in 2008. It has done so, in part, by taking a holistic approach to its business that is encapsulated in its motto: "Brewing a Better World." What that means to the company is partnering with coffee growers (rather than exploiting them), supporting the communities in which it does business, protecting the environment, promoting sustainable coffee, working with others to bring about positive social change, and creating a great place to work.[14]

GMCR communicates a purpose beyond profit at virtually every point of customer contact, even down to its product naming and tasting notes. As an example, the notes for its Heifer Hope Blend share the following: "Heifer Hope Blend was created to support Heifer International's fight against world hunger. With our support, Heifer helps coffee farmers diversify their incomes by raising livestock. We help raise awareness by showing people how their purchases can support sustainable development."[15] A product that might have seemed an indulgence is now a way to do good.

Among other values-led practices, GMCR contributes a minimum of 5 percent of pretax income to CSR activities, with an emphasis on supporting organizations that improve the quality of life for coffee-farming families. The company includes "scorecards" on its site that let visitors track such things as the number of tons of greenhouse gases emitted, the amount of resources allocated to social and environmental programs, and even workers' compensation claims and employee-retention rates. No detail is considered beyond the public purview.

Get Consumers Involved

> We came back from World War II and found our identity as Americans in conformity: IBM, the "man in the gray flannel suit," the suburbs. Then, in the 1960s, we found our identity in rebellion against conformity.... The 1980s came along, and we

found our identity in excess—having it all, the Me Generation. Now, we've found that having it all wasn't having that much. We've found the meaningful life era, a purpose larger than self. Why do we wear the little yellow wristband? Not because we want to cure cancer. We want to tell somebody we helped cure cancer. We want to be part of something larger than self. Driving a Prius still doesn't make the most economic sense in the world, but it has value to us. Why? Because it says we're good people, and we're controlling a world that's uncertain. We have a purpose larger than self.

—Alex Castellanos, political media strategist and partner, National Media Inc.[16]

The new consumer is seeking a deeper relationship with highly relevant brand partners, and a purpose beyond profit offers plenty of scope for engagement and active involvement. Social responsibility activities also afford a tremendous opportunity to remind consumers of the actual human beings behind the brand. That is of special importance at a time when people have grown increasingly wary of corporate marketing efforts.

"Leaving things a little better than we find them"

Innocent Drinks has impressed us with both its success and the extent to which it has involved consumers in building its brand. In just ten years in business, the company has managed to gain a 72 percent share[17] of the U.K.'s smoothie market. It has done so based on product quality, but also by interacting with consumers in a friendly, familiar, and fun way and by emphasizing honesty, community, and charitable values. From the very start, the three cofounders (friends from Cambridge University) asked customers to play a role in the company's growth. Before deciding to dedicate themselves full time to the new venture, the trio sold their drinks from a stall at a music festival in London. They put up a handwritten sign asking people to place their empties into either a garbage bin marked "Yes" or a bin marked "No" to indicate whether the men should quit their day jobs to concentrate on making smoothies. At the end of the day, the "Yes" bin was overflowing, and a company was born.[18]

Over the years, Innocent Drinks has stuck to its philosophy of leaving things a little bit better than it finds them; among other initiatives, it gives 10 percent of profits each year to charities in countries in which its fruit is grown, uses ecologically sound packaging, and makes ethical purchases (e.g., Rainforest Alliance certified).[19] And it continues to invite customers to be involved every step of the way. Visitors to the website are asked to "join the family" with these words:

> Hello. We are wondering if you'd like to join the innocent family. Don't worry—it's not some weird cult. It's just our way of staying in touch with the people who drink our drinks, i.e., you. Every week we'll e-mail you our news and give you the chance to win lots of drinks. We'll also invite you to nice events like the innocent village fete and maybe send you the odd present if you're lucky. Finally, we'll very occasionally ask you what you reckon we should do next, as we sometimes get confused.[20]

As of mid-May 2009, approximately 120,000 people had signed on as members of the Innocent family. In addition to receiving the weekly newsletter, many also post photos on the site, interact on the brand's Facebook page, and have even been known to gather in person. In 2007, some 60,000 people attended the first-annual Innocent Village Fete, in Regent's Park, with all proceeds from ticket sales (£150,000) going to charity. That same year, The Big Knit saw people gather across the United Kingdom to knit tiny "bobble hats" for the drink bottles; that unusual effort raised more than £200,000 to help heat the homes of the elderly in winter and support the homeless. In 2008, the company invited 100 family members to attend its AGM (Annual General Meeting, aka A Grown-up Meeting). They were treated to an inside view of the company's business and had a chance to vote on upcoming initiatives.[21]

By actively engaging people in the brand, its product and business development, and its good works, Innocent Drinks has been able to build human relationships among its customer base, the nearly 300 people across Europe who work for the company, and the corporate brand. In so doing, it has given its customers a sense of ownership over the company and reason to feel proud of their association with the brand. There is no better way to attract and retain motivated evangelists eager to help grow a business.

THE CORPORATION OF THE FUTURE
TREATS PEOPLE WELL

The corporate brands that are most successful in the future will be those that reject the notion that what is unacceptable in so-called polite society has any place in the business world. We are not so naive as to suggest naked aggression and myopic self-interest will disappear; that has and always will be part of the world of industry and commerce. However, now that the business world no longer exists on a separate sphere, it is increasingly subject to rules common throughout society. The veil of corporate secrecy that once obscured bad behavior is being pulled back—sometimes by government regulators, sometimes by NGOs and empowered consumers, and sometimes by employees communicating insider secrets with the outside world. When the chances of getting caught are so great, it is in one's self-interest to behave in a way unlikely to provoke censure.

Yvon Chouinard, founder of Patagonia sporting goods company, was well ahead of the curve in understanding the need for companies to behave humanely. In an interview with TreeHugger.com, a leading outlet for environmental news, he explained his approach to business: "It's always been difficult for us to lead an examined life as a corporation. I've always felt like a company has the responsibility to not wait for the government to tell it what to do, or to wait for the consumer to tell it what to do, but as soon as it finds out it's doing something wrong, stop doing it."[22]

Take Care of Customers

It is always a welcome surprise to come across a company that holds itself to an especially high standard. This is particularly the case at a time when service is slipping in so many industries; the Internet is awash in horror stories about abusive customer service clerks and unfair corporate practices. In this environment, companies that go the extra mile for their customers really stand out.

In the middle of the 2008 holiday season, a small Florida-based company called Bob The Fish sent this e-mail to customers who had ordered a particular item:

> Dearest Bob The Fish customer,
>
> We humbly apologize but the scheduled shipment of our NEW Bob The Fish 3-D hats has been delayed. Due to the slowdown of the U.S. economy, the factory in China has shut down a large portion of its production and unfortunately it has delayed delivery of our 3-D hats in time for the holidays. We have been assured that we WILL have our hats by January 21st.

Regrettably, we apologize for any inconvenience this may have caused. Please accept our apology and choose one of the following methods of reimbursement:

1. A FREE Bob The Fish T-shirt, to ship IMMEDIATELY
2. A FREE Bob The Fish 3-D hat (in addition to the one already ordered)
3. A full refund

Again, we apologize for the delay and any inconvenience this may have caused you during this holiday gift-giving time!

Best regards,
Robert W. "Bud" Groover, President/CEO

The e-mail concluded with toll-free and local phone numbers and a fax number through which to reach the CEO, and it was resent to anyone who did not reply to the original e-mail within a few days.

What makes this example all the more potent is that the company has a single pricing system: Whether one purchases a T-shirt, hat, visor, or pack of stickers (the current extent of the Bob The Fish product line), the item costs $25. So, rather than stick to standard corporate procedures by offering a small token (e.g., free shipping, a company mug, 10 percent off the next order) to make up for the inconvenience of a supply glitch, Bob The Fish offered a free item equal in price and in addition to the already ordered item—and with no additional shipping or handling charges. It is this sort of proactive customer service that not only builds loyalty but also reminds us this is a company run by "real people" who understand the added pressures and anxieties that accompany purchases made in the weeks leading up to the holidays.

In the words of Mark Twain (quoted in Bud Groover's signature line), "Always do right. This will gratify some of the people and astonish the rest."[23]

Be Fair to Employees

In the previous chapter, we presented data from the Future of the Corporate Brand study about areas in which companies are failing to live up to the public's expectations. The researchers were surprised to discover that corporations are seen as falling shortest in their treatment of employees. Those ratings were even lower than the scores given for environmental policies, shareholder value, and efforts to contribute to the greater good. Specifically, six in ten respondents said companies are failing to deliver on "sharing profits with all employees." And just under half (49 percent) indicated companies are falling short of expectations in terms of "respecting the rights and needs of their employees."

That first finding doubtless reflects the public's escalating frustration over the widening gap between executive and mid- and bottom-tier salaries—a frustration that existed well before the economic downturn in 2008. Twenty years ago, the ratio of CEO pay to that of the average worker was approximately 10:1; today, it is 364:1.[24] In some industries, executive paychecks could be described as obscene. In 2006, for example, the top twenty-five hedge-fund managers took home a combined $14 *billion*—more than the gross domestic product of Jordan or Uruguay that year. Three of the managers took home in excess of $1 billion for their fifty-two weeks of labor.[25]

Some values-led corporations are working to resolve this issue by boosting compensation at the lower end and constraining it at the top. For instance, Whole Foods caps executive compensation (salary plus non-equity bonuses) at nineteen times the average annual pay of hourly workers. The cap originally was set at eight times' average pay, but has since been increased to bolster executive retention.[26] CEO and founder John Mackey reduced his salary to $1 in 2007 and has forgone all future stock options and other compensation. Approximately 96 percent of stock options granted by Whole Foods have gone to employees who are not executive officers.[27]

THE CORPORATION OF THE FUTURE CHAMPIONS SUSTAINABILITY

> A single decision by the chairman of Royal Dutch/Shell has a greater impact on the health of the planet than all the coffee-ground-composting, organic-cotton-wearing ecofreaks gathering in Washington, D.C., for Earth Day festivities this weekend.
>
> —Sharon Begley, senior editor, *Newsweek*[28]

Within just a few years, the concept of sustainability has come full circle, evolving from a perceived hindrance into a "nice to have" fringe benefit and then into an essential component of companies that aim to lead their categories. This shift in attitude is partially due to the increased consumer consciousness explored in the previous chapter. However, it also stems from corporations' growing appreciation of the value sustainable practices can afford a business.

Stonyfield Farm and DuPont are among the companies that embraced some principles and practices of sustainability ahead of the curve—and for reasons that most definitely included profits. However, they were looking for markedly different types of gains. In the case of Stonyfield Farm, sustainability was both a purpose beyond profit and a way to differentiate itself in its category. As chairman, president, and CEO Gary Hirshberg told *Advertising Age*:

> Our point of view has always been that we don't really have any choice. Our gross profit structure really prevents us from doing a lot with advertising, period, and yet our green mission has really always been our [unique selling proposition]. It's been the thing that we can talk about both credibly, effectively, knowledgeably and—more importantly—genuinely.[29]

For DuPont, sustainability efforts were initially centered primarily on cost savings, to great effect: According to Andrew Winston, founder of Winston Eco-Strategies, the money DuPont saved by reducing waste and keeping energy costs flat from 2003 to 2007 equaled its net profit during that period.[30]

Many analysts agree the years 2005–2006 marked a tipping point in the movement toward sustainability. That period saw the devastation of Hurricane Katrina and the subsequent spikes in oil prices, drawing the public's attention to the issues of global warming and energy conservation. It was in this context that Al Gore's *An Inconvenient Truth* debuted at the Sundance Film Festival.

By the end of 2007, the idea that businesses should operate in a more sustainable fashion was well ingrained. At that time, just under three-quarters of respondents to the Future of the Corporate Brand study agreed: "The most successful and profitable businesses in the future will be those that practice sustainability." Most companies appear to be falling short in that regard: As noted in the previous chapter, only 12 percent of the global sample believed companies were doing an adequate job of making environmental impact a core factor in business decisions.

We are now past the point of debating whether companies should work toward sustainability. The question is how it will best be accomplished. Happily, there are important lessons to be gleaned from the frontrunners.

Be Specific About Objectives and Transparent About Progress

Multinational conglomerates GE and British department store Marks & Spencer operate on entirely different scales in entirely different industries. Yet there are similarities in how each has approached sustainability, and both serve as good examples of why it may be better to jump in with both feet rather than dipping in one toe at a time.

In announcing its broad-ranging "ecomagination" initiative in 2005, GE pledged to double investment in clean technology, to increase revenues from green products to at least $20 billion in 2010, and to significantly reduce greenhouse gas emissions. And the company proceeded immediately to take steps to accomplish those aims. In addition to earning accolades from *Fortune* as one of the world's most admired companies, GE saw global revenue growth of 22 percent in 2007, with an 18 percent increase in orders.[31] In 2008, despite global economic turbulence, the company reported an increase of 21 percent in revenues from its range of energy-efficient and environmentally friendly products and services, to $17 billion. GE has now increased its original goal of $20 billion in sales of ecomagination products in 2010 to $25 billion.[32]

Increased profitability is more than just a happy by-product of ecomagination; it was a motive from the start. In a discussion we had with Jake Siewert, vice president for public strategy at Alcoa, he commented: "I think what GE is doing right now is very interesting; they had some contentious relationships with some communities in some parts of the world, and what they're doing now is talking about the business opportunity involved in being green. They're not trying to say, 'We're doing this from some sort of moral imperative'; they're not doing it only because they think it's the right thing to do. They're doing it because they think communities, companies, customers, governments are going to be looking for clean water, clean energy, and so on. And GE wants to be the company that sells the products that produce those things."[33]

Marks & Spencer (M & S) certainly has a much more focused footprint than GE, but its ambition to be a leader in sustainability is every bit as bold. And it made clear from the outset that it expected its customers and the broader public to hold it to its word. In January 2007, the company unveiled a comprehensive initiative it calls Plan A ("Because there is no Plan B"). Rather than release a lofty mission statement that spoke in generalities about its commitment to ecological sustainability, the company detailed 100 specific actions and goals it intended to work toward over a five-year period. Clearly stated in window displays, on in-store signs, and on its website were the aims of becoming carbon neutral and sending no waste to landfills by 2012, increasing sustainable sourcing, improving the lives of people throughout its supply chain, and helping customers and employees live a healthier lifestyle. Anyone interested in further information could drill down to get to the nitty-gritty: M & S did not simply pledge greater energy efficiency; it committed to such specifics as reducing energy use in stores 25 percent per square foot of floor space, achieving 20 percent improvement in warehouses and offices, and changing over all company cars to diesel or hybrid. Rather than talk generally about humanizing its supply line, M & S introduced a benchmarking system for clothing and home suppliers, and specified that all jams, conserves, sugar, and 10 percent of all cotton sold in its stores would from thereon in be Fair Trade–certified.[34] Customers and others are able to track the company's success (and failures) in each area through regular progress reports available online.

By making its commitments public and being transparent about its actions, M & S has left itself open to criticism should it fall short. That potential for criticism serves as an ongoing source of motivation, however, and helps to ensure corporate actions live up to executives' best intentions. In an article in British newspaper the *Guardian*, Mike Barry, head of corporate social responsibility at M & S, was quoted as saying, "Four years ago fifty percent of customers said it mattered to them that M & S was a responsible business. By last year that proportion had grown to ninety-seven percent...we get the message. We are on the front foot and people now know what we stand for."[35]

By numerous measures, Plan A has proved both a competitive advantage and motivator for the company. Writing in *Your M & S: How We Do Business Report 2008*, Plan A director Richard Gillies noted:

Fifteen months into our five-year plan we're already seeing benefits in reduced energy and waste costs, savings in packaging costs and our suppliers are benefiting from these activities too. But it's not all about cost savings; industry surveys such as the Chatsworth FTSE 100 Green Survey and the Covalence Ethical Ranking show how Plan A is having a positive effect on how people regard Marks & Spencer—retaining the loyalty of existing customers and winning us new business. Plan A has also inspired new ranges of Fairtrade, organic, recycled and energy efficient products. Plan A isn't just a "nice to do"—it's a "need to do."[36]

Lead the Way

> We're starting with our own carbon footprint. Not nothing. But much of what we're doing is already, or soon will be, little more than the standard way of doing business. We can do something that's unique, different from just any other company. We can set an example, and we can reach our audiences. Our audience's carbon footprint is 10,000 times bigger than ours. That's the carbon footprint we want to conquer.
>
> —Rupert Murdoch, chairman and managing director, News Corporation[37]

Rupert Murdoch makes an excellent point: To truly diminish the impact of industry and commerce on both people and the planet, it will not be enough for humanized corporations to change their ways. The entire population will need to reconsider its approach to consumption, and make smarter and more mindful personal choices.

Wal-Mart has emerged as what some would consider an unlikely leader in this area. Former CEO Lee Scott's 2005 announcement of the company's Embrace the Earth initiative was greeted with heavy skepticism in some quarters; yet Wal-Mart has proved true to its word. Among other achievements over the past few years, Wal-Mart has accomplished:

- The recycling of tens of millions of pounds of plastic, paper, and aluminum, plus more than twenty-five billion pounds of cardboard
- The opening of a number of high-efficiency Supercenters that use up to 45 percent less energy than is standard
- The purchase of enough solar power to provide renewable energy for as many as twenty-two facilities in California and Hawaii, and enough wind power to supply up to 15 percent of the total energy load in approximately 350 Texas stores and other facilities

- The permanent conservation of more than 400,000 acres of wildlife habitat in thirteen U.S. states through the company's Acres for America program, in conjunction with the National Fish and Wildlife Foundation[38]

In a superb example of what we mean by enlightened self-interest, the company has used its eco-friendly actions as a means to both save significant money and do some damage control against detractors that had previously accused it of lapses in environmental and other areas. As of 2006, Wal-Mart had saved an estimated $3.4 billion by scoring its 60,000 worldwide suppliers on their ability to develop less-wasteful packaging and conserve natural resources.[39]

Perhaps the most impressive aspect of Wal-Mart's Embrace the Earth initiative is the impact it has had—and continues to have—on mainstream consumers. Stephen Quinn, the company's chief marketing officer, was quick to recognize the potential of such an initiative. Wal-Mart's initial goal was to double sales of products that help make homes more energy efficient. At the start of the program, the retailer pledged to sell more than one hundred million compact fluorescent light bulbs (CFLs), the use of which would prevent some twenty million metric tons of greenhouse gases from entering the atmosphere—an impact comparable to taking 700,000 cars off the road.[40] It has already exceeded that number, thanks in part to education efforts and the use of eye-catching displays and reduced pricing. Customers have also seen changes in packaging. For instance, Wal-Mart now only sells compact, concentrated versions of all liquid laundry detergents in order to conserve cardboard, plastic resin, and water. This is a change many consumers might not have made on their own; like it or not, they are being pulled on to the green bandwagon by their retail partner, to the benefit of all.

Educate and Engage Consumers in the Cause

It is not enough to do good. To derive full reputation benefits and motivate others to adopt the same behaviors, Leaders of Tomorrow have to let the world know what they are doing—and why. We are seeing all sorts of innovative solutions:

- Stonyfield Farm has hired a former journalist to run five blogs to communicate with consumers on a variety of topics related to sustainability and health.[41]

- As part of its rebranding as the eco-conscious car company, Toyota has engaged in a number of consumer-outreach efforts, including an extensive education and awareness tour, billboards touting the number of gallons of gasoline saved by hybrid drivers, and sponsorship of the Sundance Channel's (programming, "The Green," dedicated to environmental issues).[42]
- Shoppers who make a purchase from Wal-Mart's Love, Earth line of sustainable jewelry are able to trace the origins of the gold or silver from mine to market through a tracking number and website (Loveearthinfo.com). The intent is to educate consumers about the issue of unethical mining and assure customers that the raw materials in their jewelry come only from mines operated according to sustainability principles.[43]

GE is so convinced of the importance of public buy-in that it has made spreading the word to consumers the fourth pillar of its ecomagination initiative. It is accomplishing that through a dedicated website (ecomagination.com) and public events and forums. The company has even invited customers to take part in "dreaming sessions," during which they brainstorm potential solutions to specific issues.

THE CORPORATION OF THE FUTURE
RESPECTS CONSUMERS' POWER

We are looking to corporations to be societal leaders, which means they need to act as political candidates do. Before I decide who gets my vote, I am going to want to know who they are and where they are from. What is their mission? What is their purpose? I want to share in the company's rituals and icons. And I want to understand why my candidate is better than the other guy.

—Alex Castellanos, political media strategist and
partner, National Media Inc.[44]

Everything about the relationship between company and consumer has changed, from balance of power and level of familiarity to the tools each has to communicate with—and influence the behavior of—the other. This means corporate playbooks need to be revised to ensure a level of mutual engagement and trust that is optimal to both parties. It is time for companies to find a new way to communicate.

Consider the difference between two well-known advertising campaigns: "When E. F. Hutton talks, people listen" (from the 1970s and 1980s) versus Charles Schwab's current campaign, developed by Euro RSCG: "Talk to Chuck." The former is suggestive of an untouchable financial guru sprinkling his words of wisdom, as it suits him, to select members of the masses below. Communication is authoritarian and one-way. The Schwab campaign, in contrast, assumes a basic equality between advisor and advisee and welcomes the customer into a conversation. It is reflective of the new reality in which consumers insist on being both engaged and respected.

The Leader of Tomorrow (LOT) will understand these new rules of engagement:

- Keep consumers in the loop
- Let them know you "get it"
- Be part of the conversation
- Give consumers a role to play

Keep Consumers in the Loop

We have already established that today's proactive consumers are more interested in businesses and brands, and know more about them. They expect companies to respect and cater to that increased interest. The Future of the Corporate Brand found that around eight in ten respondents agreed that businesses need to maintain a dialogue with consumers and keep them informed and educated. Three-quarters think companies need to be completely open and transparent in their dealings with consumers. And six in ten actually believe public opinion should drive a company's conduct and overall strategy.[45]

Satisfying these demands will require more than simply increasing the volume of communications; companies need to reevaluate both tone and content. Today's marketing-savvy (often cynical) consumers are less likely to be seduced by slick or hollow words, preferring messaging that acknowledges their intelligence and understanding. And they are quick to recognize when actions fall short of words. It is essential, therefore, to avoid overpromising. Smart companies will either raise the level of what they deliver to match their promises or lower the level of promises to match what they are capable of delivering.

Being candid about shortcomings increases credibility and likability—both of which are vital to consumer engagement. Patagonia understands the best way to keep faith with its customers—and stave off accusations of greenwashing—is to reveal the whole truth about its products and practices. The company's online Footprint Chronicles lets visitors track a rotating set of ten products from design through delivery and highlights the "good" and the "bad" of each item. For instance, it points out that the shell of the Talus jacket is highly breathable and can be recycled through the company's Common Threads program, but it also acknowledges the water-repellent finish contains perfluorooctanoic acid (PFOA) and that the fabric, trim, zipper, and zipper pulls are not made of recycled content. Such honesty communicates the company's commitment to constant improvement and lets customers know they are working toward the same goals.

Let Them Know You "Get It"

It is never enough to fake empathy or understanding; prosumers' B.S. detectors are permanently set on high. This means it is more important than ever to understand one's customers as individuals and communicate with them as such.

There was a lot of talk in the world of marketing in mid-2008 about an experiment undertaken by a small relationship-marketing group called Unit 7. For fourteen weeks, more than three dozen employees lived their lives as though they had just been diagnosed with Type 2 diabetes. That meant three months of daily finger-prick blood tests, mandatory exercise, avoiding sweets and other proscribed foods, and becoming educated about the debilitating effects of the disease. Though some industry insiders dismissed the experiment as a publicity stunt, staffers involved claim to have come away from the experience with a far better understanding of what diabetics go through in the early stages of the disease, an understanding intended to help the agency's pharmaceutical clients better communicate with—and meet the needs of—their customers.

One senior copywriter at Unit 7 told *Brandweek* the experience has caused him to approach his job with a greater sense of humanity—and not just when dealing with diabetics. When he was later tasked with writing some hospital-discharge literature, he found he thought more about the people who would be reading his words and what they would be going through at that time: "I thought, 'These people just had a heart attack. What do they really want to hear?' I felt really connected to them. It was weird."[46]

In difficult economic times, especially, people want to know the companies with which they do business are cognizant of the pressures they are under and can relate to the attendant fears. In 2009, Hyundai Motor America began offering buyers a twelve-month protection plan, during which customers could return a car without penalty if they underwent a significant life event (involuntary job loss or personal bankruptcy, if self-employed; a job transfer overseas; or accidental death). In any of those cases, the carmaker would pay the difference between the car's trade-in value and the remaining balance on the loan, up to $7,500.[47] Regardless of how many people ultimately make use of the protection policy, it sends a clear message that the automaker understands consumers' reluctance to pull the trigger on major purchases at a time when layoffs are rampant, and it lets them know their fears are not being dismissed. Other companies in a range of industries, from GM and Ford to Virgin Mobile and Lennar home builders, soon followed suit with their own "pink slip" protection policies.

Be Part of the Conversation

The rapid growth of the Internet and blogs, in particular, has given corporations a valuable way to maintain a running conversation with customers and the general public. The smartest corporate leaders are taking advantage of that access. Approximately seventy-five Fortune 500 companies are currently producing blogs to reach the attentive public directly, typically written by a senior executive.

Procter & Gamble maintains an ongoing conversation with half a million mothers through Vocalpoint, an arm of its buzz-marketing division, Tremor. We spoke with Tremor CEO Steve Knox about the program and how its value has grown over time. In addition to using Vocalpoint for its own portfolio of brands, P & G sells the service to other companies.

"For the longest time," Steve told us, "companies operated under the assumption that they called the shots, but it was a false sense of control. The reality is, consumers have always had the last word, and today they have even more control thanks to the new tools at their disposal."[48]

The Vocalpoint unit was conceived to take advantage of the power of word of mouth. If P & G could get influential women—whom the company calls "connectors"—to chat up its products, the buzz would spark an increase in sales. It's a pretty basic premise, and one that has been proved true by companies in every consumer industry. What P & G quickly came to recognize is that, for the program to work, the moms need to be able to direct the conversation. They have to be able to choose what matters to them personally, and they need to feel some sense of ownership over the process.

Steve gave us the example of Gillette's Venus Breeze razor. As one might expect in the personal-care category, the advertising was focused on how the razor can help women "unleash the goddess within." That sort of messaging can be effective, but it is not how real women speak to one another. The Vocalpoint panelists chose instead to recommend the product to others on the basis of the quality of the shave. Once they used the sample product Vocalpoint mailed to them, these women discovered the razor was so good, it didn't require the use of lotion after shaving—a huge benefit, in their opinion.

One of the most important aspects of his job, says Steve, is to ensure his company and its panelists build a relationship based on trust and mutual respect. "The truth is," he says, "women choose not to have a relationship with most brands. Why would they want to feel connected to some product or other that plays such a small role in their lives? It is our job as marketers to make that role more significant by creating emotional connections."[49]

Creating a meaningful relationship, according to Steve, requires three components:

- There must be a *shared dialogue*, in which both sides are allowed to disagree.
- There must be *shared and remembered experiences*. "People may not remember what they talked about with a friend last week, but they can recount all the details of a shared trip to Colorado Springs ten years earlier," Steve explains. "It is these shared experiences that enable a relationship to grow. It is up to the brand to provide them."
- The final element may also be the most controversial, says Steve: A true relationship requires *shared values*. "We are not seeking a relationship with all our customers," he says, "just with those connectors who make sense for our business."[50]

Maintaining a conversation with customers is arguably even more important in industries plagued by customer-service complaints.

The cable-television industry is certainly one of them, and Comcast Corporation has been a primary target of criticism. There are a plethora of blogs in which people detail the reasons they hate Comcast, and even dedicated sites (e.g., Comcastsucks.org). Rather than ignore the online attacks, Comcast decided in 2008 to take action in a positive way. The company created a seven-person "cyberteam" in its Philadelphia headquarters and charged them with scouring the Internet for complaints against the company and then doing everything they could to help resolve the matters. Rather than be defensive, team members were instructed to accept blame, apologize, and offer their assistance. At least one formerly angry customer was won over: Bob Garfield, a columnist at *Advertising Age* who had created a site called Comcastmustdie.com, was sufficiently impressed by Comcast's efforts that he shut down the site. "My work is done," Garfield explained to *USA Today*. "They're discovering it's to their benefit in many ways to try to start conversations instead of dictating the terms of service."[51] Comcast had discovered that, in the new environment, humility trumps hubris.

Give Consumers a Role to Play

Putting consumers at the core of a brand is about more than customizing communications and soliciting feedback. More and more, consumers are looking to develop closer relationships with brand partners, whether by serving as brand evangelists, contributing to product ideation and design, or even creating branded content. LOTs will actively encourage this involvement by creating formal "ambassador programs" (as such companies as Maker's Mark and Corazonas, maker of "heart healthy" snacks, already do), offering opportunities for customization and creative input (Jones Soda lets consumers submit photos for its labels and purchase custom cases), and inviting them to take part in collaborative efforts.

It is always valuable to let customers know their opinions matter. That may be especially easy to do in the arena of CSR. American Express has enjoyed great success with its Member Project, which asks cardholders to determine the beneficiary of a large charitable contribution. Over the course of the first project, in 2007, one and a half million unique visitors went to the AmEx website to submit, discuss, rate, and ultimately vote on the project they wanted the company to bring to life. The winner: "Children's Safe Drinking Water."

Consequently, the U.S. Fund for UNICEF was awarded $2 million to bring clean water to millions of children in the developing world. In 2008, the Alzheimer's Association was awarded $1.5 million, while the other four finalists split an additional $1 million.

For companies in virtually every industry, doing business in the twenty-first century and beyond will entail a new, more humanized approach to both long-term strategy and day-to-day operations. Where once brand values were seen as an adjunct—something to append to an annual report—now they must be manifest throughout the corporate brand. In the next section, we offer direction on how companies can best achieve that goal.

Part II

REINVENTING CORPORATE CULTURE

Chapter Four

THE CORPORATE BRAND OF THE FUTURE AND THE REWARDS OF REPUTATION

What you do speaks so loud that I cannot hear what you say.

—Ralph Waldo Emerson

Emerson had it right: Today's companies are judged by the totality of their actions. Now that corporations are expected to behave as full-fledged local and global "citizens," no aspect of what they do or say can be considered beyond the reasonable scrutiny of the consuming public.

In recent years, myriad articles, studies, and books have expounded on the value of a strong corporate reputation. Reputation has been shown to affect how a company is perceived both internally and externally, and to influence such factors as:

- Employee retention and hiring
- Product and service pricing
- Investor preference
- Vulnerability (a sterling reputation can serve as a protective barrier in times of crisis)
- Credibility and trust
- Relationships with journalists, regulators, and NGOs
- Market capitalization

With regard to the latter, reputation has been found to account for as much as 75 percent of the gap between a company's book value and market cap.[1] In a fascinating study of the value of perception conducted in 2007, Communications Consulting Worldwide established that if Wal-Mart had the reputation of Target, its stock price would rise 4.9 percent, boosting its market value by $9.7 billion. Similarly, Coca-Cola would see its share price rise 3.3 percent if it had the reputation of Pepsi, and CVS would enjoy an increase of 6.9 percent if it had the reputation of its rival Walgreens.

Clearly, there is a correlation between how a company is perceived and what it can hope to achieve. American International Group found that out the hard way in late 2008 when the entire conglomerate suffered a liquidity crisis brought on by the downgrading of its credit rating. Much of the blame for that downgrade has been placed on one London-based unit of the company, but the subsequent near-bankruptcy, government bailouts, and public outrage over huge bonuses paid to executives during the collapse tarnished the entire organization, including its corporate brand.

In March 2009, Mary Williams Walsh commented in the *New York Times:*

> The problem now is not a toxic spiral of derivatives like the one that crippled the company last fall, but the damage done to A. I. G.'s brand, first by the financial troubles and then by the recent wave of hearings, subpoenas, late-night television jokes and even a bus tour past executives' homes. A strong brand is something no insurer can afford to put at risk. Insurance companies trade, more than anything else, on their image of strength and stability.[2]

At the time of this writing, A. I. G. is in the midst of rebranding its insurance operations as A. I. U. Holdings, Inc., with analysts appearing mixed on whether swapping in "Underwriters" for "Group" in the brand name will be sufficient to permit its resurrection. For now, the company stands as a cautionary tale of how quickly a giant can be felled and how the loss of reputation can wound a brand far more gravely than any financial crisis.

So, just what does it take to earn and maintain a reputation capable of offering some level of protection in times of crisis? Much has been written about the impact on reputation of such business fundamentals as product quality, customer service, and financial performance. It's inarguable that each of those components is vital to brand strength. Yet the answer also lies in how a company treats people (talent, consumers, communities) and the environment, and the extent to which it demonstrates a clear vision and purpose beyond profit. In other words, in how well it adheres to the four cornerstones we laid out in Chapter Three. Each of these factors will have a direct bearing on how the company is perceived by its various stakeholders and on the protection that will afford it in darker times.

In this chapter, we will explore the vital steps the Conscious Corporation will take to build and protect its reputation, with an emphasis on how Leaders of Tomorrow (LOTs) are turning corporate social responsibility (CSR) into a source of power and protection for the brand.

NEW GAME, NEW RULES

Take a look in your pantry or bathroom cabinet. What do you know about the companies that make the products you buy? We are willing to bet you know a whole lot more about them than you did five years ago. In all likelihood, your children and grandchildren will know even more about their favorite products, because they will make it their business to know.

In Chapter Two, we discussed the greater interest consumers are taking in the companies with which they do business. Knowing more about corporate brands creates a deeper sense of connection and, in some instances, even a feeling of ownership. As we were in the process of writing this book, one of the authors noted the pride with which his wife confided in a close friend that the matching outfits her three young daughters were wearing had been purchased at Target. In part, her pride stemmed from having found stylish dresses at an economical price—making her a smart consumer. But would she have felt the same had the clothing been purchased at a less highly regarded discount retailer? Likely not, because she and her friend might associate that brand with inferior quality, sub-par working conditions, or some other negative. Clearly, Target has done a superior job of setting itself above much of the discount category. It has done so by successfully communicating its point of differentiation ("Expect More. Pay Less"), along with the very strong underlying notion that every consumer is entitled to great design, regardless of income bracket.

Once this woman had sufficient evidence of the truth behind the brand claims, she began to internalize and convey the brand messages to others, thereby serving, intentionally or not, as a brand ambassador. By vocalizing her relationship with the brand, the ambassador, in turn, feels an even stronger sense of connection to it—and more of a stake in how the brand behaves going forward. She will want Target to justify her support by behaving responsibly, even admirably.

It would be difficult to overstate the impact engaged consumers are having on companies today. Consumers are not only more powerful, they also have more ways to insert themselves into a brand's business. Peter Sieyes, global digital and relationship marketing director at the U.K. headquarters of alcoholic beverages company Diageo, has come up with a great way to conceptualize the changed relationship between people and brands, and the effect that is having on marketing communications. In the past, he told us, managing communications was like bowling: "We would roll the ball (marketing message) at the designated target and could vary the speed and curve depending on the situation. Typically, we would hit all the pins we wanted, in essence creating a halo for the corporate brand." Within that dynamic, message diffusion was linear, and the marketer had near total control. Today, in contrast, Peter says, "marketing communications is more like pinball. Yes, we still get to release the ball, but now our messages get 'jolted' by consumer groups, bloggers, and the like. Consumers are controlling the conversation, deciding which aspects interest them and adding their own spin."[3]

On the surface, the new game format may seem like a step back for companies, but this is not how Peter perceives it. In his words, "At Diageo, we are fascinated by this new game and the opportunity it represents. There are now multipliers on the table, which means we can get more points if the context is appropriate and relevant, and if it offers a compelling message about the brand. This new ability to fuel conversations with online content and communication can prove a huge advantage for brand marketers willing to take the time—and care—to do it right."[4]

With respect to reputation management, this pinball analogy serves as an important reminder of how difficult it can be to anticipate the trajectory of any action or communication. Today's proactive consumers have all sorts of ways to assert influence and even control. And there is no guarantee an action intended to bolster a company's reputation will not have the opposite effect. As Elizabeth Spiers, founder of Dealbreaker.com, told us, it can be immensely difficult for larger, more traditional companies to adjust to these new realities. "Larger companies, in particular, are not used to being transparent about their practices," she says, "so this change has really taken them by surprise. They are used to having to manage their image with regard to a very specific class of people: professional journalists, who fact-check everything and who understand how to interact with corporations on a professional level. When you have people who are essentially amateurs doing the same thing, your ability to control your message directly is reduced immeasurably."[5]

In an era in which senior managers cite risk to reputation as the greatest threat facing global companies (above regulatory, human capital, information technology, market, and credit risk),[6] it is imperative that the Leaders of Tomorrow understand how to communicate and interact with all stakeholders and prevent corporate messaging from being twisted or ignored. This requires putting into place a reputation program that is ceaselessly proactive and integrated throughout the company.

REPUTATION MANAGEMENT IN THE ERA OF THE CONSCIOUS BRAND

There are all sorts of theories as to how best to protect or restore corporate reputation. What is now crystal clear is that reputation cannot be an adjunct priority, relegated to the care of a public relations firm or crisis-communications team. Reputation must be an ongoing focus, seen as vital to the everyday health of the company and to its chances of accomplishing its long-term mission and vision.

In our work with different industries and with all sorts and sizes of companies, we have come to view the following actions as essential to success:

- Find the right fit
- Commit the appropriate resources
- Build alliances and get your halo certified
- Be ever vigilant
- Be loud and proud
- Keep pushing forward
- Get consumers involved

At its very core, the Conscious Corporation will understand it matters less what top executives and board members intend the company to be than what internal talent and outside stakeholders *perceive* it to be.

Find the Right Fit

> The cause orientation is important. It's not enough just to send a check to the Susan G. Komen Foundation; you have to choose your enemy. If you're a pharmaceutical company, it could be disease. If you're a food company, it could be hunger. It can be poverty if you're a technology company. And then demonstrate your commitment in actuality and help people, empower people to fight alongside you. Your brand can do this, your company can do this. Empower people to be a part of the change they want to see.
>
> —Bruce Haynes, managing partner, National Media Inc.[7]

Every action a company takes—or doesn't take—has the potential to affect the regard in which it is held. Activities with a clear cause focus will not help build a brand to the same extent as such fundamentals as product quality, operational efficiency, and customer relationship management; when part of a larger purpose, however, cause marketing can be an incredibly effective way to engage consumers and other stakeholders on an emotional level. The issue, for many, is how to do it right.

First and foremost, the value of CSR initiatives will be predicated on how good a fit the cause is for the company and the business it is in. Is it a good thing KPMG and Home Depot support breast-cancer research? Without a doubt. But think how much more value Avon reaps as a result of Walk for the Cure and other initiatives aimed at eradicating the disease. The partnership fits Avon because it is a women-centered company that has long espoused female empowerment, self-sufficiency, and mutual support. The tens of thousands of women who have "walked for the cure" embody the very values on which the business has been built.

The more distant a company's cause-related activities are from its core business, the less impact they are likely to have on how the company is perceived. We can all name some supporters of the Product (RED) campaign, including The Gap and American Express, but we would be hard-pressed to connect those brands in a meaningful way to the fight against HIV and AIDS in Africa.

Done right, the socially conscious focus of a company will not simply make sense; it will actually help the corporate brand to grow bigger than the business it is in. Consider how, over the course of a few years, MTV managed to transform itself from a broadcaster of music videos into a key player—arguably *the* key player—in the "youth activism" business. Similarly, with "Just Do It" and its youth-empowerment programs, Nike has transcended the athletic shoes and apparel category to become a champion of human potential.

Larger companies with broad portfolios need to be especially careful to ensure there is no disconnect in messaging between one brand and the next. Even as many people have applauded Unilever for Dove's "Real Beauty" campaign, others have condemned it as hypocritical because of the rather opposite messaging used in the company's campaigns for Axe deodorant for men.

One final point about the "right fit": The savvy corporation will keep in mind all aspects of the environment in which it operates. Patrick Doyle, president of Domino's USA, spoke with us about his concern for the environment and steps his company has taken to be more ecologically mindful, including installing vastly more efficient pizza ovens. He told us the U.S. market is unusual in its reliance on automobiles to deliver pizzas to homes; other markets typically use more eco-friendly motorcycles or scooters. Domino's hopes the time will come when its deliverers can make their rounds in hybrid or electric cars. But Patrick does offer one small caveat: His Michigan-based company will make it a point to buy local if at all possible.[8]

Commit the Appropriate Resources

Building a genuine and sustainable CSR program takes time, money, and the motivated commitment of the C-suite. In Chapter Three, we referred to GE's wide-ranging ecomagination initiative and its publicly declared goals to increase revenues from eco-conscious products to $25 billion in 2010 while also significantly reducing greenhouse gas (GHG) emissions and improving energy efficiency.

One of the most noteworthy aspects of ecomagination is the story of its origins. In 2001, GE shareholders put forth a resolution calling on the company to report its GHG emissions and consider reducing them. The resolution was defeated, which might have been cause for celebration and a return to business as usual at a less forward-thinking company. GE took a different approach: Having already considered a GHG audit, the company decided to conduct one the following year. Three years later, in 2005, CEO Jeffrey Immelt announced ecomagination and has served ever since as the very visible face of the initiative—in interviews and marketing communications, and online.

GE has signaled its long-term commitment to the initiative in three ways: by involving top talent, by allocating sufficient funds to turn best intentions into reality, and by publicly stating very specific goals and inviting the public to monitor its progress. Each quarter, GE's vice presidents for ecomagination and environmental affairs report to the CEO about the company's progress toward its eco-goals. The company has committed to investing $1.5 billion in ecomagination research and development by 2010 (in 2007, it invested in excess of $1 billion in cleaner-technology R & D),[9] and it works to keep the public informed through an annual ecomagination report, a dedicated website (ecomagination.com), global conferences and events, and advertising.

We sat down with Beth Comstock, a longtime GE executive who currently serves as chief marketing officer. She told us, "From the start, it was clearly our CEO, Jeff Immelt, leading the charge. Thanks to his drive and the willingness of the executive team to direct sufficient resources to this initiative, ecomagination has truly morphed into far more than we originally thought possible. When we started the program, we felt we needed to inform—our investors, our talent, our suppliers, our customers, and the general public—whereas today it is all about engagement and sustaining our momentum."[10]

Given the success of ecomagination, GE announced "healthymagination" in May 2009; the new initiative is being built on the ecomagination model and is aimed at improving healthcare through the better use of technology. The company has committed $6 billion to the effort over six years, including $3 billion in R & D, $2 billion in financing for advancing healthcare IT in rural and underserved areas, and $1 billion for related partnerships, media content, and services.[11]

Build Alliances and Get Your Halo Certified

Throughout this book, we touch on the increased value of collaboration in a world that is ever more complex and competitive. When we look at the companies that have achieved greatest success in bolstering their reputations—and results—through CSR activities, we find a common thread: alliances forged with key stakeholders and organizations on the outside.

GE knew going into its ecomagination planning that opposition from environmentally focused NGOs could slow its momentum or even prevent the company from reaching its goals. Smartly, Jeffrey Immelt and other executives did not wait until after the program was developed to get buy-in from environmentalists; instead, they opened a dialogue with key influencers during the development phase to ensure the program was on the right track and to take advantage of their specialized knowledge.

"Initially, we reached out to NGOs, looking for their help," explains Beth Comstock. "Admittedly, they had some real issues they wanted us to address. At the time, there were specific concerns, such as the presence of harmful PCBs (Polychlorinated Biphenyls) in New York's Hudson River. For GE, we found that simply listening went a long way. We also built an eco–advisory board, which has been invaluable to us. This group of savvy sustainability experts and businesspeople now helps us determine which technology investments we should be making, and they help us ensure our overall scorecards are clean and accurate."[12]

One of the people GE recruited to help guide ecomagination was highly regarded environmental and business blogger Joel Makower, working with the New York–based consultancy GreenOrder. Commenting on Jeff Immelt's announcement of the new initiative, Joel called ecomagination "a textbook approach to what a major corporate sustainability effort can look like" and applauded Jeff's "willingness to put his company out front of the debate in a very visible way."[13] By inviting key influencers into the process and by working with them to address their valid concerns, GE was able to turn potential opponents into stalwart allies in a genuine and respectful way.

Allies can come in all shapes and sizes. In 2007, a company called Burt's Bees caught the attention of The Clorox Company and was promptly acquired by it for $913 million. Not a bad price for a little maker of natural personal-care products. By that point, Burt's Bees had made a name for itself as a company serious about its customers and the benefits of living life in the most natural way possible. As would be expected, its purchase by a global corporation best known for its bleach cleaners raised both eyebrows and no small amount of alarm among its customers.

John Replogle, president and CEO of Burt's Bees, took an important step to make the transition more palatable: He simply continued a practice he had instituted early in his career. When a customer calls him and leaves a phone number, he calls the person back. That's pretty astonishing for a man in his position, but John has learned that engaging with people is an excellent way to win over customers for life. He acknowledges that his call volume spiked before and during the Clorox acquisition and that most callers were eager to express their displeasure at the company's "selling out." John listened to what each person had to say and then asked him or her to judge the company not by any preconceived notions of what the sale would mean, but by its actions going forward. In the first year after the sale, John reports, most people's concerns were put to rest, and many previously disgruntled bloggers began to praise the company for staying true to its values, thereby strengthening the halo over the brand.

The strategic acquisition of Burt's Bees provided Clorox with more than a fantastic set of products; it also gave the company an inroad into an eco-conscious subculture that has grown into a broad-reaching and powerful consumer group. Through this purchase, Clorox signaled its desire to enter the rapidly growing natural-products category and to gain the benefit of Burt's Bees' experience and insights in this area. (It had outbid rivals Unilever and SC Johnson for that right.)

We watched with interest in 2008 when Clorox launched its first new brand in twenty years: Green Works, a line of natural cleaners. Two years earlier, Donald R. Knauss, CEO of Clorox, had named "health and wellness" and "sustainability" as two macro trends with the potential to grow Clorox as part of the company's Centennial Strategy, so the move to natural cleaning products was not entirely unexpected. Nevertheless, Don recognized the company would face an uphill battle and charges of "greenwashing" because it was not yet an established player in the naturals space. The Green Works line boasts of being at least 99 percent natural, biodegradable, nontoxic, made from plant- and mineral-based ingredients (rather than petroleum), and of not being tested on animals. To assure consumers and influencers these claims were genuine, Don needed backup from trusted players in the "green" domain. So, he sought the endorsement of two powerful environmental groups: the Environmental Protection Agency (EPA) and Sierra Club, the oldest and largest grassroots environmental organization in the United States. Beginning in April 2008 (just in time for Earth Day), Green Works packaging began carrying the seal of the Sierra Club (in return for which Clorox pays the organization an undisclosed fee based partly on sales). In addition, four of the five products carry the EPA's "Design for the Environment" seal, indicating they are made from environmentally preferable ingredients.

Don Knauss, John Replogle, Jeff Immelt, and other enlightened leaders take seriously the influence of outside stakeholders and make every effort to work with them rather than be forced to defend against them. With three in four consumers saying their purchasing decisions are influenced by NGOs,[14] it must be a priority of the LOT to build positive working relationships with those who would seek to influence the policies and practices of the company.

Be Ever Vigilant

> Regard your good name as the richest jewel you can possibly be possessed of—for credit is like fire; when once you have kindled it you may easily preserve it, but if you once extinguish it, you will find it an arduous task to rekindle it again. The way to gain a good reputation is to endeavor to be what you desire to appear.
>
> —Socrates

The Conscious Corporation will routinely monitor risks to its reputational health and well-being, for a reputation built over many years can be destroyed virtually overnight. Smart companies are shifting from a defensive stance to a broader, more offensive mode in which the company constantly assesses its standing and seeks out opportunities to strengthen its bonds of trust with consumers and others.

Part of staying on the offensive means monitoring the blogosphere and other channels of communication. It is becoming increasingly common for companies to spend money on image research, oftentimes hiring such firms as Factiva and Datamonitor to track databases (print publications, blogs and online forums, social networks, etc.) and search for trends in coverage and conversation. Such information gives the company early warning of any potential chinks in its reputational armor.

What happens once a chink appears? There are all sorts of ways to respond. Earlier in the book, we mentioned the proactive approach JetBlue founder and CEO David Neeleman took in speaking directly to the public via YouTube in the aftermath of the airline's 2007 PR fiasco. The video was more than an apology for passengers being stranded for hours on the tarmac; it detailed major changes the company would be making as a result of the event and even included timelines for instituting these actions.

McDonald's is another company that recognizes that damage to one's reputation cannot be corrected with PR spin or cosmetic changes; the underlying problem must be corrected. In 2004, the fast-food giant faced a version of a chief risk officer's worst nightmare. It came in the form of the release (and popularity) of the Morgan Spurlock documentary *Super Size Me*. The movie documents the deleterious physical and psychological effects Spurlock underwent while on a McDonald's-exclusive diet. Among other results, the filmmaker gained just under twenty-five pounds during the month-long experiment and experienced mood swings, sexual dysfunction, and liver damage.[15] An international discussion about obesity, poor nutrition, and the culpability of McDonald's ensued—not exactly the sort of publicity a fast-food company pines for.

What interests us about this case is what came next. Rather than simply frame the situation as "consumers' choice" (though the company did make that argument), McDonald's discontinued its super-sized fries and drinks and began adding more healthful choices to its menus. Though the company denies the former decision had anything to do with the film, it was a smart move for a business that has built its brand as a place for "food, folks, and fun," and that historically has supported children's health and wellness through Ronald McDonald House and other initiatives.

In the years since *Super Size Me* came out, McDonald's has taken a number of steps to improve its nutritional reputation. Among them, it has put into place a Global Advisory Council of independent health experts to advise the company in the areas of nutrition and children's well-being; it provides nutrition information on tray liners and in brochures in all its restaurants in its nine largest markets; and it has instituted new marketing guidelines that require that communications to children be centered on the benefits of physical activity and making balanced food choices.

Will McDonald's ever be considered the Whole Foods of fast food? Perhaps not. The point is that the company is taking positive steps in response to changing consumer needs and social and political pressures, and it is doing so in a way that is right for the brand. The Conscious Corporation does not wait for regulators to mandate change; it leads its industry in identifying and correcting problems that are holding it back.

Be Loud and Proud

In today's crowded marketplaces, retailers in particular face the dilemma of how to stand out from the crowd. How does a grocery store differentiate itself from a competitor down the street? They both carry the same six-packs of Pepsi, Sara Lee bread, and Life Savers. Price differences tend to be a matter of pennies rather than dollars. Sophisticated retailers such as Safeway step up to the challenge by offering superior in-store service and proprietary brands, and by implementing best-in-class logistics, which means fresher products for customers.

We spoke with Mike Minasi, president of marketing for this megaretailer, which employs nearly 200,000 workers. He told us, "At Safeway, the brand and the company are the same. Unlike P & G, which markets many product brands like Tide and Pampers, everything we do reflects directly on our corporate brand. Part of the DNA of the Safeway culture is our commitment to healthcare and to diversity, on both of which we continually receive high marks from the industry. Unfortunately, consumers rarely hear about it, as we walk a very fine line; typically we have not focused a great deal of our communication on our CSR efforts."[16]

So Safeway, like many other well-respected corporate brands, prefers an understated approach to corporate social responsibility and living its values. And that is to be admired. In our view, however, the brands that will derive greatest benefit (reputational and otherwise) from their values-led policies and practices are those that take a highly visible and leading role on the issues they care about.

And consumers agree. Euro RSCG's The Future of the Corporate Brand study revealed that nearly three-quarters of consumers (73 percent) think it is a positive thing for businesses to publicize their CSR activities, charitable contributions, and other good deeds. Now that social responsibility is one of the criteria against which consumers judge brands, it is only logical they want to stay informed about what their brand partners are doing. The most value goes to those companies that take bold stances and earn some degree of ownership over an issue. Think: Toyota and alternative energy or Apple and individualism.

We were impressed recently with the actions of Hiller's Markets, Inc.—a little company that acted in a big way. Jim Hiller, the CEO of this small chain of neighborhood grocery stores across eastern Michigan, decided to eliminate all sales of cigarettes because of his concerns over the health consequences of secondhand smoke. "I've agonized over this decision," he told the *Oakland Press*. "My personal beliefs are intertwined in my business ethos and to continue to sell cigarettes runs contrary to my personal commitment to this community and its future."[17] He explained: "There are all kinds of vices and unhealthy products for sale—but cigarettes aren't only dangerous to those who smoke them.... The effects of cigarette smoke can kill people who live and work with smokers. Despite the rights of those who choose to smoke, I will not make Hiller's a fellow traveler."[18]

Jim Hiller acknowledges the move runs contrary to the advice of his chief financial officer and will cost the company "many hundreds of thousands of dollars,"[19] including thousands of dollars worth of cigarettes it threw out at the start of the new year.[20] "From economic implications, this is foolish," he says. "Those of us who care believe it's the right thing to do."[21]

Keep Pushing Forward

It is one thing for a company to set socially and/or environmentally progressive goals. It is quite another to keep extending the boundaries of its reach in that regard. The Conscious Corporation will always be looking for opportunities to do more.

There are some who will never be convinced of Wal-Mart's good intentions and will invariably dismiss any social or environmental contributions the company might make. Granted, it can be easy to find fault with the behemoth retailer in some areas, but we are genuinely impressed by the extent to which it has been attempting to align itself on the side of (profitable) good as part of its sustainability efforts.

On CNNMoney.com, journalist Marc Gunther wrote about how Wal-Mart, often lambasted as a bully, is now using its clout to help the global poor and protect the planet. He cites as an example the issue of the inhumane conditions under which child cotton pickers in Uzbekistan are forced to work. In spring 2008, Marc reports, nonprofit group As You Sow, the Calvert and Domini mutual fund groups, and other activist investors wrote to more than 100 retailers and manufacturers and asked them to trace the sources of the cotton they buy and to avoid cotton from Uzbekistan. Some companies, including Levi Strauss & Company and Target, agreed to the request, while others did not respond at all. Wal-Mart stood out not only by issuing a strongly worded public statement pledging to stop purchasing Uzbek cotton, but also by stepping in and helping to organize retail trade associations to pressure the Uzbek authorities to improve the lot of these children, many of whom were forced to miss school for months at a time to labor in the fields. Moreover, where other retailers claim it is virtually impossible to trace cotton to its source, Wal-Mart is now requiring all its suppliers of apparel and home furnishings to do so. As we well know, what Wal-Mart wants from suppliers, it typically gets—the effect, in this case, being that other retailers are likely going to face strong pressure to follow suit.

Pushing forward also means recruiting consumers and others to one's larger purpose. British retailer Marks & Spencer knew its extensive sustainability goals would require the engagement of its customers, especially in the area of minimizing the use of plastic bags. So, in 2006, when it launched its Plan A initiative (detailed in Chapter Three), it gave customers shopping bags "for life." If a bag wears out, M & S will replace it for free. A month after introducing that "carrot," the company upped the ante with a "stick": The stores began charging five pence per plastic bag, with proceeds going to charity. That was enough to spur many shoppers to think about the issue and make the move to reusable bags. The result: Food carrier bag use was down 14 percent in 2007/2008 compared with 2006/2007, despite a nearly 7 percent increase in company food sales.[22]

Get Consumers Involved

> The more a corporation can make itself alive to the people it is serving, the better it is, because it's the ultimate way of forming brand loyalty.
>
> —Margaret Carlson, chief political columnist, Bloomberg News, and Washington editor, *The Week*[23]

There are all sorts of approaches a company can take to involve people in its socially and eco-conscious activities. It can be as simple as donating a portion of a product's purchase price to a cause or as complex

as involving customers in Avon's two-day, thirty-nine-mile Walk for
Breast Cancer.

TOMS Shoes makes it easy for consumers to be "part of the solution": Every single customer is a charitable donor by default. In 2006,
Blake Mycoskie, a thirty-year-old entrepreneur and former professional tennis player, was playing polo in Argentina when he was struck
by the sight of children without shoes. Upon return to the United
States, he sold his interest in his laundry business and used the proceeds to hire a shoe designer from Nike and other staff. The concept
was simple: TOMS would produce espadrille-style shoes made largely
from sustainable materials, such as hemp and recycled bottle tops. For
each pair sold, a second pair would be donated to a child in need. In
2008 alone, some 200,000 pairs of shoes were donated to children in
Argentina, Africa, and the United States.[24]

Deriving optimal benefit from a purpose beyond profit is only
possible if customers and other stakeholders feel personally invested
in the cause. It is essential, therefore, that corporations communicate
a reason to care. The TOMS website (tomsshoes.com) educates visitors about a debilitating disease called podoconiosis, or endemic non-
filarial elephantiasis, which is marked by extreme swelling, ulcers, and
deformity of the feet and legs; the condition is entirely preventable
by wearing shoes. For $1,800, customers can accompany Blake and
his team on a "shoe drop" in Argentina, at which gatherings the volunteers have an opportunity to actually place shoes on the feet of the
child recipients.[25]

eBay has taken a more multipronged approach to involving consumers in its social responsibility efforts. In the words of founder
Pierre Omidyar, the online auction house was always intended to be
a "force for good."[26] The company prides itself on creating economic
opportunity for many, encouraging the reuse of goods, and enabling
paperless transactions and energy-efficient global communications
through its PayPal and Skype subsidiaries, respectively. Anyone who
uses these services contributes to sustainability to some extent or
another. However, eBay has also created opportunities for consumers to go a step further with three businesses it calls "social ventures":
MicroPlace.com, WorldofGood.com, and eBay Giving Works.

MicroPlace is a microlending service that connects residents of the
United States with the world's working poor as a way to help alleviate
poverty. With as little as one hundred dollars, Americans can invest in

one of a number of microfinance organizations that provide loans to the working poor. These loans enable the recipients to start their own small businesses, with the objective of moving them and their families out of poverty. In its first year, investors gave more than 26,000 loans to entrepreneurs, earning an average return on investment of +2 percent while the S & P Index returned −35.97 percent during the same period.[27]

In recent years, eBay has seen an increase in the number of so-called "good" products being sold on its site—everything from Fair Trade to organic or recycled goods. To support this trend, the company created WorldofGood.com. This eBay marketplace deals exclusively in socially responsible merchandise that has been verified by third-party "trust providers" to have a positive impact on people and the planet.[28]

The third social venture is made up of two sites: eBay Giving Works on eBay.com and eBay for Charity on eBay.co.uk. Sellers on these sites have the option of donating all or part of a sale to any of more than 15,000 certified nonprofits. Those organizations may also sell directly on the site to raise funds. Charity listings are marked with a special icon, enabling people to shop on behalf of a particular cause. To date, sales have generated more than $150 million for the causes they benefit.[29]

THINK SMALL, ACT SMALL—BUT IN A BIG WAY

> We believe in happy people making happy soap, putting our faces on our products and making our mums proud.
>
> —Lush's "We Believe…" statement[30]

In the business world of yesteryear, companies would simply hold up their "Doing Good Stuff" signs as they presented oversized checks to their charities of choice. Conspicuous philanthropy was in. The problem? Donations were not tied to any sort of larger corporate purpose. More often than not, social responsibility fell under the purview of PR practitioners, and efforts to be a better corporate citizen had more to do with staving off the regulators or charming the public than with any genuine desire to act in a more conscious and conscientious way.

So, what will the Conscious Corporation of tomorrow do differently? It will move CSR out of its adjunct position, choosing instead to infuse elements of social and environmental responsibility throughout its operations, from human-resource practices and customer service to supply chains, retail venues, and packaging. And it will listen and respond to conversations taking place about the corporation and its brand equities and weaknesses.

In working with clients, we have had occasion to advise companies to "think small and act small, but in a big way." What we mean is it is not grand gestures that build a corporate reputation over time (though they can be of great value), but the individual decisions and actions that are the lifeblood of the organization. Even the most visionary corporate plans need a solid foundation—and the leadership and other talent, plus the company's policies, practices, and principles, must support the full weight of corporate promises.

We also include the directive "think small" to remind others—and ourselves—of those communities that have bred some of the most influential and paradigm-changing brands of our time. Have you ever noticed how many highly regarded businesses were born in small towns and coastal cities? To name just a few: Ben & Jerry's (Burlington, Vermont), Nike (Beaverton, Oregon), Apple (Cupertino, California), and Tom's of Maine (Kennebunk, Maine). It struck us that these companies benefited greatly from their origins in communities where people tend to know one another and take an interest in the activities of their neighbors and local businesses. It is no coincidence these brands so often refer to their roots as a key part of what makes them who they are.

Regardless of its provenance, the Conscious Corporation will behave as if it has a highly visible presence in a very small community. That means adopting such small-town values as playing fair, respecting others, and lending a helping hand as needed. As a rule of thumb, if you wouldn't want the folks down at the barber shop talking about it, you shouldn't be doing it.

The value of reputation has never been higher. Within any organization, ultimate responsibility for nurturing and protecting it must fall to the CEO. In the next chapter, we will explore how the most successful and influential Leaders of Tomorrow will prepare their companies to thrive under these new realities.

Chapter Five

WHAT IT TAKES TO BE A LEADER OF TOMORROW

Twenty-first century CEOs will be judged not only by how well they changed their industries, but also how well they led their companies to have positive impacts on the world.

—Hector Ruiz, chairman and CEO,
Advanced Micro Devices[1]

As the world changes, so do our ideas about leadership. Certain qualities that might have reaped rewards for a twentieth-century captain of industry—bravado, rigidity, an outsized personality—will likely be viewed as a detriment in the modern environment. Times have changed, and so have our expectations regarding how businesses should be run and how leaders should behave.

To divine what the future holds requires an understanding of the past and present. To that end, Euro RSCG Worldwide uses a proprietary semiotics tool, Decipher, to uncover those cultural cues and codes that, taken together, reveal patterns of actions, attitudes, and values. These patterns help us to recognize the emergence of new perspectives and behaviors, giving us powerful insights into the future.

If we use the Decipher process to look back over the U.S. business landscape since the nation's founding, we can see four clearly defined paradigms,[2] three of which have emerged in the last fifty years:

- *Paradigm One—Authoritarianism and Paternalism (1776–1950s):* The Founding Fathers (patriarchs modeled on European statesmen and monarchs) give birth to a new nation, establishing leadership qualities that will dominate the political and business arenas for the next two centuries. This is an era marked by an authoritarian management style, with an emphasis on patriotism, duty, and honor. The right credentials mean everything. Sample leaders of the era: Andrew Carnegie, Henry Ford, J. P. Morgan, John D. Rockefeller.

- *Paradigm Two—The Countercultural Revolution (1960s–1970s):* Young people rebel against the conservative norms of the 1950s, the oppression of the cold war era, and the U.S. presence in Vietnam. Socially, the call is for personal freedom, racial and gender equality, antimaterialism, and (to a lesser extent) respect for the planet. Politically, the call is for change. Sample leaders of the era: Hugh Hefner (*Playboy*), Ray Kroc (McDonald's), David Packard (Hewlett-Packard), Frederick W. Smith (FedEx).

- *Paradigm Three—American Dynasties (1980s–early 2000s):* The eighties are a time of conspicuous consumption and a business world fueled by power brokers, wealth, and excess. This era of hostile takeovers, leveraged buyouts, and mergers spawns a new breed of billionaire. Leadership is marked by cronyism, connections, and a sense of entitlement. Sample leaders of the era (real and fictional): J. R. Ewing (*Dallas*), Gordon Gekko (*Wall Street*), Leona Helmsley, Donald Trump, Ted Turner.

- *Paradigm Four—Global Visionaries (mid-2000s–?):* Starting with the high-profile entrepreneurs of the dot-com era, there is a gradual and now radical shift in leadership. Chief executives are increasingly looked to for their ability to solve complex global problems. It is no longer just about making money; leaders are expected to have vision, drive, and a capacity to inspire action. Sample leaders of the era: Sergey Brin and Larry Page (Google), Jeffrey Immelt (GE), John Mackey (Whole Foods).

That fourth paradigm, which is still in its emergent stage, has been made possible by new technologies and made necessary by society's newfound insistence on social responsibility. Technology gave us the free flow of information and ideas, citizen journalism (including a modern take on muckraking), and the power of social networking to make things happen. The push for social responsibility is a response to multiple crises—environmental (especially fear of global warming), humanitarian (refugees, genocide, poverty, health), and financial—and has been colored by the West's embrace of spirituality and volunteerism. More people have begun to think seriously about the world's interconnectedness and the imperative of looking out for one another.

At the same time, this new paradigm can be seen as a reaction against much of what we have witnessed in business and politics in recent decades. Namely: corruption, "cowboy diplomacy," sensationalism, destructive partisanship, manipulation (ruling through fear), economic disparity, and environmental abuse. The public is hungry for a new order in which character and hard work are rewarded and in which leaders motivate and engage rather than coerce.

Admittedly, it is a tough time to be a political leader, given the newly heightened expectations and seemingly insurmountable challenges. It is also an intensely challenging time to be a business leader. This chapter puts forth our vision of what it will take to be a Leader of Tomorrow in this altered environment.

THE KITCHEN IS HOT

Heavy hangs the head that wears the crown.

—Richard Parsons, former CEO, Time Warner[3]

Financial compensation aside, how many people would be interested in a job that offers the following?

- An average duration of forty-eight months
- Publicly listed compensation (subject to debate and scorn)
- The need to be on call day and night; hounded by the press at any hour
- Total accountability with less and less actual control

Being a CEO is not what it used to be. So, it may come as little surprise that nearly 1,500 chief executives of U.S. companies headed for the exits in 2008, according to data from Challenger, Gray & Christmas. That is an average of six every business day, the most since the executive-outplacement firm began conducting the survey in 1999. "CEOs are under intense pressure," comments John Challenger,

who heads the firm. "They have little room for error."[4] A majority
of these departures were voluntary, raising the question of whether
once-confident executives have a) lost their stomach for the job or b)
feel unqualified to lead their companies in such turbulent times.

In times past, corporate leaders were judged almost exclusively by
their impact on profits. For today's leaders, that would seem a luxury.
They still have to deliver stellar business results, of course, but there
is now the concomitant need to manage the so-called "softer" side of
business, including such spheres as sustainability, ethics, and culture.
To top it off, all of this must be conducted transparently, thereby opening up the executive to criticism from all quarters, inside the organization and out. As Cosmo Santullo, former head of SonicWall, put it:
"As a CEO, you have to worry about every aspect of the company and
every constituent, from analysts and the board to customers, and your
life isn't your own."[5]

As challenging as it might be to work with hostile boards, unsatis-
fied customers, and disappointed shareholders, those interactions may
prove the least of a CEO's worries. Everyone in the search industry has
heard personal horror stories about top executives and their families
being subjected to outrageous activist demonstrations. One woman
we know had to contend with "chicken rights" activists swarming her
home, picketing her community church, and even harassing her child
at school. Is it any wonder some leaders opt for an early departure?

In light of these new conditions, some might question why anyone would knowingly expose themselves (and their families) to these
pressure-cooker jobs. The draw of money, power, and position is unde-
niable, but even those benefits are losing their luster for some. Based
on the more than 500 global CEO searches it conducts each year,
the recruitment firm Spencer Stuart has found a growing reluctance
among top prospects to step in to the ring at highly visible companies.
Among their biggest concerns is the prospect of having to grapple
with increasingly powerful outside stakeholders, many of whom will
have divergent agendas.

Who are the men and women who can meet the laundry list of
expectations facing the modern-day CEO, including both growing the
business and satisfying the diverse requirements of myriad stakeholders? Throughout this book, we have referred to them as the Leaders
of Tomorrow, or LOTs. In how they act, how they think, and how
they engage people around them, these leaders are demonstrating the

value to be gained from aligning personal and corporate values, and drawing the company toward a future marked by both principles and profitability.

In this chapter, we look at some of the key characteristics that will set Leaders of Tomorrow apart—characteristics that go beyond such standard must-haves as strategic acumen, a global perspective, and operational capabilities. We are not suggesting with this list that all LOTs will move in lockstep, managing similar cultures and adopting like strategies. Without question, there will be enormous variation and individual evolution over time—such changes contribute to the strength of the capitalist system. We do believe, however, that the characteristics and behaviors we lay out in this chapter will be of increasing importance in an era in which more and more companies are recognizing the value of a more humanized approach to business.

BEYOND THE ROCK STAR: PLACING THE CORPORATE BRAND AT CENTER

Before we dive into the specific traits of the LOT, we think it is worth expressing a macro view of the space he or she will occupy within the company and the broader community. There is plenty of scope for debate over the relative value of "celebrity" CEOs versus their more media-absent counterparts. In recent years, we have seen some corporate "rock stars" run into resistance. Yet we cannot discount the tremendous value a high-profile CEO can have on the corporate brand. We think well of Berkshire Hathaway because of its enviable track record, but also because of Warren Buffett's honest and penny-pinching lifestyle. Wal-Mart founder Sam Walton had a similar impact on public sentiment. And certainly Bill Gates's philanthropic activities have cast a positive light on Microsoft, even though his humanitarian work is conducted entirely through his personal foundation.

There is a dangerous flip side, though, when the brand is all about the CEO, rather than vice versa. Bill Gates let us know early in the game that Microsoft was about far more than him and that he would not remain at the helm forever. Contrast that with Apple and Steve Jobs. Steve's almost messianic role within the tech community (despite having walked away from Apple for a dozen years) has made him arguably as big as the brand, if not bigger. It is not surprising, then, that his recurring health concerns in early 2009 sent shockwaves through the company's investor base. Even before these health issues were confirmed, *Fortune* reported: "There is only one Steve Jobs, one table-pounding visionary who can refashion whole industries with a wave of his hand. The mere hint of a Jobs health scare knocks billions of dollars off Apple's market value. (Temporary hit from a false Web post in early October about a Jobs heart attack: $10 billion.)"[6]

In our view, the optimal exposure for a LOT will strike a good balance between fame and facelessness. A CEO who occasionally appears on the cover of a business magazine and is well respected among analysts brings more strength—and less risk—to a company than an executive who hobnobs with the glitterati and is more apt to appear on Page Six of the *New York Post* than in the *Wall Street Journal*. There will always be charismatic founders who fuel their companies' momentum; going forward, however, we anticipate a shift in focus from the corporate leadership to the corporate brand. For, as we will discuss in Chapter Ten, it is the brand that must be a company's greatest source of strength going forward.

DEFINING CHARACTERISTICS OF THE LEADER OF TOMORROW

[T]he age of the authoritarian CEO is over, and chief executives today need to have the whole range of "softer skills." They need to be good listeners, consensus builders, ambassadors to the larger world, and leaders who others follow not because they have to, but because they want to.

—Joe Nocera, writing in the *New York Times*[7]

In introducing the concept of the Conscious Corporation, we have touched on companies in a variety of industries, from Ben & Jerry's to Whole Foods Market, from Marks & Spencer to GE and Burt's Bees. Thinking about the leaders who are driving these organizations toward a more conscious future, we have identified a number of characteristics that help to set them apart from leaders in more traditional, command-and-control cultures. Although this list is by no means exhaustive, we consider these four most worth noting. The LOT:

- Articulates a clear and compelling vision—and lives the brand values

- Establishes a foundation of trust
- Stays "real"
- Invites people in

The LOT Articulates a Clear and Compelling Vision—and Lives the Brand Values

> The primary task of leadership is to communicate the vision and the values of an organization. Second, leaders must win support for the vision and the values they articulate. And third, leaders have to reinforce the vision and the values.
>
> —Frederick Smith, chairman and CEO, FedEx[8]

In Chapters Eight and Nine, we will speak at length about the imperative of crafting a useful statement of a company's vision and then embedding that vision in the organization's day-to-day activities. It should go without saying that the Conscious Corporation will have a strong point of view about the business it is in and what it intends its impact to be. In order to ensure there is no disconnect between the corporate vision and reality, the LOT must not just extol that vision; he or she must embody it.

We spent time recently with Robert Redford, a man who wonderfully melds his interest in profits and his passion for the arts and the environment. Most people know Bob as the handsome Academy Award–winning actor who starred in such notable films as *Barefoot in the Park, Butch Cassidy and the Sundance Kid, The Sting,* and so many others. Some may be less familiar with the second chapter in his life: Four decades ago, Bob set in motion the Sundance group of companies. Under his careful watch and according to his vision, Sundance has grown into an innovative brand that proves the notion that a business can do well by doing good. Today, the Sundance Group oversees its founder's ownership interests in Sundance Village, Sundance Catalog, Sundance Channel, and Sundance Cinemas, as well as his involvement in the not-for-profit Sundance Institute, Sundance Film Festival, and Sundance Preserve.

We would argue that the Sundance brand benefits less from Bob's stardom than from his very personal and authentic commitment to the brand values of environmental sustainability, support for American craftspeople, and the development of new artists in independent film, music, dance, and theater. His credentials as a social and environmental activist stretch at least as far back as the early 1970s: Bob is a founding member of the Natural Resources Defense Council and has received numerous honors for his advocacy on behalf of the environment, the arts, and Native Americans, including the 1987 United Nations Environmental Programme (UNEP) Global 500 Award and the 1993 Earth Day International Award.

This is an instance in which the CEO, in some ways, *is* the brand, but the success of the business entities is no longer dependent on their founder's star wattage. The brand has grown to be bigger than the man behind it—which is precisely what Bob Redford intended. In his words: "To us, Sundance is and always will be a dream. What you see, smell, taste, and feel here is a dream being carefully nurtured. It is an area whose pledge is to people. What we offer in the form of art and culture, spirit and service, is homegrown and available to all."[9]

Since their inception, the Sundance companies have been committed to protecting the planet and promoting the welfare of its inhabitants. Though Bob is quick to admit there is still much room for improvement, it is evident the companies benefit greatly from the passion he brings and the example he sets as a private individual and as a business leader.

Few have been blessed with the public standing of Robert Redford, but every CEO must make full use of the opportunity to serve as at least the temporary face of the corporate brand. Former AT&T CEO Mike Armstrong got it exactly right when he told Entrepreneur.com:

> You've got to lead by example.... There are CEOs who get to love their office. You've got to get out into the markets. You've got to meet your customers. You've got to understand your competition. You've got to give the same speech too many times. You've got to go to the lunchbag forum with discipline. I write an article every month for the company newspaper. I do videotapes. I do company broadcasts. Communicate, communicate, communicate! You cannot be a remote image. You've got to be touched, felt, heard and believed. And you've got to stand up for what you stand for. When the company comes under attack—whether it's from Washington, the competition, or industry analysts—you've got to be out there, taking the brunt of whatever it is and lead by example.[10]

As Mike notes, it is critical for the CEO to actively embody the values and beliefs of the brand. In the absence of a strong personal connection between business goals and personal beliefs, the CEO cannot hope to bring an authentic—and motivating—passion to the brand. And that is imperative at a time when attaining the engaged commitment of internal and external stakeholders is crucial to business success.

We were struck by a comment made by Gerald Levin in announcing his retirement: "I want my identity back. I don't just want to be known as the CEO of AOL Time Warner....I'm my own person. I have strong moral convictions. I'm not just a suit. I want the poetry back in my life."[11]

But why must it be this way?

Within the Conscious Corporation, the top executive will bring his "strong moral convictions" to life within the talent and within the business and brand. We have all seen the alternative: Enron is a prime example of what can happen when the corporate leadership fails to connect a corporate code of ethics to the everyday activities of the company. Had the senior brass at Enron adhered to the company's clearly stated code, which espoused a culture of "respect, integrity, communication and excellence,"[12] and had they tied that code to employee performance ratings and compensation, a lot of retirees would not be out their life savings—and the company's top executives would have avoided prison terms.

Attracting other caring leaders into the organization
Our final point about living the brand values has to do with the hiring and management of talent. While we will delve deeper into internal policies and practices in the next chapter, we think it worth noting that the LOT must be ceaselessly cognizant of the messages he or she is sending with each and every personnel decision. As former EDS CEO Dick Brown put so nicely: "Leaders get the behaviors they tolerate."[13]

In writing this book, we had a chance to speak at length with Jim Kilts, whom Spencer Stuart placed as CEO of Gillette in 2001.[14] By all measures, Jim's impact on that company should earn him a place in the CEO hall of fame. His influence will extend well beyond his own career span because of the role he has played in shaping the next generation of leaders. Although the record books of those who have trained under him are still being written, Jim already has helped propel countless careers, including such respected names as Ricky Lenny (former CEO of The Hershey Company), Joe Scalzo (CEO of WhiteWave Foods), and Doug Conant (CEO of Campbell's Soup). These are but a few of Jim's disciples who are now creating their own positive ripple effects within the global business community.

In his recent book, *Doing What Matters*, Jim unveils many of his highly effective yet simple strategies and tactics for driving an energized culture of believers. He recognizes that with the right people, almost anything is possible, while with the wrong team, failure awaits. One piece of advice he gives up-and-coming business leaders: "Never hire a self-centered jerk—even a smart one." Arrogance and disregard for others can only lead to a contentious working environment, and that will in no way be "good for business." Likewise, the LOT will sniff out and change or remove any "Eeyores," those perpetual naysayers who find fault in every plan and who can single-handedly sap the energy from an entire department or office. There are too many good people out there to settle for executives and others who do not embody the humanized values of the brand. Enthusiasm and character matter.

In early 2009, we had a chance to attend a presentation by Tony Hsieh, the thirty-four-year-old CEO of e-tailer Zappos.com. Under his leadership, the company has seen its business grow from $1.6 million in sales in 2000 to more than $1 billion in 2008, achieved by a relentless focus on customer service. It is easy to be impressed by Zappos's success, but there is even more to admire about its approach to business and its emphasis on only retaining employees who will contribute in a positive way to its unique culture.

Infused into the company's DNA are ten core values:

1. Deliver WOW through service
2. Embrace and drive change
3. Create fun and a little weirdness
4. Be adventurous, creative, and open-minded
5. Pursue growth and learning
6. Build open and honest relationships with communications
7. Build a positive team and family spirit
8. Do more with less
9. Be passionate and determined
10. Be humble

Tony doesn't just pay lip service to these values; he expects employees to work according to the principles and be judged by them. Zappos has an unusual training process that begins with a four-week immersion in the company's strategy and culture. After the first week or so, each new employee is offered $2,000 to quit. The purpose is to weed out quickly those people who do not have the right commitment to the Zappos culture and goals. In 2008, only three recruits accepted the "bribe" and left.[15] Those employees who stay are judged by how well they adhere to the core values. As Tony Hsieh told Adweek.com, "We actually fire people if they're not living up to the Zappos core values, even if they're doing their job function. It's 50 percent of every performance review."[16]

Virgin Group was so impressed by Zappos's culture and financial results that it invited Tony for a visit to discuss his approach. His advice, as reported in *Forbes:* "Chase the vision. The money and profits will come."[17]

The LOT Establishes a Foundation of Trust

> Trust is like the air we breathe. When it's present, nobody really notices. But when it's absent, everybody notices.
>
> —Warren Buffett, chairman, Berkshire Hathaway[18]

An organization can only engender as much trust as the person who sits at its head. Over the course of its fifty-plus-year history, Spencer Stuart has installed CEOs for such leading companies as Boeing, Gillette, Starwood, and Carrefour, to name a few. As such, this worldwide leader in senior-level executive search often has a front-row seat from which to view the highs and lows of CEO placements—and the sometimes immediate impact those placements have on a company's fortune.

In 2005, Spencer Stuart saw Boeing's market capitalization increase nearly $2.5 *billion* from one business day to the next (see Chart 5.1). The reason for the marked increase in valuation? The installation of Jim McNerney, Jr. as chairman of the board, president, and CEO. Jim brought to the aerospace giant an impressive track record of growing businesses at such companies as 3M, GE, Procter & Gamble, and McKinsey & Company. By the time he took the top spot at Boeing, he had already established a reputation as someone who leads with honesty and integrity, viewing global corporate citizenship as a pathway to profits and growth rather than as an obstacle to be surmounted. This was one of those instances in which an individual's reputation

Company Name	Market Cap ($mm) [6/23/05]	Market Cap ($mm) [6/24/05]	Market Cap ($mm) [6/27/05]	Market Cap ($mm) [6/28/05]	Market Cap ($mm) [6/29/05]	Market Cap ($mm) [07/01/05]	Market Cap ($mm) [07/04/05]	Market Cap ($mm) [07/05/05]	Market Cap ($mm) [07/6/05]	Market Cap ($mm) [07/07/05]
Boeing Co. (NYSE:BA)	51,116.5	50,067.1	51,033.9	51,604.1	50,959.5	53,446.8	53,446.8	54,058.2	53,124.5	53,859.9
Announcement released 6/30/05				Change from day prior to announcement	4.88%	4.88%	6.08%	4.25%	5.69%	

Chart 5.1   The Financial Impact of Jim McNerney, Jr. Taking the Top Spot at Boeing
Source: Spencer Stuart.

and track record is so strong as to elevate the reputation of the entire organization: a vital characteristic of the LOT.

Restoring trust in Tyco

When the integrity of a single executive is called into question, the damage to the company can often be contained by separating that individual from the organization. But what if an entire organization's reputation is impugned along with that of the top leaders? Such was the case with industrial conglomerate Tyco International, which went from being one of the world's most admired companies to one of the most reviled as a result of bad decisions on the part of its once-celebrated CEO Dennis Kozlowski.

In 2002, the year Dennis Kozlowski and CFO Mark H. Schwartz resigned amid charges of theft and fraud, the board hired Edward Breen to take over as chairman and chief executive officer. Ed, also a Spencer Stuart placement, came to the company after having served with distinction as president and COO (chief operating officer) of Motorola. At that time, the Tyco board of directors was considering scrapping the company name all together. So much damage had been done that its members were unsure whether the company could be salvaged without a new brand identity. Research showed, however, that the Tyco brand still had powerful equity, especially in key categories such as electronics. The name was spared.

What happened next at the company is testament to Ed Breen and his bedrock conviction in the value of trust. Ed understood the only way to save the company would be to reestablish its credibility among three vital stakeholder groups: its retail customers, many of which no longer wanted to carry Tyco products; its employees, who had been embarrassed and demoralized by the scandal that landed their former

CEO and CFO in prison; and suppliers, who had lost faith in the viability of the former powerhouse. A lesser leader might have simply called for more stringent ethical guidelines and talked to the media about a new, more transparent era for the company. Ed Breen knew such measures would be inadequate. The corporate culture had been infected by the previous leadership's greed and ethical lapses, and that would need to be addressed before the company could move forward. Ed decided the best way to get rid of that infection would be to cut out the affected "limb." As there was really no way to determine which executives had been most deeply involved in the misdeeds of the former regime or could not make the necessary changes in culture, Ed and his team took no chances and fired the company's top 290 employees—clearly not a scenario for the faint of heart.

Although much of the blame for the company's financial woes was appropriately directed at the former top executives, serious questions were also being posed to the board: How could they have witnessed such out-of-control spending and not taken action? At the time Ed Breen came on board, GovernanceMetrics International, a director watchdog group, scored Tyco's board a 1.5 out of 10, the lowest score of any public company.[19]

Enter Jack Krol.

Ed had determined that putting together a stellar board with impeccable credentials for honesty and integrity was vital to ensuring Tyco's future—though it would not be an easy task given the company's diminished reputation. Atop Ed's wishlist for the new leader of the board: Jack Krol, the highly regarded former CEO of DuPont. Jack told us the humorous tale of how this partnership came to be. After politely declining several invitations from board members to join the Tyco board, Jack took a personal call from Ed Breen. Ed invited Jack in for a meeting in his office. Jack accepted, but, as he was leaving for the meeting, he assured his wife, Jan, that he was just "going through the motions" and had no intention of actually joining the board, as he was far too busy. Jack told us his wife responded, only partly in jest: "That's good. Because if you take the position, I'll leave you."[20]

During the now-legendary meeting, Jack and Ed delved into a philosophical discussion about what needed to be accomplished at Tyco over the first thirty, sixty, and ninety days in order to pull the company out of its mess. Jack shared his perspective on what he believed needed to occur, outlining eight critical to-do items. At some point in the meeting, Ed opened his top desk drawer and pulled out what has been described as a tattered sheet of paper containing his master strategy for saving the company. Six of the eight items matched Jack's list exactly. The rest is history. As the story goes, Jack, having accepted the position, returned home and begged his wife for forgiveness, claiming to have been "outsold by another salesman."[21] Another trait of the LOT: the ability to sell ideas with passion!

Once Jack was lead director of the board, he and Ed knew they needed to get to work quickly to restore faith in the company—as well as the pride and morale of its talent. Beyond focusing on a step change in business performance, the new leadership undertook a number of bold moves, the most important of which was instituting a new values system that demanded honesty and integrity in all the company did. The team also set about correcting the previous regime's lack of overt focus on the environment, health, safety, and social responsibility. They recognized improvements in these areas would be crucial to their efforts to rebuild the corporate brand. With an almost entirely new management team and working closely with the board, Ed put into place new and specific measurement criteria that ensured the new company and its leaders were living up to the newly established values of the company. Then, as we predict will become increasingly typical, the company publicly declared its new values and principles, revealed its progress to date, and outlined its goals for the future. To help ensure compliance and identify major risks, Jack Krol instituted, with Ed Breen's enthusiastic support, a complete enterprise risk assessment process whereby two or three directors make an annual visit to each of the business units. This "SWOT team"[22] of sorts meets with each unit's senior management team to review the business's major risks and discuss mitigating actions. This very public and formal process sent a clear signal of the zero tolerance the new leadership had for anything other than consistent and appropriate behavior.

In the years since Ed Breen "cleaned house" at Tyco, the results have been truly impressive. In 2006, GovernanceMetrics International rated the new Tyco board a 10 out of 10, placing Tyco in the top 1 percent of companies assessed.[23] According to Jack Krol, much of the credit must go to Ed Breen and the systemic approach he took to restoring trust and supporting a leading-edge governance process.

The LOT Stays Real

In a 2007 survey of 1,500 U.S. senior managers and executives, business-management website BNET found that CEOs were rated quite highly for such qualities as "passion for the business," "intelligence," and even "ethics." Where they fell short was in the area of interpersonal communications and connection. Even high-level executives gave their CEOs lukewarm scores on such measures as "accessibility," "communication," "compassion," and "approachability." When given a list of a dozen words to describe their CEOs, only one in five executives picked "caring" or "warm."[24]

Tomorrow's top-performing companies will be led by genuine and approachable leaders. The distant and authoritarian approach that was so popular in earlier decades is not adequate in an era in which the most sought-after talent thinks nothing of moving from one company to another or even from one field to the next. LOTs will expose their human side, as spouses, parents, and members of the community. Employees want to know their company is in capable hands, but they also *need* to know those hands are attached to an actual human being.

In the next chapter, we will delve more into the realities of managing members of the Millennial Generation, a generation marked by a desire for a more equitable work-life balance. For now, suffice it to say that the Leaders of Tomorrow will need to tread a delicate line in balancing company performance and employee happiness. In tomorrow's more humanized companies, different skill sets will be required to engage, motivate, and retain top talent.

Richard Tait, cofounder of the Cranium, Inc. board game company, has kept it real by creating a culture that is more in keeping with employee lifestyles than a traditional, buttoned-up working environment would be. For starters, the talent get to select their own job titles, allowing them to express their views of themselves and what they do. Richard himself is known within the company as the Grand Poo Bah (a title he carries with appropriate self-effacement), while his cofounder, Whit Alexander, is Chief Noodler. The CFO? Professor Profit, naturally. The individualized titles contribute to an atmosphere in which people are appreciated for who they are, not just what they do. As Richard noted in an interview with *Fortune:*

> Fun is always at the core of our culture. I find it very frustrating when I go to the offices of other toymakers, and I see they've

chosen to paint their walls beige. It costs the same to paint them red. It's perplexing to me. You have to create an environment for people to be creative and innovative. My office has a glass wall, and I'm right near the front door, so I'm the official greeter. The walls are brightly colored, and we have music playing everywhere. Even the way the offices are arranged is incredibly collaborative— there's no sense of departments.[25]

Stay off the pedestal

One of the advantages of staying "real" is that the media, shareholders, and the broader public come to recognize the CEO as an actual human being, rather than as some infallible icon. Although he was not in a business leadership role, who could forget the tale of New York's rising political star Eliot Spitzer? The governor and former crusading state attorney general had earned the nickname "Mr. Clean" by waging battle against corruption in whatever form he found it. One call-girl scandal later, and Mr. Clean was in the gutter. His opponents could not have dreamed of a faster or steeper fall from grace.

The LOT Invites People In

Even someone with the imagination, vision, and "small world" philosophy of Walt Disney might struggle to envision how closely connected the world is today—and, as we have explored in this book, how closely consumers, brands, and businesses are intertwined. Leaders of Tomorrow will make it a priority to build bridges between their organizations and the outside world, encouraging both communication and collaboration.

While CEO of Procter & Gamble, A. G. Lafley was at the forefront of the collaboration trend for a number of years, having publicly decreed in 2000 that half the company's future innovations should come from the outside. Since that time, the company has made good use of its Connect and Develop research program, which taps into science and business networks; its VocalPoint consumer panel; and a team of technology entrepreneurs tasked with scouting out innovative products the company can adopt. A. G. also made it a point to spend three full days a year with the company's Design Board, a group of outside consultants who offer perspectives on P & G products in the pipeline. P & G recognizes that no matter how brilliant and creative its own people are, their work will benefit greatly from exposure to outside ideas.

At Zappos, CEO Tony Hsieh has established a channel of communication with a decidedly modern flair: He uses Twitter.com to "tweet" numerous messages a day to whomever might be interested. (For those readers unfamiliar with Twitter, users respond throughout the day to the question, "What are you doing?" Their answers are limited to 140 characters.) Importantly, Tony sees Twitter communication as a way not just to connect with customers but also with his own internal talent: "Prior to Twitter," he told one publication, "a lot of employees were curious what a day in the life of a CEO was like, and there was no good answer because every day is different. With Twitter, employees can follow along and learn about all the different things that I do, and feel more of a personal connection with me."[26]

Tony tweets about what he is doing ("Presented at Employee Engagement conference & just noticed random holes in my shirt. I think I'm being stalked by ninja moths"), what his colleagues are up to ("Alfred dropped & broke his iphone an hour ago so can't twitter. He is starting to get the shakes, needs to find a methophone clinic"), what he is thinking ("About to fly to DC. Reading 'Predictably Irrational,' but hoping pilot is predictably rational. Oh, and also hopefully he's not reading."), and even what he is eating ("Enjoying pomegranate margaritas & guacamole made tableside w/ @adam_miami at Rosa Mexicana!"). Other tweets engage his "followers" (people who have signed on to receive Tony's Twitter posts) in company business. For instance, one tweet read, "New Zappos TV commercial—what do you think? How would you rate it on a scale of 1–10?" Another said, "Cool new experimental way to browse Zappos! Please twitter @zappos your feedback, thanks!"[27] In both cases, he included a link people could click on to get to the referenced content. As of the time of this writing, Tony had 133,619 followers. Not a bad-sized focus group.

Whether using Twitter, blogs, large-scale consumer panels, or some other mechanism, the LOT will make it a priority to increase linkages both within the company and to outside stakeholders. The information that will find its way back to the LOT and other executives, as well as the deeper connections forged with consumers and others, will prove an ongoing source of competitive advantage.

CMOS, START YOUR ENGINES

Thus far, we have framed our view of the Leader of Tomorrow within the context of the CEO position. That makes sense, given the ability of a powerful and charismatic chief executive to drive a company toward a new vision of the future. We do believe, however, that there is one executive position superbly suited to helping the CEO push the company to become a more humanized version of itself. That person is the chief marketing officer, or CMO.

As an organization strengthens its embrace of the four cornerstones of the Conscious Corporation—a purpose beyond profit, a people-centered culture, a sustainable approach to business, and respect for consumers' power—the CMO will be uniquely positioned to translate the boss's vision into tangible actions both within and outside the company. More and more, we are seeing the chief marketer serve as a company's primary "consumer disciple," charged with pushing brand messages to outside stakeholders and then bringing information and insights back into the organization from the outside world. The CMO is also well suited to help institute macro changes because he or she is in the unusual position of being both a direct report (typically) to the CEO and having daily interaction with nearly every business function. This provides a unique platform from which to promote change and measure progress.

Recently, we sat down with David Wilkie, who leads an exclusive network of CMOs called the Marketing 50 (M50). This group of star marketers, which meets twice a year, is truly a "who's who" from companies such as HP, Visa, Philips, McDonald's, Nike, and Nokia. Thanks to his work with these leading-edge thinkers, David has a unique vantage on how the position is changing over time and the impact the right CMO can and should have on corporate strategy.

The most successful marketing officers, in David's view, behave less like CMOs than like CGOs (chief growth officers) and CCOs (chief customer officers). When it comes to sustainability and corporate consciousness, marketing officers who think like a CGO will explore how shifts in customer values and priorities are going to influence demand for items in the company's current product and service portfolio. Furthermore, a growth officer will use insights into consumers' environmental and social concerns (and the extent to which they drive behavior) to help envision a portfolio that will prove even more compelling in coming months and years. Of course, foreseeing such opportunities requires keen customer insights, and that is where thinking like a CCO comes into play. Putting on the customer officer hat, marketers can play a crucial role in ensuring the company's brand, products, operations, et al., exceed customer expectations in an increasingly transparent world. The chief customer officer must take into account not only what a product is and how it works, but also how it was manufactured or grown and what impact it has had—and will have—on the planet.

We are no longer talking only about staving off PR nightmares or reputation hits. Instead of thinking defensively about their brand's image, today's best marketing officers realize future profits will rely more heavily on the ability of their brands to engender trust and build emotional connections over time. Those officers able to bring together an understanding of the customer base, a compelling vision for growth, and the skills to establish brand trust will be best positioned to help their organizations generate legitimate growth opportunities in two contexts: profits and customer relationships.

CMOs on Sustainability and Corporate Social Responsibility

David Wilkie confirmed that M50 is seeing increased interest in sustainability and corporate social responsibility as part of a broader movement toward corporate consciousness. "As recently as two or three years ago," he tells us, "there was a notable ramping up of interest in the topic of sustainability. Today it seems it is better understood across organizations. We are moving past the point where CMOs have to persuade their CEOs of the financial value of sustainability. Now we are seeing CEOs leading the charge."[28]

From David's perspective, the approach to sustainability has become more holistic. Instead of being centered on particular products or services that are earth or society friendly, interest has moved toward making the organization itself represent the values that are increasingly important to target customers. "In a transparent world, consumers are taking ecological and social factors into account when evaluating purchase decisions," he says. "As consumers have become more empowered in their dealings with companies, brands have to prove they are worthy of their customers' trust."[29]

David agrees head marketers are in a great position to help evolve their organizations in a way that makes sense for these times. "CMOs are sort of chief everything officers," he explains, "seizing whatever new opportunities the marketplace presents. Since the concept of sustainability is relatively new to many organizations, it's not surprising it has largely been pushed into companies by proactive CMOs. These are the people most responsible for knowing what is on the minds of customers, and being more conscientious about personal consumption choices is clearly on the rise."[30]

David has this advice for corporate heads looking to hire a marketing officer to help push a values-based agenda: "CMOs who have a personal passion for sustainability—having come to it on their own or even having picked it up from their children—seem to have greater success in building momentum within the organization. Their zeal for the subject translates into an energy that can prove infectious. If I were advising a CEO who wanted to consider sustainability in the hiring of a new CMO, I would suggest that, in addition to exceptional customer-insight skills, the CEO look at how passionate candidates are about sustainability in their personal lives."[31]

Spencer Stuart recently surveyed the M50 members to get their points of view on the move toward corporate consciousness. They confirmed what we have been seeing in our own work with corporate clients: The group was nearly unanimous in stating that corporate social responsibility is important to their companies' overall business strategies. CSR is also important to their overall marketing strategies, with around one-third calling it "extremely important." When we asked whether CSR initiatives were more or less important to their companies today compared with three years ago, the vast majority said "more important," while just one in six said it has remained about the same. Despite the difficult economic climate (the survey was conducted at the end of 2008), not a single person said CSR had declined in importance at their organization. And most said social responsibility initiatives would be the same or even more important in the coming year.[32]

As detailed in Chart 5.2, the environment, healthcare/employee wellness, and social change are the top CSR priorities for these leading companies at present. In contrast, what used to represent the bulk of social responsibility activities—charitable giving—came in dead last. Writing a check simply does not offer the strategic advantage today's companies require.

Stop Marketing and Start Leading

At the start of this chapter, we detailed the pressure-cooker environment in which today's chief executives operate. We could make the argument that chief marketing officers are under as much pressure internally as the CEO faces externally. In 2008, Spencer Stuart's annual CMO Survey found that chief marketers in the top 100 most-advertised

1. Environmental sustainability
2. Improved healthcare and employee wellness
3. Driving social change
4. Fair treatment of companies/workers in supply chain
5. Diversity
6. Positive working environment
7. Education
8. Fair compensation
9. Pro-bono services/volunteerism
10. Charitable giving

Chart 5.2   CSR Priorities Within the M50 Member Companies

Note: Ranking is based on responses to the question, "Which of the following are your company's top three CSR priorities? (Please rank 1, 2, and 3)." The results are ranked according to votes cast, with first-place votes garnering three points; second-place votes, two points; and third-place, one point.

Source: Marketing 50 Gauge Questionnaire, December 2008.

companies had an average tenure of just twenty-eight months in the job. So, just as the CMO role is becoming more vital within the C-suite, companies are losing out on the advantages of having a single professional in that position over a term of any truly meaningful length.

The job of the chief marketing officer is increasingly broad and complex. What is now required is not so much great marketing skills as superior leadership skills. After all, CMOs at the largest companies have marketing teams that number as high as 1,000. Those are the people who should be doing the day-to-day marketing, while the chief officer is informing the overall business and brand strategy. GE's Beth Comstock, cited in the previous chapter, is an example of the direction in which we think the CMO position should be moving. As a former general manager (she served as president of GE's NBC Universal Integrated Media group), Beth is ideally suited for the CMO position at GE corporate. As that role becomes more pivotal to strategic growth, we expect to see more proven general managers step into the position.

The Conscious Corporation cannot come into being without the active, even passionate commitment of the Leaders of Tomorrow within the company. The executives driving this change must include the CEO, should include the CMO, and will need to involve others at all levels and functions of the organization. In the next chapter, we will explore how the top leadership can ensure their commitment to a more conscious future while influencing decisions and actions throughout the organization.

Chapter Six

CREATING A CULTURE
TO ENGAGE THE TALENT
OF TOMORROW

Our first priority should be the people who work for the companies, then the customers, then the shareholders. Because if the staff is motivated then the customers will be happy, and the shareholders will then benefit through the company's success.

—Richard Branson, chairman, Virgin Group[1]

For most of the boom years over the past few decades, many companies found it challenging to recruit suitably qualified staff. And virtually every company struggled with the challenge of unlocking the value of employees once hired—engaging them and motivating them to give their best effort from day to day. *Talent management* moved out of sports and entertainment to become a business buzzword. The "man in the gray flannel suit" was encouraged to change into khakis or jeans and bring his dog to work.

Now, as the economic crisis grinds on, the situation has changed in some respects. Corporations are shedding staff, and there are more qualified jobs seekers than job openings. So, does this herald a return to management by diktat and a return to the buttoned-up workplace? The Greek philosopher Aristotle was of the opinion that "Pleasure in the job puts perfection in the work," but he was running a school, not a business competing in a tough economy. Do fun, frills, and perks have a place in companies now? Or should employees just hunker down and be grateful they have a job at all?

Some shortsighted companies may decide the downturn is an ideal opportunity to play hardball with staff and cut back on those extras intended to breed job satisfaction in flusher times. To be fair, it may be that some of the more whimsical employee-benefit initiatives were better suited to boom times and should be trimmed back at least for the time being. But it makes no sense to sacrifice long-term growth for short-term savings. Committed employee engagement and purposeful talent management cannot be regarded as good-time gimmicks. These elements are essential to creating a culture that maximizes value for all stakeholders in tough times as well as in good.

GENERATIONAL SHIFT: THE NEW WORKFORCE

Underlying all other considerations in this chapter is one simple fact: With each passing year companies will be relying ever more on the rising generation of Millennials (aka Generation Y, aka Echo Boomers) to staff them and create their value. This is the generation born roughly between 1977 and 1995; it represents the biggest shift in the U.S. workforce since the Baby Boomers came of age. Eighty million strong in the United States alone, this generation will soon account for the majority of the country's workers.

Millennials' expectations of work have been shaped by the abundance of the boom years, the pervasive spread of powerful technology, and the blurring of work and leisure, public and private. And this is the case not just in the United States, but also in most of the developed world. This generation is distinguished by an attitude that represents a marked shift from previous ones; generally speaking, they are more motivated by values in action than by the traditional incentives of money and status.

Early reactions to this new workforce included accusations of laziness and lack of focus and commitment—accusations that would be familiar to the Generation Xers who came before them. Jack Krol, whom we discussed in the context of the Tyco case in the last chapter, served as vice chairman and then CEO of DuPont for most of the 1990s. He recalls the issue of life-work balance cropping up among younger employees during that period:

> When I was a young executive coming up the ranks, I don't recall ever hesitating for a second if my boss asked me to go somewhere or

do something. If I needed to pack my bags and be in Ohio tomorrow morning, I would do it without question. Back in the nineties, we began to hear young executives say, "I would love to make the trip, but I really need to check in with my spouse to ensure we have everything covered on the home front."[2]

What began with the Xers has intensified under the millennials. To some extent, it is reasonable to say this new generation is simply wired differently; after all, they have grown up in a far different world from the one their grandparents and even parents experienced. There is at least one additional reason for their unwillingness to sacrifice all for career advancement, however: Members of this generation have no expectation that they will stay with a single company—or even in the same industry—for their entire career, and so they are more calculating in terms of the benefits they seek in a job. In the search industry, we are seeing many young executives maximize their time with a company by learning and earning as much as they can before moving on to the next opportunity. They are simply not interested in staying in one place for the duration, even if that were feasible. And companies are doing a lousy job of giving them reason to stay.

We would also note that this is a generation set apart by its emphasis on finding work within an organization that is both socially and environmentally conscious. A 2007 Net Impact survey of 2,100 MBA students in the United States found that 81 percent thought businesses should work to improve society, and 78 percent wanted corporate social responsibility to be a part of their university curricula.[3] A 2008 survey of college students and recent college graduates found 81 percent wanted to work for a company that is green-friendly, green-conscious, or green-certified, and 79 percent would be more likely to accept a job offer at a green company over another company when evaluating two similar job offers.[4]

Only time will tell how much Millennials' attitudes and expectations will remain shaped by the boom years and how much they will be modified by the economic downturn. What we do know for now is how Millennials are at this time—always bearing in mind that talking about an entire generation is bound to be a gross generalization. From our joint perspective in marketing, search, and strategic consulting, we offer the following point of view on how mindful organizations will derive optimal benefit from this next generation of talent.

Understanding the Millennial Mindset

It is perhaps all too common for members of older generations to deride today's youth for having grown up cosseted by overprotective and always-there "helicopter parents." Older people bemoan the fact that every young sports competitor today is handed a trophy at the end of the season, making the award meaningless and depriving both stellar and lesser athletes of one of the tough lessons of life. Others speak of the fact that bowling alleys now come with "bumpers"—meaning an entire generation has grown up not knowing what it sounds or feels like to bowl a gutter ball. Directors of school plays are instructed that everyone who shows up gets a part, regardless of commitment or talent.

Beyond these emotionally protective measures, many young people have been praised all their lives for the simplest accomplishments, whether for drawing with chalk on a sidewalk ("Such natural talent!") or simply turning in a homework assignment on time. If they run into trouble at school or work, their parents rush to bail them out. College professors and deans have complained of parents calling to make excuses for a student's late work or to argue for a better grade. We have even heard of parents calling human-resource departments to lobby for a better benefits package for their adult children.

One of the consequences of having grown up in the care of such hands-on adults is that this generation requires a lot more input and guidance than was the norm in workplaces a decade or more ago. In a 2008 survey, 65 percent of Millennial workers at Ernst & Young said being provided "detailed guidance in daily work" was moderately or extremely important, compared with 39 percent of Baby Boomers who said the same. Moreover, 85 percent of Millennial employees said their age-group peers want "frequent and candid performance feedback," while only half of Boomers agreed.[5] A few years ago, in response to this generational shift, Ernst & Young launched an online "Feedback Zone," a place where employees can ask for and submit feedback. The firm also assigns younger workers a mentor.[6] At IBM, managers are counseled in Millennial-appropriate behavior, such as using open-ended questions to prompt a dialogue and being specific about expectations.[7]

Millennials want more than simple direction, however. They expect encouragement and inspiration, and want to feel they are being taken seriously and are making a difference within the company. (Funnily enough, encouragement and inspiration work well with other generations, too!) Organizations from Global Hyatt Corporation to P & G to IBM are encouraging cross-generational collaboration and learning by pairing older and younger workers on team projects and in traditional and reverse mentorships. (In a reverse mentorship, the younger employee mentors the older in areas such as technology adoption and cultural trends.)

IBM has found that the various age groups respond best to different methods of training and professional development. Whereas Baby Boomers prefer the traditional structure of a classroom and teacher, members of Generation X typically opt for online courses that are self-paced, while Millennials derive more benefit from social learning, through blogging and the like. The company offers training in a variety of formats to accommodate these divergent needs.[8]

Beyond differences in how they like to work, Millennials also stand out in regard to *why* they work and what motivates them to put forth their best effort. This is a generation that values both personal achievement and communal success. They like to feel they are a part of some larger cause—whether that cause is meeting second-quarter projections or helping solve a social problem.

Also setting Millennials apart are their heightened expectations of how they will be received in business. Up to this point in their lives, these young men and women typically have not been asked to compromise on very much. They have come of age at a time when everything seems possible if one is sufficiently persistent. When they arrive at a new job, they have every expectation that their contributions will be valued and that they will automatically be accorded the respect of older colleagues. Should this prove not to be the case, some Millennials will choose to go elsewhere rather than stick it out until they earn their stripes. That can be a real drain on organizations that depend on a constant influx of the best and brightest to grow.

The Conscious Corporation of tomorrow will put aside notions of how things "should" be or used to be and embrace what made the young workers worth hiring in the first place. They will learn that collaboration can reap rewards beyond the grasp of traditional command-and-control cultures. Finding just the right ways to engage employees and give them a sense of long-term ownership over the corporate brand will prove a vital competitive asset.

The workplace is changing. That much is apparent. And success will depend on how well an organization changes to meet the new

realities. An article in *The Economist* warned of the fine line employers must walk between balancing company performance concerns and
creating an environment in which young employees can do their best
work. The author concluded:

> Younger workers will have to accept that in difficult times deci-
> sions will be taken more crisply and workloads will increase. Their
> managers, meanwhile, will have to make an extra effort to keep
> [Millennials] engaged and motivated. Firms that cannot pull off
> this balancing act could see an exodus of young talent once the
> economy improves. That, to borrow from [this generation's] text-
> message shorthand, would be a huge WOMBAT: a waste of money,
> brains, and time.[9]

WHY IT PAYS TO ENGAGE

Though their body art might occasionally suggest otherwise,
Millennials are not some separate species of human being in the
workplace. They are just more open in expressing what they want and
need as compared with older generations. What worker wouldn't want
clearly expressed goals and expectations, a sense of being valued, and
acknowledgment of his or her individuality and basic humanity? These
are core desires of any age group. The difference today is that companies are beginning to figure out that providing these things benefits the bottom line. So, regardless of which generation has prompted
the move toward more people-conscious management styles, every
employee ultimately will benefit.

There are arguably dozens of ways in which companies derive
value from the active engagement of their talent. We will focus here
on the three we consider of greatest import:

- Higher magnetism and lower turnover
- Stronger financial performance
- Better customer relationships

Higher Magnetism and Lower Turnover

As we have moved from an industrial economy into an intellectual-
capital economy in which great ideas propel growth, it has become

more important to attract and retain precisely the right sort of talent. Virtually anyone could be trained to operate a printing press; it is quite another thing to have the skills and aptitude to envision and design the next-generation search engine or mobile phone. Those that make it a priority to engage their internal talent in positive ways earn a reputation that allows them to draw from a far broader pool of applicants. Consider the example of Southwest Airlines: Having earned a reputation as a company that places a high value on employee happiness and well-being, Southwest has become a "destination employer"—a company where so many people want to work it can afford to be choosy about whom it hires. In 2007, Southwest received 329,200 résumés and hired 4,200 new employees.[10] How many other organizations have the luxury of hiring only the most promising 1.3 percent of job applicants?

Once hired, employees who are highly involved in the business and brand experience are less likely to want to leave. According to Gallup, companies that truly engage their employees experience 50 percent higher employee—and customer—retention.[11] That represents a big savings given that the turnover cost of a single midlevel position in the United States is now estimated at $40,000 to $100,000, according to The Great Place to Work Institute.[12]

Stronger Financial Performance

> The financial success of great workplaces is not a hit-or-miss proposition, but rather an affirmation of the long-term benefits that come from helping people to cooperate with each other and commit to the vision and future of the firm.
>
> —Amy Lyman, cofounder,
> The Great Place To Work Institute[13]

Organizations with higher levels of talent engagement and commitment are more productive and profitable than their lower-engagement counterparts. Companies on *Fortune*'s annual "100 Best Companies to Work for in America" list between 1998 and 2005 returned 14 percent per year, compared with 6 percent for the overall market, according to Alex Edmans, a finance professor at the University of Pennsylvania's Wharton School. Writing in Knowledge@Wharton, he said: "One might think this is an obvious relationship—that you don't need to do a study showing that if workers are happy, the company performs better. But actually, it's not that obvious. Traditional management theory treats workers like any other input—get as much out of them as possible and pay them as little as you can get away with."[14]

Part of the problem is rooted in managers being rewarded for short-term results, which encourages short-term thinking. Investing in employees is a long-term proposition, but it is one that has been proven to pay off. Research from Hay Group Insight found that not only are engaged employees two-and-a-half times more likely to exceed performance expectations, they also improve business results by up to 30 percent.[15] Insufficient engagement is a real issue for companies. One study found that only about 25 percent of employees are engaged (and only 12 percent are fully engaged).[16]

Better Customer Relationships

An obvious reason for increased profits at engaged companies is the resultant improvement in customer satisfaction. The Container Store attributes its success in large part to the way it trains and treats employees, and how that then leads to improved service. Since its founding in 1978, the retailer has seen average annual growth of 20 percent;[17] it has made *Fortune*'s annual list of "100 Best Companies to Work For" for the past ten years in a row. Among other policies, the company offers flexible schedules to accommodate family needs, pays sales employees 50 to 100 percent above the industry average, provides a medical/dental/vision insurance plan to part-time as well as full-time employees, and offers a generous 40 percent merchandise discount.

That employee discount is particularly meaningful, given that many of its workers are former customers. "We have almost never needed to use [a professional] recruiter; we rarely run newspaper ads," The Container Store's recruitment director, Karyn Maynard, told *HR Magazine* in 2007.[18] Instead, the company trains employees to keep an eye out for potential candidates and talk to them about employment opportunities with the company. All store employees carry in their aprons "recruiting cards," which provide basic information and instructions for applying for a job online. It is part of the company dress code.

Diane Berry, a managing vice president with Gartner Executive Programs, told *HR* that hiring regular customers can help employers realize substantial efficiencies. "They are engaged by the brand, it's a place that they align with, they see value," she explains. "That's absolutely helpful in attracting and retaining folks."[19]

Zappos is another company renowned for employee engagement and its impact on customer satisfaction. In fact, customer service is considered the larger purpose behind the brand. Zappos focuses its recruitment and training efforts—and its entire corporate culture—on engaging employees in its quest to continually wow customers with its outstanding service ethic. CEO Tony Hsieh and the top team give employees the creative freedom and autonomy they need to provide great service.

We spoke with Aaron Magness, who oversees business development and marketing at Zappos. He told us that, in a departure from the industry standard, call-center employees are not given a script and are encouraged to take the time to interact with customers in a personal way. The company makes it a point to hire representatives who are outgoing and caring, and who genuinely are interested in assisting the people whose calls they take. In a policy lifted right out of the classic film *Miracle on 34th Street*, call-center employees have been known to search rival sites on behalf of customers if Zappos doesn't have the required shoe style or size in stock.[20]

"Customer service could be construed as a one-way type of thing," Aaron noted, "but it's really more about customer experience—it's doing stuff outside of what is just good, standard service. Like when you pay for standard shipping, and we upgrade to free overnight, that's part of the experience. Or when you place your order and you just happen to talk about your wedding or your friend's wedding, getting what you need for the event is good service, but receiving a handwritten card in the mail hoping that the wedding went well, that's the experience."[21]

Zappos is able to contain its advertising expenditures in part because repeat sales account for approximately 75 percent of its revenue.[22] People know and like the brand, and recommend it to others. "Most companies will put millions and millions of dollars toward advertising," Aaron told us. "Instead, we say, 'How much better can we make the customer's shopping experience? And the way to improve that experience is to focus on our company culture.'"[23] In 2008, he said,

Zappos spent just $3 million on television advertising, while racking up $1 billion in gross sales.[24] Not bad.

ENGAGING THE WORKFORCE OF TOMORROW

Understanding the need to engage the internal talent is one thing. It is quite another to be able to pull it off on a consistent basis and over time. In the Conscious Corporation of today and tomorrow, it is imperative that talent at all levels consider themselves a vital part of the organization's operations and success—and that requires that they have an emotional stake in the corporate brand. This is best accomplished by giving them a role to play in the company's purpose beyond profit, offering opportunities for learning and growth, promoting the pursuit of personal passions, and recognizing the actual human beings who make up the ranks of workers.

Give Talent a Role to Play in the Purpose Beyond Profit

The great majority of people have to work for a living; the most fortunate ones work at something in which they really believe. But that needn't be limited to a lucky few. An opportunity to make a larger contribution can and should be part of the work culture. With today's hectic and demanding lifestyles, many people find they have neither the time, energy, nor imagination to make a social contribution in their personal lives. Sure, they may write the occasional check or drop off a few cans during a food drive, but they are not involved in good works to an extent they consider of any significance. This makes it all the more important—and motivating—to find meaning at work. If "making a difference" sounds a bit too warm and fuzzy, remember the clincher Steve Jobs used to persuade John Sculley to quit PepsiCo and join Apple: "Do you want to spend the rest of your life selling sugared water or do you want a chance to change the world?"[25]

Google is an example of a company that means serious business but also has a sense of being galvanized by a bigger purpose. Googlers across all levels and departments are connected by a single powerful thread that infuses their work: the feeling that this thing they are a part of has the capacity to change the world. "Philanthropy doesn't resonate with me," twenty-four-year-old Dan Siroker, an associate product manager at Google, told BNET.com. "What motivates me is working on products that I think help people's lives."[26]

Chuck Salter, writing in *Fast Company*, describes Google's sense of its broader mission as follows:

Google's singular worldview sees information as a natural resource, one that should be mined and refined and sorted and universally distributed. Information is a necessity, like clean water. That idea stands at the center of all Google does, unifying what can appear to be wildly disparate projects: mapping the world, searching the Web on a cell-phone screen, providing an early-response system for epidemics and natural disasters, developing cheap renewable energy.[27]

Google employees are made to understand that what they are doing today will have a direct impact not just on how people find information, but on how people live and work. They are actually helping to shape the future of human communication and data management. That's pretty heady stuff for a kid just out of college.

In Chapter Three, we spoke about Innocent Drinks and its larger purpose of "leaving things a little better than we find them." Most of the 10 percent of profits the company donates to charity each year are funneled through the Innocent Foundation, which funds rural development projects in the countries where the company's fruit ingredients originate. To help build connections between employees and beneficiaries—and bring the foundation's work to life for the talent—the company has instituted a scholarship through which one employee a year is sent on a two-week, all-expenses-paid visit to one of the communities in which the company is making a difference.

In 2007, the scholarship recipient visited the south of India, where she designed a website for the Irula Tribe Women's Welfare Society. During her stay, this employee had a chance to visit some of the villages the organization is helping and saw firsthand how her employer, through its support of the welfare society, is helping to improve the lives of Irula women.

Like Innocent Drinks, the Conscious Corporation will find ways to make employees feel connected to the good works of the corporate brand.

Offer Opportunities for Continuous Learning and Growth

In our fast-changing world, who would want to employ someone who has learned nothing since the completion of his or her formal education? Lifelong education isn't about whiling away spare time, it is now about keeping up with a changing world. And that requires learning beyond what one typically picks up on the job. Workers today are acutely conscious that they are competing not just against people across town, but also against people on other continents. They need to keep their skills sharp and continually look for ways to improve their marketability in tomorrow's anticipated environment. For some, opportunities for personal and professional growth will supersede financial compensation as a priority in choosing—and staying with—an employer. Loyalty will be gained through learning, not just earning.

People-centered cultures don't consider workers disposable. When they make a hire, they invest the time and money necessary to ensure the employee has the tools and motivation he or she needs to thrive on the job. Google views itself almost as an academic institution. As the company's human-resources manager Anne Driscoll told *Fast Company:* "Our philosophy is providing all the great things you would have in a Ph.D. or graduate program. That's how you're going to attract people who are interested in working in a collaborative environment."[28] We mentioned earlier the $2,000 "bribe" Zappos offers new hires to quit after the first week of training. If a person is not a good fit for the company and is not interested in adhering to its core values, Zappos seeks to sever the relationship quickly. That frees the company up to focus on the development of those people who will be there over the longer term.

The ultimate goal of most professional development is to help employees move beyond their current positions to a higher level within the organization. At the starting point, however, individuals need the proper care and training to ensure they are equipped to handle the demands of the immediate position. One of the factors that has allowed The Container Store to establish such loyal employees and stellar customer service is the extensive training the company provides. Every full-time salesperson undergoes an average of 241 hours of training in the first year; this compares with a retail average of just 7 hours.[29]

Innocent Drinks makes development an ongoing focus, including both formal training programs (e.g., Innocent Academy, Innocent Business Academy) and continual "craft development" aimed at building professional depth. This might include studying for professional exams or building an external network within the industry. To ensure the U.K.–based company becomes a truly European business, Innocent makes every effort to fill office openings internally, with three- to six-month transfers. Sending staff on assignments in other countries helps them feel more connected to the other cultures in which the company operates. As stated on its website: "We take the development of our people pretty seriously. Why? First of all, we know it's a reason why great people join and stay at Innocent—to further their careers, to become a better version of themselves, and to play a part in growing a successful business. Secondly, it makes sense for us to have a team of engaged, talented, high-performing people at the top of their games. Pretty obvious, really."[30]

While many businesses encourage the building of external networks, McKinsey & Company takes the concept a bit further. It encourages departing employees to remain in touch through regular "alumni" events. Each year, the strategic consultancy holds more than one hundred gatherings around the world, ranging from informal cocktail parties to full-blown conferences. An alumni website also helps current and former consultants stay in touch. Maintaining connections with and offering support to former employees pays a dividend when ex-McKinseyites assume leadership positions at top corporations and nonprofits, and subsequently become McKinsey clients themselves.

Too often today, employer and employee part ways with acrimony or at least some level of resentment. Others are simply indifferent when the relationship ends. In light of the more frequent job changes of today, it will behoove businesses going forward to be as thoughtful in creating an exit strategy as they are in planning the "on-boarding" process. Keeping the door open to former employees opens up the possibility of future collaboration and mutual support.

Promote the Pursuit of Personal Passions

When employees were working more-regular hours and taking at least a couple of weeks of vacation a year, it might not have been so important to love one's work. The workday finished at a specific hour, and people had both the time and energy for leisure pursuits. But times have changed: Hours are longer, expectations are higher, and new technologies are making it less clear where work stops and one's personal life begins.

Americans, in particular, are notorious for their relentless focus on work. Almost 40 percent of U.S. workers log more than fifty hours a week, despite the well-ingrained notion of a forty-hour workweek.[31] Moreover, the average U.S. worker is permitted just 8.1 days of paid vacation a year, as compared with a legal minimum of twenty-eight days in the United Kingdom and thirty days in Germany. Worse yet, half of Americans don't use their full allotment of vacation days,[32] and those who do go on vacation may find it difficult to leave work behind. A study by travel-services company Expedia found that 29 percent of workers surveyed had trouble coping with stress from work at some point in their vacation cycle. And nearly one-quarter check work e-mails or voicemail while on vacation, up from 16 percent in 2005.[33] With two-thirds of people who work more than forty hours a week reporting being highly stressed, it is little wonder job stress costs U.S. businesses in excess of $300 billion a year on account of such things as absenteeism, mistakes and accidents, reduced productivity, and substance abuse.[34]

It should go without saying that the Conscious Corporation will recognize the benefit of paid time off on employee stress levels, morale, and focus. Beyond that, enlightened businesses will seek to help their talent maintain a more balanced lifestyle even when on the job. In looking at the hundred companies on *Fortune*'s 2009 "Best Companies to Work For" list, we found that eighty-three permit telecommuting, seventy-five offer compressed workweeks, sixty-one allow job sharing, thirty-two provide on-site child care, and nineteen offer fully paid sabbaticals. That says a lot about these companies' recognition of their talent's need to maintain at least some semblance of life-work balance.

Toward that end, more companies are offering such convenience-oriented perks as on-site concierges, dry-cleaning drop-off and pickup, car detailing, and even medical services. Employees typically pay for these things, but they reap the benefit of being able to get their car serviced or have a medical checkup without spending an hour or more driving there and back and waiting in line. Not only do these amenities contribute to productivity by reducing absenteeism, they also support the notion that one's personal life should be about more than catching up on errands and chores.

Taking a lesson from 3M's storied "15 percent rule," Google permits its engineers to devote 20 percent of their time to working on something company-related that interests them personally. This is more than a motivational tool; it has proved a fertile source of new business ideas. Many valued technologies and practices have their origins in 20 percent time, including Gmail, Google News, and even the shuttle buses that bring people to work at the company's headquarters in Mountain View, California.

Innocent Drinks values a workforce that is about more than sales, marketing, and accountancy. So, it gives out scholarships to support employees who would like to study something new. As stated on its website, "Three £1000 scholarships are up for grabs every quarter, so if you've ever wanted to learn the Japanese art of origami or would like to take moped lessons, you can apply for a scholarship. Everyone then votes for who they think should receive it. Obviously bribes can be accepted."[35] The company also sponsors a variety of clubs that reflect employee interests. At present, there are clubs for wakeboarders, martial artists, climbers, tennis and squash players, and cheese lovers. If enough employees are interested in starting a new club, the company will consider adding it to its roster.

Zappos seeks to create a more humanized environment by encouraging managers to spend between 10 and 20 percent of their time with team members outside the office, whether going out for a meal or enjoying a morning hike. The company even provides a life coach to help employees manage their personal and work lives. CFO Alfred Lin justifies the expense by saying, "You can't provide great service if you're upset about something in your life. [The coach] easily pays for himself."[36]

Outdoor outfitter REI considers time off an important part of its culture. In addition to paid vacations, employees may request up to twelve weeks of unpaid leave a year to pursue a personal interest, volunteer, travel, or attend school. After fifteen years with the company, employees are given a paid four-week sabbatical. Every additional five years earns another sabbatical that includes one additional week of paid time off. To encourage a shared love of the outdoors, the company provides "challenge grants" that fund employees' personal outdoor goals, such as climbing Mount Everest or a long-distance bicycle trip. And, on a day-to-day basis, employees at the company's headquarters in Kent, Washington, are encouraged to enjoy lunchtime activities such as yoga, running, bike rides, basketball, and Ultimate Frisbee. It is all intended to help the talent maintain lifestyles in keeping with those of the company's target audience of outdoor enthusiasts. As stated on the company website:

> We encourage each other to enjoy all aspects of life....Perhaps more than most companies, the degree to which our employees lead balanced lives impacts our bottom line. Most of our employees are enthusiastic about the outdoors—and when our employees spend time in the outdoors, they are connecting with the core of this company.
>
> —REI's Culture & Values[37]

Recognize the Human Being Behind the Title

Being turned into a soulless zombie, clone, or robot is the stuff of horror movies. It is human nature to want to be recognized and respected as a unique individual—to be called by name rather than by number, to not be confused with other people, and to have both one's innate humanity and achievements acknowledged in some meaningful way.

In the old way of doing business, companies would recognize the superior efforts of an employee by granting a better title, job function, and/or paycheck. All of these things are important, of course, but they are not necessarily sufficient to motivate the employee to stay with a company today. Compensation in and of itself does not necessarily foster emotional bonds, and those bonds are increasingly important at a time when employee loyalty cannot be assumed.

What talent is craving in these hyper-fast, high-tech, disconnected times is a sense that the employer sees the person behind the employee identification number. Innovative companies are finding it pays to restructure the workplace in a way that is more "homelike" and cognizant of the human beings who populate the cubicles and offices. Google's headquarters—aka the Googleplex—is well known for its casual style and recreational amenities. Many other companies have created similar environments. In Santa Clara, California, NetApp's headquarters comes complete with two cafeterias, a gym, recreational areas for volleyball, a putting green, and complimentary snacks. The data storage company, which raked in $3.3 billion in sales in 2008, has been included in *Fortune*'s "Best Companies to Work For" list six years running.

Just about any good-sized company can equip a game room or offer Beer Fridays. What sets companies such as NetApp apart runs deeper than physical-plant facilities and employee perks. *Fortune* cites NetApp's "down-to-earth ethos" as making the organization feel like a small startup instead of a big company with some 7,000 employees. One example of this ethos can be seen in the company's travel policy. Early on, executives scrapped their dozen-page written policy in favor of this simple injunction: "We are a frugal company. But don't show up dog-tired to save a few bucks. Use your common sense."[38]

Too often, companies treat even senior-level employees as children, scolding them with companywide memos and forever adding new rules and restrictions to control their behavior. The more humanized businesses of tomorrow will recognize that most employees respond as they are treated. Accord them basic human respect and consideration, and they will likely respond in kind.

Taking a more humanized approach starts even before the job interview at some businesses. Talking about his company's hiring process, Zappos's Aaron Magness told us, "Even right down to the job application, we've made it very Zappos-y. We have questions on there like, 'If you were to walk into a room to a theme song, what would that theme song be?' Or 'How lucky a person do you think you are?' We all could walk into a standard interview and do a pretty good job because we know the questions. When we throw people for a loop and ask these other kinds of questions, the real applicant comes out. Part of the interview process is a crossword puzzle, a word find, or a maze. It's just a fun way to show that Zappos is a different kind of company."[39]

When it comes to more senior-level hiring, the Zappos recruitment process is extensive. An emphasis is placed on ensuring the applicant is going to be a good fit for the other employees. "The person will come out with us for dinner and drinks," Aaron says, "it's not just sitting in an office talking about stuff. And there's a group there. The person will be looked at by a bunch of different people in a bunch of different settings. We're democratic in interviews—no matter who you are you're expected to have an opinion, and a strong opinion at that."[40]

At Whole Foods, team cohesion is considered of such importance that teams are empowered to do their own hiring. After a trial period with the company, each new store employee is voted on by his or her team. If the person doesn't receive the approval of at least two-thirds of the team, he or she is let go.[41] In addition to fostering better teamwork, this policy sends a clear message to employees that they are valued and their well-being matters to their employer.

WHAT IT MEANS FOR LEADERS

Traditional models of leadership have favored the technical (quantitative) over the emotional (qualitative) dimension of leadership. Ironically, as technology grows geometrically more powerful and machines manage more of the analytics, our leaders must become more human, perhaps more humane.... To excel today, business leaders must master both quantitative skills such as finance, statistics, and accounting, and those less easily quantified, like communications, people development, and team-building.

—Glenn Hubbard, dean of finance and
economics, Columbia Business School[42]

The Conscious Corporation recognizes that, while it is important to get pay programs right, money is typically not the driving factor in employee engagement. The Towers Perrin Global Workforce Study has consistently shown employees are generally more motivated by intrinsic factors such as opportunities for personal growth (improving skills and capabilities), feeling part of an organization that is socially responsible, and working for a company that values and supports its employees' well-being.[43]

As more companies recognize the value of engaged talent, they are giving new thought to how they treat and motivate employees at all levels. Part of the process of creating a more engaging culture is seeing the company less as an institution or machine, and more as individuals working together in a complex group. The frame of reference is human, not abstract. Whereas institutions ignore external influences, people react to the world around them. Whereas institutions have guidelines, people have beliefs. Whereas institutions are rigid and unfeeling, people have moods and likes and dislikes. And whereas institutions like repetition and rules, people like to tell and be part of stories that evolve over time.

The Conscious Corporation will behave less like an institution and more like the people who together *are* the company. Among the key questions Leaders of Tomorrow will ask themselves as they strive to create a mutually beneficial corporate culture:

• What is making employees look forward to going to work in the morning?

- What are we doing to support and encourage our talents' passions and learning?
- How are we living the culture—and how are we helping our talent to do the same?
- What changes need to be made to create a workforce in which 100 percent of our talent are fully engaged at all times?

Critical to building this culture is knowing the alternative one wishes to avoid. The Zappos culture we have discussed in this and the chapter prior came about in part as a consequence of CEO Tony Hsieh's earlier experiences. When Tony was just twenty-four years old, he sold his first company, LinkExchange, to Microsoft for $265 million. He did so, in part because he simply could not stand to work there anymore. In an interview with *Fortune*, he explained, "When it was just five or ten people, it was a lot of fun. We were working around the clock, no idea what day of the week it was, sleeping under our desks. We hired all the right people in terms of skill sets, but by the time it was one hundred [employees] or so, I dreaded going to the office."[44]

Aaron Magness talked with us about the impact this experience had on Tony—and, consequently, on Zappos. "When Tony left LinkExchange, where he didn't like coming into work every day, that's where a lot of his mentality comes from. He would think, 'Next time I do this, I've got to get the company culture right. How do we get the right talent in place?'" He adds, "A lot of outsiders think that all of our focus is on customer service, but it's really all about the company culture. As Tony often says, if you get the company culture right, the rest happens on its own."

Chapter Seven

EMPOWERING EFFECTIVE BRAND MESSENGERS IN A SECOND-OPINION SOCIETY

The challenge for business is they need to communicate credible actions through multiple channels using multiple sources multiple times. We're in a second-opinion society now.

—Laurence Evans, CEO, StrategyOne[1]

Everything communicates, especially in today's hyperconnected environment. The question is how much of what a company communicates is intentional. An organization may have the noblest aspirations and most inspiring mission. It may invest heavily in slick, smart, and compelling paid communication to build up its reputation and goodwill among external audiences. But paid messaging is merely the deliberate, structured part of brand communication. More often than not, these messages are then amplified—or undermined—by people within the business. We judge a company not so much by what it says, as by what we see its people do—and, increasingly, what we see them post online.

Before the world got wired, there was limited scope for internal talent to share their views about their employers. Now anyone with Internet access can reveal the inner workings of a company to the outside world with just a few keystrokes. It may be insiders themselves opening up online, or it may be their family, friends, and/or acquaintances relaying insights that have been passed along. ("You're not going to believe this memo...")

Some companies still aspire to manage all external communication. Apple Computer, for one, reportedly tries very hard to control what its people say; it is strict about preventing unauthorized communication with the outside. Yet even its best efforts have not made the company leakproof. A few years back, Apple filed suit against the website ThinkSecret.com for allegedly revealing confidential information about a not-yet-released Apple product.[2] The reality is, no business—or organization of any sort—can retain absolute control over its information. Whether deliberately exposing a trade secret or simply sharing an anecdote from work, employees' speech adds to a company's communication, for good or for ill.

In Chapter Six we looked at the benefits of creating an internal culture that motivates and inspires—a culture with which employees can identify and in which they can justly take pride. In this chapter we explore how what takes place within the company can shape brand perceptions on the outside, thereby bringing the brand to life externally through direct experience and word of mouth.

The Conscious Corporation will recognize the potential value to be gained when employees serve as conduits of communication. By what they say and how they interact, they can add richness and texture to perceptions of the brand. In some cases, they can create experiences and tell stories more effectively and more credibly than paid communication can. And they can help to build up stores of goodwill that will allow the company to thrive in good times and survive when times get tough.

A key takeaway from Edelman's 2009 Trust Barometer is that employees are among the most credible sources of information about a company, behind only industry analysts and articles in business magazines. This means consumers, investors, and others trust what employees are saying more than they trust the words and perceptions of their own friends and family, traditional media, corporate communications, and all other information sources. Commenting on this finding, CEO Richard Edelman said: "Companies had better tell their own employees what's going on first. They're typically the last priority for information... But employees are the people who are in the best position to go either on the offensive or defensive for your company. Transparency is the new green. Say what you're going to do and say why, then actually do it."[3]

BRINGING THE BRAND TO LIFE BEYOND COMPANY WALLS

We all know that we are more likely to commit to a task if it excites or motivates us, if it gets our pulse racing. So it should come as no surprise that employees and consumers will connect more readily with their company or their brand if their "heart is in it." To deliver business success in any form you have to have your people committed to the task. By involving employees in the future of the business you are allowing them to recognize their part in making it happen. By getting agreement on your promise to your consumers you allow all employees to realize their individual responsibility to deliver it.

—Graham Massey and Steven Fuller,
cofounders and codirectors, The House[4]

What is an organization aside from the people who are in its employ at any given time? Yes, an organization is also an "idea"—an entity marked by knowledge and perceptions of its history, its values, its output, and its mission. But those perceptions may be altered by the behaviors of current executives and other talent. From the perspective of people outside the company gates, every employee has the potential to make them think good or ill of the organization. In the most obvious way, all customer-facing employees (from retail clerks and customer-service representatives to the CEO and paid spokespersons) are the "face" of the company. In a less obvious way, all employees potentially represent the company when they are off-duty, whether in face-to-face contact or in online interactions.

Consider these employee statements culled from JobVent.com[5]:

- "Run away from this company! Pay is only good if you are a cheater and lie/steal/bait-switch people into buying policies....Executives turn a blind eye to corruption to preserve their bonuses for putting up big sales numbers. Who cares if the policies are good and profitable, just bind it!"
- "I've worked for Starbucks for almost 8 years....In the end this company has raised me to [be] who I am today. I have learned discipline, responsibility, delegation, multitasking, teamwork, leadership, courage, patience, and much, much more."
- "This company is just awful....We get no support and are constantly dealing with rightfully irate customers."

- "This company is pathetic....I can't believe that [company name] is the largest company in the industry. This company is in disaster mode."
- "Teavana is beyond awesome—pay, benefits, opportunity, and senior management cares about you as a person. Thank you to the founders and mgmt for building such an amazing place!"

Whether one wants them to be or not, employees are de facto brand representatives. The question for Leaders of Tomorrow is this: To what extent should a company deliberately train its talent to carry brand messages into the outside world? Should corporate policies encourage employees to represent the company in their personal lives—and, in particular, online?

As we have gotten to know more about some of the leaders spotlighted in this book, we have been impressed by how heartily they have embraced the notion of transparency and have made it easier for talent to communicate with outside stakeholders, including the general public. These LOTs recognize that their employees are uniquely qualified to spread company messaging in a way that is highly personal and compelling. Of course, this is only effective to the extent that it is self-motivated and genuinely felt; marketing-savvy consumers will be sensitive to the slightest whiff of insincerity or manipulation.

In the following pages, we will look at several ways in which companies are harnessing the power of employees to bring the brand to life.

Make Brand Values an Everyday Reality

It is common for companies to expend millions of dollars on branding campaigns intended to differentiate them in the marketplace. However much money is thrown at the effort, that branding can only be as effective as it is real for the people behind the company and the brand. Months of flawlessly executed television, print, and Internet advertising can be negated by a single interaction between a customer and an employee whose behaviors or attitude are in opposition to the brand promise.

We talked in the last two chapters about e-retailer Zappos.com and how its business has been built on ten core values, including "deliver WOW through service," "create fun and a little weirdness," "build open and honest relationships with communication," and "build a positive team and family spirit." When we asked Aaron Magness, who heads up business development and marketing, how Zappos has managed to make these values an everyday part of employees' work, he told us the values are easily embraced because they came from the inside in an organic and meaningful way.

"Our core values work," Aaron explains, "because they weren't dictated. It wasn't the sort of thing where [CEO] Tony Hsieh and [COO and CFO] Alfred Lin said, 'These are the core values you will live by.' They reached out to the entire company and said, 'We want to come up with a set of values we can all live by. What do you think those are?' Then they took all of these employee responses and fit them into buckets. Our values were created and are driven by the employees and they're embraced by senior management, so both key pieces are there. Everyone knows we hire and fire by these values."[6]

To keep the values alive, Zappos must constantly guard against complacency. Company leaders focus on the existing team and make sure every new hire will enhance the culture. "I can bring in a superstar," Aaron says, "but frankly, if the person's a jerk, in the end it's not going to help us. We need to make sure everyone's mindset is focused: What am I doing to improve the culture, lift morale, etc.? If you get that right, there is really not much else to worry about."[7]

The Ritz-Carlton Hotel Company is another organization that lives its values in a way that is both genuine and ever present. Every employee carries in his or her pocket a card imprinted with the company credo, along with a dozen service values, ranging from "I build strong relationships and create Ritz-Carlton guests for life" and "I am always responsive to the expressed and unexpressed wishes and needs of our guests" to "I am proud of my professional appearance, language and behavior."[8]

Every day, the entire staff—from custodians to the president and COO—gathers in what the company calls its daily "lineups." For fifteen minutes at the start of each shift, Ritz-Carlton's "Ladies and Gentlemen" hear stories about exceptional service, discuss the content of their credo cards, and share information that will help them to improve their customer interactions in the day to come.

At first glance, it might be difficult to find commonality between Ritz-Carlton's corporate culture and that of Zappos. "Ladies and Gentlemen Serving Ladies and Gentlemen" might seem incongruous with the Zappos pledge to be "just a little bit weird." Yet at their core, both companies hire and train people to make customers' experiences the best they can be. For Ritz-Carlton, that means impeccably groomed and discreet staff. For Zappos, it means bad puns and marshmallow-eating contests. In their own way and in their own environment, they both work.

Creating Connections in a Disconnected World

The approach Zappos and Ritz-Carlton are taking to make employees responsible for communicating their company values and culture to customers is of special value in this age of disconnect. Businesses' dedication to maximizing profits and creating shareholder value doesn't always align with customers' interests. Cost-cutting has led to irksome developments such as the dehumanized automation of trial by phone menu ("Please listen to the following options"), lengthy waits for a service operator to answer ("We are experiencing heavy call volumes—your call will be answered in the order received"), and automated reassurances that sound increasingly hollow ("Your business is important to us"). Then, when the call finally gets through, there is the prospect of a conversation with someone incapable of helping (whether because of attitude or lack of training) or somebody halfway around the world whose thick accent makes communication difficult.

Even before the economic crisis, such experiences were making consumers frustrated with business in general. "Why do they make it all so difficult? Why can't I just talk to a live person?" A few years ago, consumers began to band together and share information about how to bypass corporate technology roadblocks and get in touch with an actual live human being. There are now websites where one can peruse business listings to figure out how to crack the code at a particular company. For instance, the GetHuman Database site (www.gethuman.com) tells us that to connect with a human being at Sunoco, one should press "00000" and then mumble when prompted for an account number. People seeking to converse with a live person at SunTrust should call the main number and then "press # rapidly and repeatedly." For DirecTV, it is best not to "press or say anything," while callers to Sony's main number are advised to say "agent" no matter what question is being asked.[9] Other tips being bandied about the Web for reducing call-waiting times include raising one's voice, calling a sales or account-collection number and then asking to be experiences are chronicled in the book *Punching In: The Unauthorized Adventures of a Front-Line Employee* (Collins Business, 2007). In the article, Alex cites the Apple Store as one of two retailers (the other being The Container Store) to make a strong point of hiring people who are passionate about the brand. He notes that Apple employees are trained to interact with customers in a three-part process: "They explained to customers that they had some questions to understand their needs, got permission to fire away, and then kept digging to ascertain which products would be best. Position, permission, probe."[14] This back-and-forth with customers is one of the reasons Apple Stores are able to boast of annual sales in excess of $4,000 per square foot, compared with less than $1,000 per square foot for multibrand retailer Best Buy.[15]

The Apple Store has been so successful in bringing the brand to life for a broader audience that rival Microsoft has announced a similar initiative. The purpose of opening stores, according to Microsoft, "is to create deeper engagement with consumers and continue to learn firsthand about what they want and how they buy."[16] Exactly what the new consumer demands.

Making virtual seem "real"

As more businesses become virtual, companies will need to figure out how to maximize the impact of "customer facing" employees who never actually share face time with any customers. Interactions by phone and e-mail also shape perceptions of the brand.

In an Internet environment in which most services are free, Silicon Valley–based Smugmug.com is one of the few photo-sharing sites that actually charges for all its services, even the most basic. Founded by a father-and-son team in 2002, it is popular among amateur and professional photographers alike. It has been described as "an unusual success story among Internet companies…family-owned, bootstrapped, profitable, and thriving."[17]

Besides doing a very good job with the technological aspects of photo hosting, Smugmug counts as a key to its success its highly responsive customer service, delivered entirely by e-mail. As with The Container Store and Apple Store, company policy is to select customer service staff from among existing users. Smugmug also makes a point to hire people in all time zones around the world. The result is impressively fast, informed, and enthusiastic responses—not transferred to the correct department, or selecting Spanish language (the operators will be bilingual). In this general business context, it is easy to see the increased impact a positive interaction with a "live" employee can have.

Taking a brand "live": The Apple Store

Apple turbocharged its comeback by adding human interaction to the brand experience. It accomplished this by opening dedicated retail stores, designed with the brand's distinctive flair, filled with its must-have products, and, crucially, staffed by Apple experts keen to share their knowledge and enthusiasm. The stores—more than two hundred of them as of early 2009—have been hugely successful in winning over converts to the brand (an estimated 40 to 50 percent of computers sold at the stores go to previous non-Mac users[10]). The employees are typically friendly and helpful, able to adjust the conversation to suit newbies and longtime technophiles, and willing to set up customers' purchases as required. The whole experience is truly "high touch."

Understandably, the Apple Store hiring process is highly competitive and thorough. According to IfoAppleStore.com, an unaffiliated online resource about everything related to Apple's retail operations (yes, even the stores have a fan site!), the company receives an average of two hundred applications for each open store position.[11] Apple judges applicants less on what they know than on who they are and how well they will fit into the store culture. According to the site:

> More than anything, [the] personal interview attempts to judge your suitability to the team, not your technical or sales skills. If Apple hires you, they will train you in both topics, according to their needs. At this point the manager is looking for an Apple advocate or enthusiast who can fit into the store experience that Apple has created....If they find that spark, they can teach you how to repair a Macintosh or sell a computer. It's almost impossible to do the reverse.[12]

To ensure it is drawing from a pool of Mac enthusiasts, the company is known to recruit through fan sites and user groups.

In an article in *Fast Company*, journalist Alex Frankel detailed his experiences as an Apple Store employee. For two years, Alex went "undercover" in a series of entry-level retail jobs to better understand "the world of commerce and the corporate cultures that drive it."[13] His all that common in the world of online services. As one Epinions reviewer put it:

> Smugmug has some of the best customer service I have ever seen. I am almost convinced these people do not leave their desks. I have sent e-mails through all times of the day, morning up to as late as 1:00 a.m. and managed to get replies usually in 30 minutes or less. Once I even got a reply in under 10 minutes. They are always extremely helpful [in] answering questions and are always open to suggestions. I have yet to stump them, and always leave those e-mail back-and-forths feeling wiser and appreciated as a customer. Without a doubt, two thumbs up.[18]

Online or off-, great service leaves the customer feeling valued and connected to the human beings on the other side of the transaction.

Each of the companies we have highlighted in this section has managed to turn employees into brand builders in a way that does not feel forced or artificial—a good thing, since brainwashed drones would be a sure turnoff. Through careful staff selection, internal communication and interaction, and an organic process of aligning staff values and company values, these businesses have made it easy and natural for their employees to live the brand values in every interaction with customers and other outsiders.

Lift the Veil of Secrecy

For companies that have retained a command-and-control mentality, the Internet is a scary place. Rather than consider how informal communication online can be of benefit to the brand, these organizations focus on potential risks, including the damage an employee might do by posting something negative about the company or by acting in a way that is contrary to company thinking and values. A former colleague recounted to us the tale of how his daughter—then aged eleven or twelve—and some of her friends used his e-mail account in the early 1990s to post derogatory messages about people in a public chat room. To them, it was a harmless prank. This man saw it differently, not least because his screen name broadcast the identity of his employer, and so every post the girls made seemed to come from within the company. Needless to say, he spent part of the following evening in the chat room, explaining what had happened and apologizing profusely for the behavior of the girls who had used his account.

So yes, things can go wrong online—and the damage to a company can be very real. However, employee communications can also be of tremendous benefit to the company and its reputation. A survey by Edelman found that employees who blog are twice as likely to present their jobs in a positive light as to denigrate them.[19] In a competitive economy, such positive PR can create an advantage.

Smart corporations are focusing on the upside of free-flowing interactive communication, while also taking steps to manage the inherent risk. Over time, they are becoming more proficient at using employee communication as a way to engage the public in the inner workings of the organization's culture and values. Not surprisingly, companies in the technology space have been leading the way.

Mahesh Murthy, founder and CEO of search-engine marketing firm Pinstorm, says it normally is more traditional companies that seek to control or prevent employee communications online, while IT firms such as Google and Microsoft encourage employees to be active bloggers. A typical approach is to have "insiders" (either from agencies that represent the company or company employees themselves) engage with the wider world through open consumer forums. Their task is to spread the company's viewpoint, while also defending it, calmly and reasonably, against attacks. "At Pinstorm itself, one of the twenty-six parameters for performance assessment is how active the employee has been in publishing blogs and being a part of social communities," Mahesh says.[20]

Great value can be derived from interacting with everyday consumers, but also with specialists such as scientists, advocacy groups, and the technology community. Mobile phone maker Nokia and tech giants IBM and Microsoft are among the companies encouraging their employees to interact with the Web-developer community, offering them assistance and solutions over and above what would be considered within their regular job parameters.[21]

For a company and a corporate brand that has truly transformed itself from the inside out, it is hard to beat IBM. In the early 1980s "Big Blue" was the archetypical corporate behemoth, implicitly attacked by the revolutionaries of Apple in their famous "1984" commercial. In the intervening years, as Microsoft displaced IBM as the tech giant in the spotlight, Big Blue transformed itself into an all-around player in global IT solutions. Beyond that, it has managed to revamp its public persona. Long famed for the caliber of its workforce (employees have earned five Nobel Prizes, six Turing Awards, seven National Medals of Technology and Innovation, and five National Medals of Science[22]), Big Blue was also seen as uptight and stuffy. No more. The company has taken steps to loosen up its buttoned-up image, including establishing a relationship with open-source software Linux and its geeky community in 1999.[23]

IBM has also undertaken a number of innovative communications initiatives geared toward motivating employees to build the brand themselves. One such initiative was ValuesJam, an online gathering of tens of thousands of IBM employees. First held in 2003, the seventy-two-hour event was intended as a way for the internal population to shape its own values. Anyone could add to the ongoing conversation. The following year, more than 57,000 IBMers gathered online to determine how those values could best be applied to improving the company's operations, workforce policies, and relationships.[24]

In a 2008 issue of the *Journal of Business Strategy*, Jon Iwata, IBM's senior vice president of marketing and corporate communications, spoke of the value of two-way collaboration and communication now available through Web 2.0:

> These new media models give us additional ways of reaching audiences with messages. Most challenging is that you have to be willing to allow others in the company—I'd say everyone in the company, eventually—to engage with each other and the external world without continuous monitoring and oversight by "authorized spokespeople." But it starts with recognition that we are no longer in control of our company's messages and channels. Once we liberate ourselves from that illusion, we can begin to adopt new ways, tools and approaches.[25]

It is worth pausing to reflect on the significance of one of the world's biggest and most powerful brands coming right out and saying it is no longer in control of its messages and channels.

For a number of years now, technology pioneer Hewlett-Packard has allowed talent at various levels and functions within the company to maintain their own blogs. Beyond hosting employee business blogs, the HP website also includes an index of links to the personal-interest blogs of its employees. All interactions are guided by a code of conduct that is no more onerous or intrusive than any noncorporate blogging guidelines would be. The company recognized early on how critical this new channel would be in establishing more meaningful relationships with customers and other external stakeholders.

In Chapter Five, we talked about how Zappos CEO Tony Hsieh communicates with employees and customers by sending SMS messages through Twitter. That's just the tip of the communication iceberg for the company. At the time of this writing, 435 Zappos employees are communicating with the world via Twitter. Sample employee tweets from the first week of March 2009:

- "Ooh free hamburgers served up at Zappos today, yep we are spoiled/blessed. Thank you!!!"
- "Heading into Zappos History Class!"
- "Just did an AWESOME parade at Zappos! We're 'Doing More with Less' and saving soda can pop-tops for charity!"
- "Wow! Poker pro Phil Hellmuth is touring Zappos right now. Took a dozen photos with him."
- "New Callaway Hyperbolic golf shoes are live on Zappos! http://tinyurl.com/d43ub5."
- "Meeting at White House tomorrow to discuss ways to help economy that administration may not have thought of yet. What are your suggestions?" [Tweet by Tony Hsieh]
- "Zappos on Celebrity Apprentice this Sunday March 8 on NBC! http://bit.ly/16MRB."
- "About to meet with 43 local high school students to talk about Zappos culture and hiring."
- "Another beautiful day at Zappos!"

The Zappos culture encourages total exposure, through employee tweets, but also through blogs, Zappos TV (posted videos), Facebook, and its annually published (and sold) *Culture Book*. The latter is a collection of hundreds of short essays written by Zappos employees and business partners, explaining what makes the company culture unique and successful. One employee, posting on the book sales site, commented:

Best Book Ever! As an employee at Zappos, I take great pride when I write my annual entry for our *Culture Book*. I would recommend that everyone take a look and see how Zappos has made changes in all of our lives, customers and employees alike. It's exciting to see so many people excited about the same thing, and it's not a billion dollars! :) You never know, reading about our culture may make you step back and take a look at your own life to see if there are any changes that you could make to Wow your own family and friends! Enjoy!

Granted, this employee is shilling a company product, but that level of enthusiasm is not hard to find among Zappos employees. This is not a crowd that shies away from the use of exclamation marks.

We asked Aaron Magness why the company makes such a point of opening itself up to the outside world. He told us that doing business out in the open is not just a positive thing; it is also a necessity in this day and age:

> The days of dictating your brand to the populace are gone. People outside the company can get information faster than you can. They'll find out if someone's being shady or not treating customers well. That is why we embrace transparency. Using the *Culture Book* as an example, it is our chance to say what we really think and to see what everyone else thinks. The public and those outside of the Zappos organization are allowed to see inside our culture and that we're regular people.[26]

Aaron noted that Zappos has begun to take a more formal approach to sharing the secrets of its success with other businesses. "We were getting more and more visitors for company tours every day," he said. "And we were finding that a lot of these people were asking the same questions. That made us wonder how many other people had these questions but weren't asking. We're not interested in guarding the secret sauce; we just want to make all business better. If we can help in that effort, that's great. We've made a lot of mistakes along the way, so if you're starting your business or are in a business, you don't have to make the same mistakes."[27]

At the end of 2008, the company rolled out a new consulting service, Zappos Insights. For just under $40 a month, members get instant access to every update Zappos makes on its site, videotaped interviews recorded in response to user questions, downloadable products for inspiration and training, discussion forums, a library of employee-written articles, and a list of recommended reading.

Expand the Talent Base

Getting people to work together toward a common objective is one of the most powerful ways to align values. And getting consumers to contribute ideas and feedback is one of the smartest ways to drive innovation. Put the two together and you have a potent formula for creating new products, forging bonds between the company and the outside world, and bringing the corporate brand to life.

In the early 2000s, software company Adobe Systems started work on a product aimed at the burgeoning market of digital photographers. A small group of employees went around interviewing photographers to find out where the current pain points were and to design innovative solutions to address them.[28] In a move that is becoming increasingly common, Adobe released a downloadable beta version of the resultant product, Photoshop Lightroom, and set up a forum in which consumers could exchange experiences, feedback, and criticism with the company and with one another. Ongoing interaction on this forum (and others) fed into the product development process leading up to the release of the full 1.0 version in January 2007. The insider-outsider interaction was so effective that it was also used to develop a major upgrade to the company's flagship product, Adobe Photoshop.[29]

As Adobe found, this kind of open interaction can become quite robust, particularly where outspoken prosumers are involved. Criticisms can be harsh, and there is nowhere to hide when news of key staff departures or internal conflicts becomes known. But the payoffs are many: bugs exposed and fixed, a more stable and better-rounded product, greater innovation, and a high level of engagement between insiders and outsiders. Through their actions and responses during intense, ongoing interactions with consumers, employees reveal the company's values and brand DNA. It is probably no coincidence that since 1995 *Fortune* magazine has consistently found Adobe to be one of the best U.S. companies to work for; it ranked eleventh in 2009.[30]

It is not only technology companies that are fostering insider-outsider interaction to drive innovation and spread the brand message. Denmark-based LEGO, founded in the 1930s, is synonymous with the colorful interlocking plastic "bricks" familiar to children all over the world. But the company has had to move with the times to compete in the electronic era. Its Mindstorms programmable bricks were a big hit when first released in 1998, and their fan base was not limited to children. Soon after its release, the original Mindstorms RCX brick (the computer "brain" of the system) was hacked and reverse engineered by enthusiasts, who created a whole raft of ingenious products and applications for it. Initially alarmed by this breach of IP, LEGO ultimately realized that rushing in with cease-and-desist notices would be foolish and that limiting the hackers' creativity would be contrary to its mission of encouraging exploration and ingenuity. So the company actually wrote a "right to hack" provision into the Mindstorms software license, and soon communities of enthusiasts were busy inventing and swapping ideas and code online.

Having seen firsthand the power of customer interaction, LEGO decided to kick it up a notch when developing the third generation of Mindstorms NXT in 2004. It recruited a small group of hard-core enthusiasts to be the Mindstorms User Panel; these unpaid panelists worked with each other and with LEGO to create the product. LEGO later expanded the group to one hundred participants.[31] Clearly, at least in the Mindstorms space, the boundary between LEGO employee and nonemployee has been blurred, to say the least. Between them, through their interactions, they are co-creating the brand.[32]

Foster a Big-Picture Mindset

In Chapter Four, we explored the push away from corporate philanthropy toward a more holistic approach to corporate social responsibility (CSR). And we talked about the importance of involving customers in those initiatives, giving them ways to be part of the "solution" in partnership with brands. On a broader scale, we are seeing Conscious Corporations infuse their workforces with a more global outlook on their work and the impact it has on others, near and far. It is about creating a larger social consciousness and sense of interconnectedness. And while it begins with employees, it invariably extends into the outside realm, as well.

Ritz-Carlton does something really interesting with its Community Footprints program. Rather than simply involve its own talent in "giving back," it recruits guests to work alongside employees—and to pay for the privilege. Through its Give Back Getaways program, hotel guests can devote a few hours to hunger and poverty relief efforts, environmental conservation, or promoting the well-being of disadvantaged children.[33] Guests in Washington, D.C., for instance, can help prepare food for the homeless and others at the DC Central Kitchen, while visitors to Beijing may sign on to plant trees with the Greener

Beijing Institute. Guests staying at the Ritz-Carlton in Istanbul have the option of participating in a children's music-therapy session that has its roots in ancient Turkish-Islamic medicine. Importantly, these programs are open to children as well as adults. It is a great way for the luxury brand to build stronger links between itself and its customers, while also reminding employees of the company's people-centered service culture.

Amsterdam-based logistics company TNT keeps its employees connected to the broader world through a partnership with the World Food Program called Moving the World. The company makes available a fifty-person disaster-response team that is ready to help out anywhere in the world on very short notice.[34] In 2008, for instance, the team shipped 127 metric tons of high-energy biscuits, rice, and ready-to-eat paste for infants, plus clothing and other materials, to villagers displaced by flooding in Bihar, India.[35] This program is obviously a great way to put the specialized skills of TNT employees to use, but the benefits to the company extend beyond pride of accomplishment. The hands-on experiences of TNT employees afford them an expanded world view. Moreover, by blogging about their experiences on the company's website, these employees are spreading the good word about TNT and its corporate values.[36] Reading about how the disaster response team comes to grips with the challenges of overseas assignments is a world away from carefully crafted PR statements. The blogs effectively communicate how employees are busy applying their knowledge to good works and how that enriches their professional and personal lives.

Spreading the word

When CSR didn't extend beyond writing a check to charity, it may not have mattered quite so much whether a company publicized its good deeds. Traditional corporate philanthropy was not typically seen as an avenue for elevating the corporate brand in the eyes of talent, customers, or other stakeholders. As a consequence, it was sometimes carried out relatively invisibly, with little to no thought given to its potential to build stronger brand loyalty, either inside or outside the organization.

It is a different situation today: Consumers are holding their brand partners to higher standards, and they absolutely want to know what brands are doing to solve social and environmental problems. As noted in Chaptr Four, 73 percent of respondents to Euro RSCG's Future of the Corporate Brand study agreed "It is a positive thing for businesses to publicize their corporate social responsibility works and charitable contributions."[37]

Among some companies, the mindset has been that publicizing one's good deeds is somehow gauche or takes away from the spirit of altruism that underlies them. As a consequence, these companies hide their light under a virtual bushel basket and prevent customers—and sometimes even employees—from taking an active role in the good works.

We had an interesting conversation with two executives at Global Hyatt Corporation: John Wallis, chief marketing officer, and Brigitta Witt, vice president for environmental affairs. They talked about how Hyatt has been actively involved in sustainability efforts for the past decade, with five areas of focus: energy, waste, supply chain, sustainable construction, and employee awareness/engagement.

Brigitta told us that when she joined the company in early 2008, she thought she was going to have to build a sustainability program from scratch. As an outsider up to that point, she had not been privy to all the steps Hyatt was already taking to reduce its energy use and negative impact on the planet. "When I arrived," she said, "I soon realized there were already a lot of efforts happening in the field—and there already was tremendous enthusiasm and passion among employees for sustainability. So that wasn't the hard part. Now we are working to fundamentally transform the DNA of the company to champion sustainability."[38]

Every Hyatt employee is receiving green training, courtesy of an on-site team at each hotel property. John explained, "Training is given not by 'corporate' but by the Green Team in each hotel to the other staff. The key ingredient to our success is that the evangelists are managing the process. They are passionate about it."[39]

The Green Teams typically are made up of one person from each department, according to Brigitta, "because this is something that really does impact every aspect of the business—it's not just a housekeeping issue or an operations issue."[40] Headquarters gives the teams a blueprint to follow, including communication guidelines and an online forum in which employees can communicate and collaborate on sustainability efforts. "I've been surprised and humbled by how many employees are engaged in this initiative," she added. "They are contributing their individual passions and personal time. We simply mobilized them by giving them permission to act creatively to follow their passion."[41]

One way Hyatt measures employee engagement in sustainability processes is through the creativity that comes out of individual hotels. Every market is different, and some employees are facing unique challenges. For example, in Santiago, Chile—a city with minimal environmental awareness—employees had to figure out how to recycle in the absence of any sort of public infrastructure. The solution: The hotel got three local charities to provide them with recycling bins; when they're full, the charities pick them up and are able to sell the contents and keep all proceeds. The program has proved so successful that the city government has asked the local Hyatt Green Team to come into schools to teach students about recycling. "Although there are cultural differences around the world, the notion of doing the right thing unites everyone," Brigitta said.[42]

As should be the case for any company, Hyatt is engaged in sustainability out of enlightened self-interest. According to Brigitta: "We're doing it because it's the right thing to do. We have an impact in every single community in which we are located, and it's our responsibility to ensure we're making a positive contribution to those communities. But it also makes good business sense. Whatever we can do to make sure we're operating more efficiently will have a positive impact on the bottom line."[43]

Up to this point, Hyatt has not used sustainability as a marketing tool. That was a conscious choice, John told us, because the company had made a commitment that this would be more than just some PR effort. However, that policy may change now that external stakeholders have become more demanding. "Our customers—individual travelers and large corporate clients—want to know more about what we are doing. Do we have a CSR statement? What is our recycling policy? And so on," Brigitta explained. "We are going to need to start communicating more with the public about it, because that's something they expect today. But if and when we do communicate, it will be in a meaningful way. We're not going to issue a press release to say we're using recycled pens in all of our rooms; if we did that, we would be sending out press releases all day."[44]

Now that the talent has bought into the company's sustainability efforts, John sees customer engagement as a next step: "We have set out to awaken the environmental consciousness of eighty-five thousand employees around the world. Our belief is that if we educate ourselves first, our staff will tell our customers, and, in turn, customers will get engaged."[45]

Cultivate Brand Ambassadors

It would be difficult to overstate the potential financial value of building a sense of community among customers and talent. A 2006 study of more than 140,000 registered eBay users found that members who were active in one of their discussion communities won up to 25 percent more auctions and spent 54 percent more total dollars.[46] Furthermore, a study by Jack Morton Worldwide found that 70 percent of consumers said participating in a brand experience increases their likelihood of purchasing that brand's products; 75 percent of those who had participated in a live marketing experience said they were now more receptive to the brand's advertising.[47]

We spoke in Chapter Three about the value of involving consumers in corporate initiatives. The truth is, many consumers are every bit as hungry to connect with brands as the brands are to connect with them. It is an irony of our modern world that the more tools of connectivity become available, the more isolated we feel. People are craving more meaningful connections, and the Conscious Corporation is responding by helping its customers forge human bonds—with the company, with each other, and with their communities—and in so doing is helping to create fiercely loyal brand ambassadors.

There are all sorts of ways to engage consumers in a brand-based community. One of the pioneers in this area is iconic motorcycle brand Harley-Davidson, which has made membership in the million-strong Harley Owners Group (H.O.G.) a major brand benefit. What other company has developed sufficiently strong brand loyalty to get more than 200,000 customers from all over the world to travel, at their own expense, to a hundredth anniversary party in Wisconsin?

If any company could come close to matching Harley-Davidson in terms of brand devotion, it probably would be Apple. The biannual Macworld conferences have been compared to religious revival meetings, with Steve Jobs in the role of charismatic cult leader. Mac users think of themselves as a distinct subculture—people bound by loyalty to a brand that connotes nonconformity, liberty, and creativity. In the words of a Mac fanatic, as quoted in *Wired*:

> If you see somebody in an airport in London, or someplace down in Peru or something, and you see an Apple tag on their bag, or an Apple T-shirt, it's like the Deadheads...you have an instant friend. Most likely, you share something very core to your being with this person, which is a life outlook, a special vision.[48]

Nike may not enjoy quite the same devotion in its loyalists as Harley-Davidson and Apple do, but the company has done a tremendous job in building communities around its "Just Do It" ethos. As one example, the Nike+ initiative makes excellent use of new technologies to harness the passion of the running community. Through a wireless system created in partnership with Apple, runners can track distance, speed, and calories burned on their runs and log the cumulative info on Nikeplus.com. The site also offers all sorts of opportunities to retrieve information, get support, and interact with other running enthusiasts (and novices). There are tips on training, route information shared by runners, and opportunities to come together in races sponsored by Nike and others. Members can even issue specific challenges—e.g., eight miles a day for a week, most miles in a month, fastest three-kilometer run—and monitor each others' participation and progress. As of this writing, the Nike+ community had logged a cumulative 120 million miles...and counting.

Nike+ may not be a formal brand ambassador program in the way that some other companies have dedicated programs involving product sampling and the like. Yet it would seem at least as effective in building brand loyalty and esteem over the long term. For some participants, the program has proved life changing. As one new running enthusiast posted on the site:

> I am so grateful to Nike+ for everything it has done for me; it gave me the little incentive to get off the couch and go out and run. I bought the shoes, the sport kit, and got running. First, I ran just 1.5 miles, and now I am up to 13.2 miles. I love hearing the feedback and my pace. Why do this, you ask? I tell people it's because I got tired of being fat, being out of breath. I want to be thin and healthy, and I have lost over 30 pounds. I am sore, tired, fatigued, hungry, and so happy. How is that possible? Run and finish and you will know. March 3rd 2008 I am running a marathon with Nike+.

On August 31, 2008, Nike held the Nike+ Human Race, the biggest one-day running event in history. Runners converged on twenty-five cities across the globe for a ten-kilometer race, followed by concerts by such well-known artists as Kanye West, Moby, Ben Harper, and Fall Out Boy. More than a million runners participated in the event, raising some $3 million for the U.N. Refugee Agency, the Lance Armstrong Foundation, and the World Wildlife Fund.[49] So, maybe the folks in Beaverton, Oregon, *are* giving Harley-Davidson a run for its money!

Whether seeking brand ambassadors, unpaid advisers, or active participants in brand initiatives, there is huge potential for companies to stimulate and harness the energy of employees and customers. Treated right, these people will willingly and energetically carry the brand's values and "vibe" into the wider world. The smartest companies will enjoy the multiple benefits of engaging their best and brightest talent in growing the corporate brand, attracting their first choice of new talent, and projecting the brand in tangible and meaningful ways to customers and investors.

We have moved past the point at which this might be considered some sort of risky "bleeding edge" thinking. There are more than enough examples with a track record to show that employee- and customer-mediated branding works well—and more than enough examples for companies to find inspiration for their own initiatives.

In the next two chapters, we will share insights into how leading companies of today are creating the sorts of core values and missions capable of engaging both internal talent and external stakeholders, while also growing the business and the brand.

Part III

ACCELERATING THE MOMENTUM OF THE CORPORATE BRAND

Chapter Eight

VISION, SHMISION—GETTING REAL WITH A USEFUL STATEMENT OF DIRECTION

Obstacles are those frightful things you see when you take your eyes off your goal.

—Henry Ford, founder, Ford Motor Company

We have talked in broad terms about the forces pushing us toward a more humanized business culture and the new imperatives for interacting with stakeholders. Yet we have also seen that every company that is leading its industry in these areas has its own blueprint. Whereas some businesses have been built on the principles of humanized conduct, others have made a more gradual shift from traditional capitalism to enlightened self-interest. Where some Leaders of Tomorrow (LOTs) steer their businesses in the direction of their own personal passions (think: Robert Redford, Richard Branson), others gradually develop an affinity for someone else's vision of a purpose beyond profit. What each successful business has in common is a single-minded vision or unifying objective that serves as a benchmark against which to judge individual business decisions. Will the decision move the company closer to or farther away from the desired goal? Is the decision in keeping with the values central to the company's view of itself?

FROM BEST PRACTICE TO THE BUTT OF JOKES IN A DECADE: THE MISSION STATEMENT

It is difficult to imagine anything that has given birth to more puffery, confusion, and conceit than the corporate mission statement. All too often, committees piece together a hodgepodge of high-minded statements of intent and impossible-to-attain "visions" that bear little relation to the actual workings of the company. Once the statement has gotten an executive sign-off, it is circulated to the corporate masses and printed and reprinted on every report, press release, and other material intended for public or shareholder consumption. Yet the statement rarely has a clear impact on the corporate brand or on how the company conducts its business day to day or over the longer term.

There is nothing inherently wrong with the concept of a statement of mission. In fact, we would argue such a statement is essential to corporate success. The problem is, the majority of these statements are neither well conceived nor properly embedded and executed. This is partly due to their near-universal use: Everyone feels they must have one, but too few know how to do it right.

Mission statements have been around for quite some time, but the practice really exploded in the 1990s. Numerous books were published about the concept, including such popular titles as Patricia Jones and Larry Kahaner's *Say It and Live It* (1995); John W. Graham's reference tome *Mission Statements: A Guide to the Corporate and Nonprofit Sectors* (1994); and Joseph V. Quigley's *Vision: How Leaders Develop It, Share It, and Sustain It* (1995). This spate of literature and all that came after illustrates how a worthwhile concept can actually lose strategic relevance as it spreads.

Ultimately, the mission statement moved beyond the office and into popular culture, but as an object of derision rather than respect. Scott Adams's "Dilbert" comic strip, which so hilariously chronicles the bureaucratic ineptitude of many workplaces, regularly lampoons jargon-filled corporate statements. For a time, the Dilbert.com website even featured the Dilbert Mission Statement Generator: Users could make selections from a list of adverbs, verbs, adjectives, and nouns, and generate such doozies as: "Our mission is to continue to efficiently facilitate diverse methods of empowerment and professionally disseminate performance based deliverables to meet our customer's needs." Sadly, that statement is not all that far removed from some of the ones we have spotted in the real world. As evidence of how bad it has gotten, a woman in an online message board posted this statement: "It is our mission to dramatically initiate performance based opportunities as well as to proactively leverage existing quality leadership skills to meet our customer's needs." A colleague of her husband was charged with writing a corporate mission statement and had jokingly put this one together and left it on his boss's desk. He expected his employer to laugh and instruct him to write a "real" one. Imagine his astonishment—or, perhaps, horror—when he discovered his boss had actually taken the statement seriously and had it framed and mounted near the office entrance.[1]

Given the superficial, convoluted, and/or jargon-filled nature of so many mission statements, it can come as no surprise that the internal stakeholders—the talent—have grown cynical about their worth. (This cynicism is particularly prevalent among the new generation of employees, the so-called Millennials, for they are less apt than their older counterparts to "drink the Kool-Aid" without first scrutinizing the ingredients.) As a consequence of such disregard, many corporate visions enter neither common parlance nor common practice within the organization.

As we move into this new era of the Conscious Corporation, it will fall to the top executives to address and amend the dichotomy between the need for organization-wide strategic alignment and the cynicism that too often prevents it. These leaders will achieve this by replacing false promises and vague objectives with a carefully crafted, unquestionably meaningful, and, most important, *useful* embodiment of corporate vision and values. Stripping it of all subtlety and sophistication, we have come to call it a Useful Statement of Direction (USOD). When embedded and sustained within the organization, that statement becomes a guiding light that illuminates strategic decisions and actions year after year, whether in boom times or in bust.

ASSESSING THE CURRENT STATE OF PLAY

In our combined decades of experience as consultants, marketers, and heads of business, each of us has had an opportunity to work with organizations at all stages of evolving business plans, strategic plans, and mission statements. Cavas Gobhai, in particular, has been a leader in this area, having spent more than thirty years working with organizations ranging from startups to Fortune 500 companies, from fiercely profit-oriented corporations in the private sector to cities, towns, and nongov-ernmental organizations in places as diverse as Boston, Bombay, and Berlin. A trusted resource to LOTs, Cavas and his services are widely regarded as the gold standard in strategic, creative, and collaborative thinking. He often characterizes his practice as "top teams creating out loud." Many of the insights and terms introduced throughout this chapter and the next are taken from his practice, although the thinking of all the authors is represented in these pages.

Before we get into best practices, we thought it would be useful to identify four rungs in the progression toward a viable statement of direc-tion. The job of the LOT is to get the organization to that final rung.

First Rung: What USOD?

- No USOD, period: Within these unguided organizations, tactical decisions are made in the absence of any compelling directional context. We are glad to report this end of the spec-trum has become much less populated of late.
- An incomplete USOD: One that lacks all the components of a truly useful statement of direction. This typically is the result of an aborted effort begun around a conference table and then abandoned for lack of ability, leadership, or prioritization.
- No "real" USOD: This vision is intended for framing in the conference room or foyer, as proof the corporate leadership have done their duty and can now get back to what really counts: the company's day-to-day activities, albeit rudderless and without any clear destination.

Second Rung: That's Classified, Buster!

- Only the boss knows: The syndrome is all too familiar: "What do they mean they have no direction? I must have said it a hun-dred times!" (When told his employees' number-one complaint is "unclear objectives," Dilbert's pointy-haired boss replies, "*My* number-one complaint is that it takes too much effort for me to be clear.... Why are they so selfish?"[2] A response that would ring all too true in some workplaces.)
- Only the consultants know: They had better know; we paid a lot of money for that presentation! The boss, having

recognized the need for a vision, has cleverly outsourced this vital activity.

- Only the cool crowd knows: A high-level team keeps the USOD close to the vest, driven either by a failure to communicate (due to lack of skill or will) or, to greater detriment, by a command-and-control culture that regards information as power. (This tendency may become more marked in difficult times. When the prospect of layoffs looms, some top teams retreat into their lairs and lose transparency, just at the time when it is needed most to engender and sustain trust.)

Third Rung: We're Getting There

- The basic package: A LOT-driven, well-crafted USOD, owned by the top team, is spread through one-way communication alone.
- The upgrade: The above, plus an opportunity for Q&A—though only for clarity. This is an exercise intended to elicit but one response: "Yes, I understand."

Fourth Rung: EUREKA!

- The LOT package: This stage includes not just a well-written and thought-out USOD, but also a series of carefully planned forums held organization-wide. In rare instances, thanks to new media, they might even be extended to encompass key segments of the stakeholder community. These forums serve to embed the USOD not merely in a way that speaks to the head, but also in a compelling way that speaks to the heart—a combination that moves the talent from passive acceptance to engaged ownership and commitment. Over time, the USOD evolves from a written statement into a living, breathing force that powers the company's growth—a force that is firmly yet flexibly embedded into the Conscious Corporation. (We will address this rung and the seeming paradox between firmness and flexibility in the next chapter.)

At this final stage, it becomes the job of the LOT and other top executives to sustain the USOD activity, in formal and informal ways, on an ongoing basis. Virtually every communication must be viewed as an opportunity to spread strategic alignment—clarifying the "why" behind each "what." Indeed, as we will later see, this simple device of including the why in each communication becomes an effective way of informally spreading the USOD within the organization.

CREATING THE FRAMEWORK FOR THE USOD

We have already established that in the new business environment, both the internal and external constituencies care about and are moved by the company's long-term vision. As an organization becomes more transparent and accountable, it must anticipate that its stakeholders will take an interest in all it does. Where once the words and assurances of a charismatic leader might have been taken on faith, now there is more of an insistence on a written unifying direction that is clearly understood within the organization and easily communicated to interested parties on the outside.

Before we get into the individual characteristics of an effective USOD, it will help to set out a framework that explains the various components it must incorporate. For a USOD is not just a simple statement of mission or vision (though that is part of it). Such statements—particularly what we would call the "bumper sticker" variety—typically lay out the "what" ("We're going to own the category!"), less often the "why" ("based on the emerging 'x' trend and our clear 'y' strength"), and most often leave out entirely the "how." A genuinely useful statement of direction, in contrast, covers not just the ends, but also the ways and means.

LOTs may find it helpful to think of the USOD as a journey—which makes sense, given it is intended to get an organization from where it is to where it wants to be. There are four basic components to that journey:

- The Destination: A description of the company's desired state. (Where do we envision ourselves in our optimal future?) More and more, as the Conscious Corporation continues its ascent, we will see this destination infused with a higher purpose—an increasingly essential element in winning over shareholders and the newly empowered consumer.
- The Path: The avenues (strategies) and streets (tactics) that will lead to the destination.
- The Engine: The capabilities, assets, resources, and structure that will propel the organization down the Path and toward

the ultimate Destination. Most often, these will include not just means that are currently possessed, but also means that need to be developed or acquired.

- The Lighting: These are the streetlights and traffic lights (and some stoplights!) that illuminate and guide the path. In other words, the organization's values and beliefs. The Conscious Corporation cannot exist in the absence of this kind of light. Certainty of these values—including nimbleness, creativity, and collaboration—are what enable the flexing of some of the key elements of the USOD in response to changed external scenarios, while also allowing the organization to remain true to its Destination and Path.

Using Ben & Jerry's as an example, we see how these components work together and affect each other and both local and corporate operations.

The Destination

This is expressed in the company's three intertwined missions:

- The Product Mission: "To make, distribute and sell the finest quality all natural ice cream and euphoric concoctions with a continued commitment to incorporating wholesome, natural ingredients and promoting business practices that respect the Earth and the Environment."
- The Economic Mission: "To operate the Company on a sustainable financial basis of profitable growth, increasing value for our stakeholders and expanding opportunities for development and career growth for our employees."
- The Social Mission: "To operate the company in a way that actively recognizes the central role that business plays in society by initiating innovative ways to improve the quality of life locally, nationally and internationally."

Central to these missions is the belief that "all three parts must thrive equally in a manner that commands deep respect for individuals in and outside the company and supports the communities of which they are a part."[3]

The Path

Strategies and tactics that lead toward the Destination are various and ever growing. They include, among many others:

- Emphasizing values-led sourcing (Fair Trade and organic ingredients; supporting local and values-based suppliers)
- Rejecting milk from cows treated with recombinant Bovine Growth Hormone (rBGH)
- Supporting social and environmental progress through the Ben & Jerry's Foundation; the Ben & Jerry's PartnerShop Program (under which select scoop shops are independently owned and operated by community-based nonprofit organizations); the Lick Global Warming education and action campaign; and such promotions as Global Free Cone Day.

The Engine

Powering the company are such things as:

- The global reach afforded by its $326 million acquisition by Unilever in 2000
- Its successful franchising system.

The Lighting

The progressive orientation of Ben and Jerry's founders, Ben Cohen and Jerry Greenfield, is well known. Among the values that guide the company:

- Creating economic opportunities to narrow the gap between rich and poor
- Minimizing any negative impact on the environment
- Using and promoting sustainable and nontoxic methods of food production
- Supporting nonviolent ways to achieve peace and justice
- Showing a deep respect for human beings inside and outside the company.

All these values are in keeping with the four cornerstones of the Conscious Corporation.

The strategic alignment that binds each of these elements has proved sufficiently strong to keep the company true to its founders' mission and values even under new leadership and ownership by a multinational conglomerate.

PRINCIPLES TO KEEP IN MIND

In addition to understanding this very basic framework—and the essential nature of each component of the journey—the LOT and other executives will keep the following basic principles in mind when working to devise a USOD.

"Simplify, Simplify, Simplify"

It is a paradox of the modern business world that the more complex an organization becomes, the simpler its brand vision need be. As a company's internal and external constituencies grow larger (and, typically, more scattered), it becomes increasingly important to provide a unifying sense of direction and purpose that is easily, even intuitively, understood by all stakeholders within and outside the organization. This means the USOD must be simple in both concept and language. As a simple statement of mission, it would be hard to beat this directive from Fujifilm: "KILL KODAK." Point taken.

"Open It Up"

There is little sense in hiring smart, creative people if one is not going to use them to maximum benefit. Nor does it make sense to develop a USOD in a vacuum. Creating a Useful Statement of Direction is an opportunity to focus the smarts and the hearts of one's entire talent base and, in some cases, even to solicit input from interested outsiders, including top customers. Uniformly, true LOTs will enlist the active assistance and perspective of outside resources, benefiting from their wide-angle view of the external environment and their tough-minded and objective evaluation of the company's internal strengths and weaknesses. As President Woodrow Wilson so smartly said, "I not only use all the brains I have, but all I can borrow."

There is no formula for identifying whose ideas and insights will be most valuable in creating a USOD at any specific organization. What is important is that the LOT and others within the organization be open to the possibility that sometimes the people with the clearest, least biased perspective might be those with a distant view of the forest rather than those tending to the corporate trees. There potentially is much value to be gained by tapping into external constituencies—whether consumers, NGOs, or some other group—rather than viewing them as a threat to be contained.

"Aim 'Em, Don't Tame 'Em, and Get Out of the Way"

We will discuss this notion at greater length in Chapter Nine. For now, suffice it to say that creating and embedding a Useful Statement of Direction will require leadership based on direction, motivation, and empowerment rather than the traditional reliance on command and control. At a minimum, this means creating a meaningful USOD, selling it through to the talent and eliciting their genuine commitment to infusing it into their work and mindset, and then giving the talent the space and resources they need to bring the USOD to life. At many, if not most, established companies, this will necessitate removing barriers both hard (e.g., antiquated legacy systems, counterproductive bureaucratic controls) and soft (e.g., outmoded institutional beliefs that may have been important to a company's past success but now are impeding its future growth).

PREPARING TO CREATE THE USOD: BASIC STEPS

Before any discussion of Destination, Path, or Engine can take place, the company must lay sound groundwork:

First, the organization will need to define its space, the other players in that space, and a commonly held, unflinchingly accurate view of the current state of the company. How is it perceived and received? Everyone knows that getting to a destination is far easier when the starting point is clear. Before the process begins, the current reality must be understood, blemishes and all.

Second, the team needs to take an outside-in approach. By this we mean looking at the implications of various external forces and boiling them down to those critical factors that anyone in the space must do excellently to win. (We call those Future Success Factors.) For the Conscious Corporation of tomorrow, these will include the four cornerstones outlined earlier in the book: purpose beyond profit, people-focused culture, championing sustainability, and respect for consumers' power.

And third, the company will take some time to look in the mirror—the "inside" factor of the outside-in approach. This is the time to identify organizational strengths and weaknesses, as viewed in the context of the earlier two steps. When analyzing strengths, the LOT will keep the team honest by first asking, "Is that strength relevant to the shortlist of Future Success Factors?" And then, "Compared with whom (i.e., against which competitors can it be considered a strength)?" and "According to whom?" The latter questions serve as a reminder of the competition (from both inside and outside the category) and, of critical importance today, the newly expanded and activated stakeholder community. Those working on the inside and judging from the outside may have vastly different perceptions of a company's strengths.

It is only after these issues have been addressed that the team has earned the right to explore collaboratively and creatively a range of alternatives that will lead to what we might confidently call the "right" USOD. As we will see in the next chapter, this creativity and collaboration will stand the Conscious Corporation in good stead, especially when the going gets tough.

DEVELOPING THE USOD: KEY CHARACTERISTICS

Now that the company has done the prep work needed to begin the statement-development process, it is time to apprise the working team of three essential elements to keep in mind. These characteristics will ensure the USOD is broadly usable and adaptable.

Back when we first began talking about USODs with clients, we took a certain pride in the subtlety and sophistication we were able to bring to the task. We came to the table with more than a dozen criteria—all different and, we thought, important—against which every potential USOD should be measured. All appeared to be going well until we were brought up short at one meeting by a read-my-lips type of interruption: "I said THREE, not TWENTY-THREE," shouted the LOT, as we were midway through the list of criteria. He knew then what we have since discovered and mentioned earlier: that the complexity of the current environment demands a simplicity of approach and communication.

We soon pared down our list to three absolutely critical, don't-even-think-about-ignoring-them criteria. Granted, we did fudge a bit by folding a number of our original criteria into these double-barreled three. (You see, even we the authors have adopted the principle of transparency!)

The First Characteristic: Memorable Focus

There is no sense in creating a USOD that lacks focus. That much is obvious. If the statement of direction does not contain a clear mission of purpose and objective built on concrete and specific goals, it is not useful—and, by definition, cannot be considered a USOD. Successful companies are not built on abstractions.

A quick Internet search turned up these gems of mission statements (identities have been shielded to protect the unimaginative):

- "To supply outstanding service and solutions through dedication and excellence."
- "To improve and enhance the lives of those whom we touch, by leveraging professional competence and by being relevant to all who are impacted."
- "To produce innovative, value intensive products by cultivating the creativity and capabilities of dedicated employees who support the common goal of creating and maintaining satisfied customers."

Would you have any idea what industries these businesses are in? (Any reader who guessed construction materials, human-resource services, and lighting products, respectively, should close this book immediately and open up shop as a psychic or freak-show attraction. You'll make millions.) Looking at those mission statements, would you be able to divine what these companies see as their optimal futures? If you were an employee of any of these organizations, would the mission statement provide clarity and guidance to your everyday work? Our guess is your answer is "no" to all of the above.

Now consider these statements, which represent the first "catchy" and memorable parts of a subsequently fleshed-out USOD:

- "We are Ladies and Gentlemen serving Ladies and Gentlemen." (Ritz-Carlton)

- "Dogs rule. Everything we do is for the love of dogs, from the dog food we make to the dog adoption drive we support." (Pedigree)
- "To build a place where people can come to find and discover anything they might want to buy online." (Amazon.com)

Each one of these statements of mission provides a specific focus for internal talent, as well as a clearly articulated message of purpose for customers and other stakeholders. They vary in the degree to which they might be considered memorable, though none of them fails on this score.

Our directive that a USOD should be *memorable* as well as *focused* stems from the simple fact that highly memorable statements are more apt to permeate both minds and hearts, and drive the actions of internal stakeholders: the talent. If employees have to flip through a three-ring binder or check the corporate website to remind themselves of the company vision, it is all but certain the vision is not having any measurable impact on corporate behavior—or results.

Even in a fairly complex USOD, there need to be certain core concepts and verbiage that can easily be recalled by all stakeholders and consistently applied by talent across functions. Steve Knox, CEO of Procter & Gamble's Tremor marketing division, tells us every single one of P & G's more than 130,000 employees can recite the company's mission to "provide branded products and services of superior quality and value that improve the lives of the world's consumers."[4] That commonality of vision serves as a great recruiting tool for the company.

Whole Foods Market is a company we have already held up as a superior example of the Conscious Corporation. The core values by which it operates are clear, focused, and of great relevance and importance to stakeholders (whether internal talent, customers, or shareholders):

- Selling the highest quality natural and organic products available
- Satisfying and delighting our customers
- Supporting team member happiness and excellence
- Creating wealth through profits and growth
- Caring about our communities and our environment
- Creating ongoing win-win partnerships with our suppliers.

In introducing these values on its website, Whole Foods explains:

> The following list of core values reflects what is truly important
> to us as an organization. These are not values that change from
> time to time, situation to situation or person to person, but rather
> they are the underpinning of our company culture. Many people
> feel Whole Foods Market is an exciting company of which to be
> a part and a very special place to work. These core values are the
> primary reasons for this feeling, and they transcend our size and
> our growth rate. By maintaining these core values, regardless of
> how large a company Whole Foods Market becomes, we can pre-
> serve what has always been special about our company. These core
> values are the soul of our company.[5]

As noted earlier, Whole Foods is one of those companies that affixes
its list of values on the walls of at least some retail locations. They are
proudly proclaimed for retail customers and frontline staff alike to
see. That's all to the good, but taken together, are those values necessarily memorable? We would argue that certain of them are; it would
be easy for store employees to remember their mission of "satisfying
and delighting customers." And managers are likely reminded by their
underlings from time to time of their mission to "support team member happiness and excellence." It might be difficult, on the other hand,
to recite all six values in their entirety or to remember each one in the
process of making a business decision. That does not matter, because
the company has come up with a very straightforward (yet comprehensive) statement of principles that incorporates each of these values
in a way that is highly memorable and useful: "Whole Foods. Whole
People. Whole Planet." Now that is what we call memorable focus.

With just half a dozen words, the company clearly states its reason for being, the vision of the future it intends to help achieve, and
the criteria by which every business decision must be judged. If the
decision falls outside the parameters of whole foods, people, or planet,
then it is contrary to the mission of the business and potentially deleterious to its growth.

We are the first to admit how difficult it is to achieve a mission
statement as simple yet meaningful and memorable as that of Whole
Foods. Few companies will be fortunate enough to match it, but,
once a vision has been established, there are certain tricks that can be
employed to make the statement more memorable (and, hence, more
widely remembered and used).

Sometimes wordplay—such as the use of an acronym, alliteration, or rhyme—can serve as an important aid in retention and use. Some of these may sound a bit corny to the uninvolved critic, but that matters little if they are effective. One of our clients—a small, private equity–funded quick-service food chain—was determined to grow its business without losing sight of the values and traits that set it apart in its category. Working with the CEO and others, we helped devise a USOD that included, at the top, a simple mnemonic: "Company X is the place to be because Company X's…GOT ME!" (Later on in the embedding process, the company added, "It starts with ME!")

Though "Company X's…GOT ME!" might sound like nothing more than an employee rallying cry, it actually encapsulates important information about the company's operations and mission. Each letter in "GOT ME" stands for a one-word strategic objective: Growth, Operations, Team, Marketing, and Environment. (We should note this mnemonic was simply the first layer of the USOD. Each of those objectives was augmented by a memorable one-line statement of the intended Path, and then near-term goals and tactics were enunciated for each Path.)

In the aggregate, "because Company X's…GOT ME" reflects the sense of pride the company works hard to instill in its employees, as well as the extent to which the leadership values the individual contributions of the talent. This is critical in every industry, but is perhaps even more so in retail businesses, where store-level employees are the customer-facing front line of the company—they make it happen. Ultimately, this wordplay became a vital part of a fully formed USOD that will shape this company's business decisions going forward, while also ensuring managers and employees at all locations are committed to a common vision.

A point to remember is that a unique and clearly differentiated Destination may pale in usefulness and ultimate impact compared with one that appears pedestrian or trite when viewed on a stand-alone basis. Once carefully defined and embedded—and viewed in the context of the USOD—virtually any set of words can be extremely powerful.

The Second Characteristic: Credible Stretch

Done right, the USOD will be simple enough to enunciate to—and be understood by—the various stakeholder communities. It will be bolstered by some sense of credibility, whether that stems from a charismatic and trusted leader (e.g., Paul Newman and Newman's Own), a cultural or historical association (e.g., IKEA's Swedish heritage), or some other differentiating strength. Yet the USOD must also be sufficiently inspiring to engage hearts and minds and sufficiently aspirational to keep employees on their toes.

A common mistake we see is to stray too close to either end of the attainability spectrum: When stating their mission, some companies do no more than describe where they already are. (Isn't it great? We've made it!) Others aim so high—perhaps only because they enjoy the self-indulgence of soaring rhetoric—that their stipulated goals cannot possibly be achieved. In our experience, the most successful USODs are those that balance credibility and aspiration, motivating talent with shared goals that encourage them to stretch as individuals and as a team without being so lofty they are dismissed out of hand.

If one asks people familiar with Google to name the company's mission, they will likely respond, "Don't be evil." That is, in fact, one of its mottos, but the search giant's formal mission is "to organize the world's information and make it universally accessible and useful." It is a mission that already incorporates a whole lot of "stretch," but it is well within the scope of what Google seeks to accomplish from day to day. Importantly, Google's USOD (regardless of whether the company terms it as such) is given added granularity and focus by an overarching corporate philosophy ("Never settle for the best") built on these ten "truths":[6]

- "Focus on the user and all else will follow." Google's decisions are centered not on what is best for shareholders but on what is best for the end user.
- "It's best to do one thing really, really well." By having an unrelenting focus on creating the "perfect" search engine, Google is continually finding new solutions and user-centered products (e.g., Gmail, Google Desktop, Google Maps) that fuel the company's growth.
- "Fast is better than slow." All efforts must be geared toward minimizing the time users spend on search. Or, as the company website says: "Google may be the only company in the world whose stated goal is to have users leave its website as quickly as possible."[7]

- "Democracy on the Web works." The company's page-ranking mechanism relies on the power of millions of users to assign value to sources of information.
- "You don't need to be at your desk to need an answer." Google is dedicated to offering search to everyone in every place, whether at home, in the office, on the road, or off the beaten track.
- "You can make money without doing evil." The integrity of search results will never be compromised for financial gain.
- "There's always more information out there." Google's researchers continuously look for new ways to bring all the world's information to those who seek it.
- "The need for information crosses all borders." The company is committed to facilitating access to information in every part of the world and virtually every language.
- "You can be serious without a suit." Google's talent-centered campus and corporate culture (perhaps "noncorporate culture" would be more apt) are built on the idea that "work should be challenging and the challenge should be fun."
- "Great just isn't good enough." Google considers being the best in its category a starting point, not an endpoint. It continually strives not only to improve existing products and services, but also to anticipate and meet needs that have not yet been articulated by customers.

Leaders of Tomorrow will recognize the value of incorporating into their USODs those fundamental truths that bolster the corporate mission and force the company to stretch in positive ways. Articulating these truths and making them a part of the internal conversation will help to ensure none is sacrificed on the altar of short-term (and short-sighted) financial gain.

The Third Characteristic: Compelling Linkage

The final vital characteristic of a Useful Statement of Direction is linkage. There must be *vertical linkage* among the various elements of the USOD. In the case of the talent, especially, it must be apparent how the Destination was derived from the analysis of external and internal factors. Further, it must be clear how the company's Engine (capabilities, assets, etc.) will be used to propel the company down the envisioned Path (strategies and tactics) toward the agreed-upon Destination (the company's optimal future). And, for the conscious corporate brand of tomorrow, it must be equally clear how the corporate Lighting (values and beliefs) will illuminate the entire journey. A disconnect anywhere along the way will ensure the Destination remains out of reach.

There must also be *horizontal linkage* across the various elements of the USOD. The corporate values (aka Lighting), for instance, must be complementary and in no way in conflict with one another. Nor should the paths be moving the company in divergent directions. Pretty obvious stuff, but we have all seen businesses with units operating at cross-purposes.

And finally, and perhaps most important, there is the *inward linkage* between the USOD and the internal talent. This is where the word "compelling" comes into play. Ideally, all employees, no matter their rank or title, will understand what their function is in relation to the USOD and in what specific ways they are expected to push the company toward its declared Destination. (We will talk more about this particular linkage in the next chapter.)

Starbucks is an example of a corporate brand whose journey has been interrupted (at least temporarily) by faulty linkages. The company is by so many measures a role model for the Conscious Corporation, having been built on such core values as respect for employees, Fair Trade participation, diversity, community support, and environmental responsibility. Its mission is both clear and compelling: "To inspire and nurture the human spirit—one person, one cup, and one neighborhood at a time."

There is no shortage of analysts eager to explain Starbucks's fall from grace (and plummeting profits), but we believe that Howard Schultz, the original force behind the brand who has now returned as CEO, was correct in attributing the problems to too-rapid expansion and the "watering down" of the Starbucks experience. In a memo that was leaked and circulated widely online in early 2007, Howard shared these concerns with then-CEO Jim Donald:

> Over the past ten years…we have had to make a series of decisions that, in retrospect, have lead to the watering down of the Starbucks experience, and, what some might call the commoditization of our brand.…

For example, when we went to automatic espresso machines, we solved a major problem in terms of speed of service and efficiency. At the same time, we overlooked the fact that we would remove much of the romance and theatre that was in play with the use of the La Marzocca machines....We achieved fresh roasted bagged coffee, but at what cost? The loss of aroma—perhaps the most powerful nonverbal signal we had in our stores; the loss of our people scooping fresh coffee from the bins and grinding it fresh in front of the customer, and once again stripping the store of tradition and our heritage? Then we moved to store design.... One of the results has been stores that no longer have the soul of the past and reflect a chain of stores vs. the warm feeling of a neighborhood store. Some people even call our stores sterile, cookie-cutter, no longer reflecting the passion our partners feel about our coffee....

We desperately need to look into the mirror and realize it's time to get back to the core and make the changes necessary to evoke the heritage, the tradition, and the passion that we all have for the true Starbucks experience....

Let's get back to the core....We have built the most trusted brand of coffee in the world, and we have an enormous responsibility to both the people who have come before us and the 150,000 partners and their families who are relying on our stewardship....[8]

Having retaken the corporate reins at Starbucks, Howard Schultz is now seeking to rehumanize the brand by reigniting the emotional attachment it once shared with its customers. We noted with interest his plans to redesign stores with furniture made from reclaimed materials and communal tables intended to encourage customers to put away their laptops, PDAs, and newspapers and reconnect as human beings. Some may argue it is too late for Starbucks to regain fully its emotional connection with its customers, but these and other steps Howard has laid out will go some way toward repairing those compelling linkages that have been severed at such a high cost to the brand.

Now that we have introduced the basic elements of, and criteria for, the Useful Statement of Direction, plus the basic steps in the process of crafting one, we turn to the next chapter, in which we discuss the critical art and science of embedding the USOD both firmly and flexibly within the organization—arguably the most important task facing the Leader of Tomorrow.

Chapter Nine

LIVING THE USOD: HOW TO EMBED AND SUSTAIN IT

If you want to build a ship, don't herd people together to collect wood and don't assign them tasks and work, but rather teach them to long for the endless immensity of the sea.

—Antoine de Saint-Exupéry, French aviator and writer

As difficult as it is to craft a statement of direction that is useful and unifying, compelling and effective, what comes next is far more challenging: embedding it into the organization and ensuring it permeates both the overall corporate culture and individual strategic decisions. It is a task that has got to be a priority of the entire C-suite, but most especially the chief executive.

DEFINING THE CEO'S ROLE IN THIS CRITICAL TASK

We have already noted that some chief executives outsource the vital task of creating a clearly articulated mission statement. Bringing in a consultant can be of immense benefit, adding process insights and a broad view of the business environment, but it is an absolute imperative that the head of the company and other leadership *own* the process—and the result. It is this ownership that helps to separate the Leader of Tomorrow from a run-of-the-mill boss.

Why are some CEOs hesitant to involve themselves in this essential task of strategic alignment? Sometimes, it is simply a matter of overloaded schedules and poor prioritization. Other times, this reluctance stems from what Cavas Gobhai calls the "Boss-in-the-Box Conspiracy."

What is a Boss in the Box, and why do we call it a conspiracy? Simply put, it is a top executive so hampered by a command-and-control culture that he or she is unable to operate as anything other than the omnipotent CHIEF EXECUTIVE. On their way up the corporate ladder, these high achievers were likely well regarded for such qualities as visionary thinking and innovation. Once they are perched on the top rung, however, their creativity becomes muted. Why? Because too few chief executives have the luxury of being able to bat around ideas and make off-the-cuff suggestions. What might be a random musing or a thought-starter for creative give-and-take is perceived by the talent as having the gravitas of a command simply because of who uttered it. How many bosses have tossed out a half-baked idea only to discover that some eager beaver has gone and implemented it in the CEO's name? The consequence in some cases is that the boss becomes overly cautious about what he or she says, potentially depriving the organization of one of its most creative thinkers. Thus the talent "conspires" with the boss in keeping the boss securely in the "box."

Happily, there are solutions to the Boss-in-the-Box Conspiracy. True Leaders of Tomorrow manage to build a corporate culture that places the chief executive at the center of the organization, rather than teetering alone at the top. These executives surround themselves with creative and strategic thinkers in an environment that values both collaboration and productive dissent. This is the sort of environment Google strives to maintain. In the *McKinsey Quarterly*, Google CEO Eric Schmidt described his company's philosophy thusly:

If you don't have dissent, then you have a king. And the new model of governance is very much counter to that. What I try to do in meetings is to find the people who have not spoken, who often are the ones who are afraid to speak out, but have a dissenting opinion. I get them to say what they really think and that promotes discussion, and the right thing happens. So open models, beyond input from outside, also have to be inside the corporation.[1]

Before we share an example of another LOT who encourages such dissent, we should note how difficult it can be, within a traditional corporate culture, to integrate the CEO back into the pack once he or she has been designated top dog. The rest of the pack knows who is boss and responds accordingly. It was just this problem that faced the head of a major supermarket chain during one of Cavas's "creating out loud" strategy sessions. Like several of Cavas's clients, this LOT uses these recurring meetings with his top team as an opportunity to step away from the minutiae of everyday work and produce those big ideas that will influence the larger culture over time. The LOT wanted to be a full and active participant in the discussions, unhindered by the baggage that comes with the ability to fire virtually everyone else in the room. At the same time, he wanted to reserve the right to make executive decisions and proclamations as he felt warranted throughout the event. To accommodate these twin desires, Cavas provided a very simple visual device: a cardboard table tent with the word BOSS emblazoned in black marker. For most of the session, this chief executive would be regarded as the equal of every other participant, capable of expressing his very strong opinions without fear they would go unchallenged. When he wanted to put on his boss hat, all he had to do was hold up the table tent (which he thereafter tended to do with a self-effacing chuckle).

After Cavas explained the system that first time, the LOT exclaimed, "Oh, I get it. When I want to be the BOSS, I wave this tent so everyone can see where I'm coming from—my position of authority. But the rest of the time I get to be [and here he turned the cardboard upside down] a Super SOB like the rest of you!" A great icebreaker, even if the remark fell well outside the parameters of political correctness.

What this grocery-chain executive and other LOTs have come to recognize is that there is great benefit to be reaped by loosening the reins and creating a culture built on collaboration and mutual respect rather than rigid control. Or, as Cavas would say about the LOT relaxing his grip: He knows how to "lose it to use it." No matter how good a Useful Statement of Direction top executives commit to paper, it will have no value in the absence of buy-in and genuine commitment on the part of people throughout the corporate pyramid. This chapter looks at how to do that the right way.

EMBEDDING THE USOD WITHIN
THE ORGANIZATION

In what we termed the largely inadequate "state of play" in the last chapter, we spoke of a midtier rung we called "That's Classified, Buster!" At this stage, the corporate leadership has developed a USOD but has failed to communicate it in any meaningful way to the talent. The good news is there is now at least some level of strategic alignment among key decision makers. The bad news: These people cannot propel the company to its intended destination on their own.

Eventually, the executive leadership will decide the time is right to announce the USOD to the rank and file. Rather than engage employees and secure their enthusiastic commitment, however, the CEO or committee head will address the talent through some form of one-way communication (a memo or video, perhaps) or, one step better, through town hall–type meetings that offer a limited question-and-answer period at the end but are not intended to provoke substantive discussion or any clear follow-through.

The Power of a Push-Pull Approach

The only effective way to create a living, constantly evolving USOD is to get everyone in the organization fully engaged. This is best accomplished through a push-pull technique, though the ratio of pushing to pulling will vary from company to company and may well change over time.

The top team will *push* down certain key aspects of the USOD, making it known there is no room for negotiation or resistance. In more humanized cultures, the LOT will be transparent with the talent about the grounds for this seeming intransigence, explaining why certain elements are a done deal for reasons of core values, brand consistency, shareholder commitments, and so on. This information must be transmitted with compelling clarity and a sense of drive and determination.

There is much to be gained from taking a "big bang" approach to the initial announcement. In larger companies, especially, it may take a certain amount of pyrotechnics to capture people's undivided attention. We were amused and not a little incredulous when we heard Microsoft chairman Bill Gates had released a swarm of *mosquitoes* into the audience at TED2009, the Technology, Entertainment, and Design conference held in California. During a presentation on malaria education and eradication, he released the (non–malaria carrying) insects with the words, "Not only poor people should experience this."[2] While we would not advise this same antic, we are certain Bill Gates made his point—and got his audience's attention. Announcing a USOD in a big way will drive home the fact that this is not yet another in a long line of corporate initiatives that will be forgotten by the following quarter.

And now back to the *pull* part of the push-pull approach. Once the LOT has their attention, he or she and the top team must compel the talent to move past their role as audience and become active players in giving life to the USOD. (We would note that by *compel* we mean engaging and motivating the talent, not coercing their participation.) It is now the talent's task to take ownership of the mission and vision, and become the primary contributors to the evolution of the more local and specific aspects of the USOD within their business units, functional areas, and throughout the entire organization.

In the last chapter, we discussed the key components of the USOD: Destination (optimal future), Path (strategies and tactics), Engine (capabilities, assets, etc.), and Lighting (values and beliefs). When considering which elements require "pushing" versus "pulling," it might be helpful to view these components in another way: as the What, Why, and two kinds of How.

The "What" is the content of the USOD. In virtually all cases, the essentials of the Destination and the major Paths will be *pushed* through the organization by the LOT and top team. The "Why" is the strategic rationale for the content. This, too, will be pushed out to the talent, alongside the What. It will include a clearly articulated argument that helps the talent understand how this particular USOD was derived (What were the external considerations, Future Success Factors, and strengths and weaknesses that caused us to aspire to this choice of Destination?). Where a purpose beyond profit is integrated into the USOD, it will also be necessary to articulate the reasons behind this focus. Those reasons should address both the "enlightened" part (Why is it good for the world?) and the "self-interest" part (Why is it good for the company?) of *enlightened self-interest*.

The Hows address the means of execution—first broadly and then, over time, more specifically. Whereas the What and Why components can be generated around a conference table and may involve just a handful of people, the Hows require the long-term commitment of all internal stakeholders. We say there are two kinds of How, because certain strategies, tactics, and actions will need to be universally adopted regardless of location or function. These Hows are integral to the brand; everything communicates and any incongruence will confuse stakeholders (internal and external) and damage the brand integrity. The second kind of How can and should be tailored to local realities (taking into account cultural differences, for instance) and functional roles. A shipping clerk is going to have different responsibilities under the USOD compared with a purchasing agent or engineer—even though their actions are all propelling the organization toward the same Destination.

The LOT will *push* (prescribe) some Hows when introducing the USOD to the talent. (It would be difficult to draft and communicate a grand plan without outlining the intended Path to achievement.) But the bulk of the Hows will be *pulled* by the talent and refreshed over time, with new or adjusted Hows continually adding relevance and more fuel to the Engine. These Hows are evolved and embedded by the talent; this is what engenders true ownership. To offer some context, we will now move on to a real-life example: Burt's Bees.

Educating and engaging the talent: Lessons from Burt's Bees

In Chapter Four, we touched briefly on Burt's Bees and its president and CEO, John Replogle. We take another look at the company now as an example of how to strike a good balance between pushing the USOD into the organization and encouraging talent to take a leadership role in pulling the company toward its Destination. The natural personal care company is guided by a core set of principles it calls "The Greater Good Business Model" (GGBM). These principles include an unwavering commitment in three areas[3]:

- Natural ingredients and processes as a path to well-being
- Environmental stewardship as it relates to sustainability in operations, supply chain, and packaging
- Humanitarian efforts that support the well-being of all of the company's constituents

In Chart 9.1, you will see that each of these principles is tied to the company stakeholders (whom Burt's Bees calls "constituents").

THE GREATER GOOD™ BUSINESS MODEL

Operating our company with the highest level of social responsibility

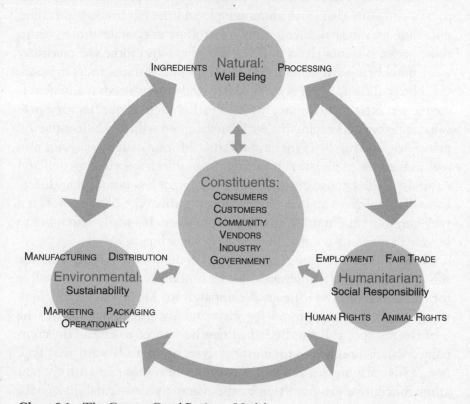

Chart 9.1   The Greater Good Business Model
Source: Burt's Bees, 2009.

The two-way arrows indicates the collaborative nature of these relationships. Even as Burt's Bees is meeting the needs of its customers and others through its products and socially responsible practices, it is also continually processing their input so as to continue to grow and change in ever more positive ways.

The company website digs deeper into the business model, revealing components of a well thought-out USOD that incorporates each of the key characteristics we laid out in the previous chapter: memorable focus, credible stretch, and compelling linkage.

The primary tenets of the GGBM are pushed throughout the organization. The company is not going to brook discussion about its fundamental commitment to "making people's lives better every day...naturally."[4] However, there is also a very clear pull component at work, as Burt's Bees seeks to actively engage employees in its efforts to be a company that cares about people and the environment. It does not want its internal talent simply to follow corporate directives in these areas; it wants them to drive initiatives and force the company more quickly toward its intended Destination, as stated in its mission.

The pull component is particularly evident in the company's environmental efforts. We spoke with John Replogle about his very personal approach to keeping the company aligned with its environmental principles. Noting he is the proud father of four daughters, John told us: "I take a lot of pleasure in raising my children's environmental and natural-product consciousness, and my approach is not all that different with employees and customers. Raising this type of awareness is a very tangible benefit in my life and in my work. It's really satisfying to be able to do some good in the context of our business."[5]

John joined the company three years ago, after having run the skincare business at Unilever, where he and his team were responsible for launching the "Real Beauty" campaign for Dove and establishing the Dove Self-Esteem Fund for girls and young women. When he took the top spot at Burt's Bees, he knew he wanted to extend the company's social- and eco-consciousness even further. Toward that end, one of his early moves as CEO was to put into place an entirely new annual incentive program tied to the company's sustainability goals. Significantly, this bonus program applies to every employee, regardless of function or level within the company.

John and his top team also recruited a group of employee volunteers to develop companywide programs and initiatives that educate employees, customers, and others about sustainability issues and how they can make a positive difference, while also pushing the company more quickly toward its environmental goals. The group is called ECOBEES (Environmentally Conscious Organization Bringing Ecologically Empowered Solutions), and it is a driving force behind the company's lofty objectives of delivering zero waste to landfills and being fully powered by renewable energy by 2020. (Impressively, the latter goal means getting the company completely "off the grid," rather than just offsetting its power use with energy credits.)

John fully intends to have 100 percent employee engagement in the company's sustainability efforts. He sets the tone by giving each employee a copy of the book *It's Easy Being Green*, by Crissy Trask. The ECOBEES team reinforces that learning by continually educating employees about steps they can take to live a more sustainable life at work and at home. As one example, the talent got a close-up view of corporate waste (and how to reduce it) during a "dumpster dive" event, in which employees combed through every inch of the company's refuse. Based on the learning from that day, Burt's Bees has expanded its recycling program to include various new materials and has even installed composting bins in every break room. Additionally, the employee benefits package includes a number of so-called "ecobenefits," including financial incentives for alternative transport, hybrid vehicles, and carpooling or biking to work. The end result is a workforce motivated to come up with new Hows to make the What of the Destination possible.

In speaking about his employee-engagement efforts, John told us, "Consumers can see right through a company. It is my job as shepherd to ensure our activities are a pure reflection of our brand. I'm proud of what we've achieved and keen to move forward to do even more—to fulfill our potential to be a company that helps define the evolving relationship between business and community."[6] The fact that his personal mission is aligned so completely with his company's mission makes John a model Leader of Tomorrow.

A Tiered Approach

There are many ways to announce a Useful Statement of Direction and begin the process of bringing it to life. The most effective approach within any organization will be predicated on such factors as number of employees, geographic spread, corporate culture, and structural organization. Suffice it to say, embedding the USOD is a lot easier to pull off in a five-person shop than in a company with tens of thousands of employees spread out across the world. We will share with you details of one methodology, put in place by a major food retailer. It is illustrative of the sort of tiered approach that will allow a company to ultimately involve and engage every segment of talent.

The LOT in this case was a young CEO of a multi-outlet retailer with nearly 100,000 employees spread across a region of the United States. This man had impeccable Ivy League credentials, but his desire to evolve and implement a USOD stemmed not from a business-school case study but from his wish to replicate the sort of people-centered organization his parents had created in their own small neighborhood business. Granted, he needed to do this on a staggeringly larger scale.

Armed with his goal of creating a more humanized—and profitable—company, our LOT decided to take a multi-tiered approach, with each tier being made up of a carefully selected group of people:

Group One

From the outset, the LOT recognized the need for outside resources and expertise. So, he assembled a team of about twenty people (primarily his direct reports, but also including some talent one level below) and gave them the task of bringing in outside experts and supervising the overall process. A research company was hired to ensure the LOT and his top team (including, importantly, the head of operations) had an accurate, unvarnished picture of the current state of the organization as seen through the eyes of its external and internal stakeholders. Another group of consultants was brought in to help identify the macro and micro trends affecting the grocery and general retail categories, the customers who shop (or don't shop) at the company's stores, and the overall business environment. Such trend research is essential to establishing the broader context in which the corporate brand and its individual businesses operate. It also provides a valuable opportunity to assess where the organization stands in regard to the four cornerstones of the Conscious Corporation: purpose beyond profit, people-centered culture, championing sustainability, and respecting consumers' power. The company can then use that point-in-time picture as a benchmark against which to measure its progress in each of the four areas over time.

Group Two

A smaller, six-person team was made up of the LOT and one other member of the lead group, plus relatively junior talent selected on the basis of their skills in synthesizing information and translating it into usable (easily understandable) language. This team digested the research findings and used the resulting insights to identify possible Destinations (missions and visions) and Paths (strategies and tactics). The LOT and Group One considered each recommendation and, after much discussion and debate, made their highly informed choices.

Group Three

The LOT and his team recognized that, in an organization of this size, it would be critical to enlist another broader tier to spread the USOD quickly and effectively throughout the company. The top team identified a few hundred employees suitably positioned to serve as key leverage points throughout the company. These men and women were pulled from all parts of the organization (functionally and geographically) and were given the charge of driving the USOD throughout the company—ultimately engaging all of the nearly 100,000-strong talent. The LOT made clear to this group which elements of the USOD were sacrosanct and fully formed (the What, the Why, and some of the Hows) and which were intended to be shaped and grown by the talent (the more local Hows).

To further engage the talent, small but meaningful incentives (employee discounts) were provided to those internal stakeholders who helped to activate the USOD, over and above the satisfaction they derived from seeing their ideas come to life. At each store, progress is monitored on a weekly basis by small, task-oriented groups.

As the USOD evolves, the various business units and functions add granularity to the statement. The LOT and his top team keep an eye on the aggregate activity and identify potential synergies and opportunities to replicate successful strategies and tactics in other locations and functional areas. At the same time, they watch for disadvantageous overlaps and conflicts that must be addressed.

REFRESHING AND SUSTAINING THE USOD

Properly embedded, the USOD will serve as a compass, motivator, and accelerant, provided it is coupled with clear accountability. Will it have a permanent impact on the company and the corporate brand? That typically depends on five factors:

- First, to what extent do the talent feel ownership of the mission?
- Second, how explicit is the linkage between the actions of individuals, teams, and the company as a whole and progress toward the Destination? Is it clear that Action X would move a company closer to the Destination, while Action Y would have

the opposite effect? Such linkage must be felt on a personal level and must also be clear enough to be objectively perceived by others both inside and outside the organization.

- Third, how skillful and insistent is the LOT when it comes to refreshing and sustaining the USOD? If the leader is not fully committed and engaged, it is highly unlikely anyone else will be.
- Fourth, how much visibility does the USOD have day to day and over time? Does the talent perceive it as sitting at the core of their work?
- Fifth and finally, is the USOD revisited periodically for discussion and potential modification?

The first two factors will have been addressed by a well-crafted USOD. If the third factor—a skilled and motivated leader—is not in place, then it is unlikely the process can move forward in any meaningful way; in fact, it is unlikely the process will even have been begun. Most often, it is the fourth and fifth factors that prevent an organization from realizing the full worth of the USOD it has taken the time and care to create.

In addressing the fourth factor, we talk to clients about making strategy a natural part of everyday conversations, rather than something relegated to scheduled meetings. Every communication should be viewed by the LOT and the top team as an opportunity to spread strategic thinking—and gain strategic alignment. Our approach is centered on two deceptively simple devices: The first is a process Cavas has termed the "Why and By game." Whenever people are discussing actions, the top team will draw the conversation into the strategic arena by asking, "Why?" When skillfully wielded, this tool helps the talent articulate the strategic underpinning of the proposed action and possibly reshape it for greater effect. Conversely, when the conversation becomes overly abstract, asking "By?", as in "By whom?" will lead to more tactical responses. Over time, this modeling of how to "speak strategy" in informal ways will filter down through the organization, helping to ensure that any potential misalignment is spotted and corrected before it has had a significant adverse effect.

The second device—the "added-value paraphrase"—is a useful variant of the first. Here, we seek to ensure clarity by having the listener in an action-oriented conversation repeat back what was said by the speaker but in different words. This ensures actual comprehension, rather than the parroting back of phrases the listener did not truly comprehend. For added value, the listener will be asked to speculate on our old friend the "Why" to ensure his or her understanding of the strategic reasoning behind the action. Virtually anyone who has been in business for a while can recall a time when participants in a meeting all nodded their heads to acknowledge their understanding and acceptance of a new strategy and then proceeded to work in opposition to one another because of confusion over the relevance of the strategy to each others' day-to-day actions. The humanized corporation understands this frailty and makes every effort to minimize it.

As for the fifth factor, we counsel clients to take a disciplined approach to revisiting and refreshing the USOD. Typically, this means holding an annual meeting with the top team, at which time key elements of the USOD are reexamined in light of changing external and internal realities. As we work through the "What stays the same and what needs to change?" exercise, we find it is especially common for clients to fine-tune their pull-type Hows. Being by nature more specific and local, the value of these activities tends to fluctuate in the upturns and downturns of markets. By undertaking this refreshment exercise periodically, the LOT ensures the sustained relevance and positive impact of the USOD. One of the LOTs we know who heads up a major division of a Fortune 500 company goes one step further, assembling his top team monthly for a brief check-in to see whether the newer elements are "taking" in the embedding process. The team then institutes any needed course corrections.

THE USOD IN TURBULENT TIMES AND THE "PARADOX OF PERMANENCE"

We have used various forms of the word *embed* throughout this chapter. The term carries the connotation of something that is firmly (and permanently) rooted within the totality of the organization— and that is true of the USOD. What is also true, however, is that the value of what is embedded depends wholly on its *sustained relevance*. As noted in the previous section, that will require ongoing revisions to ensure the statement of direction remains both useful and highly effective. So, to be permanent the USOD must constantly change— hence the paradox.

When the business environment is changing rapidly and in unpre-
dictable ways—as was the case in 2008 and early 2009—the de facto
scenario on which the USOD is based may no longer apply. Where,
then, does that leave the worth of the embedded USOD? For some
companies, especially in a severe downturn, the temptation may be to
abandon the statement of mission and vision as inapplicable and revert
to tactical fixes—linkage be damned. In so doing, the organization
risks losing its way.

Within a properly conceived and constructed USOD, the LOT
and the top team will have embedded softer cultural aspects—namely,
the values and beliefs—along with the harder policies, practices, and
tactics. Among the most important softer elements are nimbleness,
creativity, and collaboration. The latter two enable the first.

The strategic response of the Conscious Corporation in turbulent
times will be to flex the USOD in order to achieve the optimal balance
of its various components. What matters more in a flush economy may
matter less when times get tough, and vice versa. What is essential is
that the organization not throw out the proverbial baby with the bath-
water. The need for a USOD is every bit as vital in a down economy—
arguably even more so—than in good times.

When the decision is made to tweak various emphases, the LOT
and the top team must communicate these changes—and the reasons
for them—throughout the organization. In the absence of such communication, the talent may find some C-suite decisions incongruous
with their sense of the USOD. Everyone needs to understand the situation in full so as to be in a position to spot relevant new opportunities
that are inherent in challenging times.

We have previously commented on the imperative of collaboration, the shift enlightened businesses have made away from a bitter
and divisive zero-sum game between "us" and "them" and into a more
synergistic effort that benefits all. Keeping an eye out for potential
partners is vital at any time in the new environment but is even more
so when entire industries face unforeseen challenges.

Creativity will come into play at several points in the process of
refreshing the USOD. Smart companies will have increased the frequency of their monitoring activities to stay a step ahead of market
changes (to the extent possible). Such ongoing surveillance will allow
for the uncovering of opportunities that can be activated through creatively fashioned responses.

Keeping in mind the "paradox of permanence" inherent in any USOD while in the process of first evolving it, the LOT and the top team will find it useful to identify a number of possible and probable scenarios at that early stage so as to prepare for their impact. This preparation will include the establishment of mechanisms through which the organization will monitor leading indicators to detect movement toward and away from the various scenarios; in so doing, top executives will be better prepared to make a preemptive move or response ahead of competitors.

So, now we have seen how Conscious Corporations evolve and embed their values-centered missions throughout their organizations. In our final chapter, we will take a look at how some of the leading businesses of today are creating profits and growing their businesses and industries by creating corporate brands built on the humanized principles we have covered.

Chapter Ten

MAXIMIZING TOMORROW'S BRAND VALUE BY LIVING CLEAR VALUES TODAY

Many commentators have noted that the Wall Street meltdown marks the end of the Reagan era....A huge amount of populist anger is brewing as the Wall Street meltdown spreads to Main Street. Already there is a growing consensus on the need to re-regulate many parts of the economy.

—Francis Fukuyama, U.S. philosopher and economist[1]

When the world eventually emerges from the crisis that started in 2008, the economic landscape will have changed. And so will the attitudes of governments and citizens toward business.

From the 1980s onward, free-market capitalism ruled. An increasingly business-friendly political and social mood supported lower taxation, deregulation, and globalization. Corporations were free to decide for themselves how they wanted to maximize profits and shareholder value and remunerate themselves. They could relocate production and operations to wherever in the world offered the lowest costs, the lightest regulation, the most attractive incentives, and the lowest taxes. There was an implicit deal between business on one side and consumers and their political representatives on the other: We will provide jobs and income and affordable goods if you will buy those goods and let us get on with making money as we see fit.

At one extreme the most single-minded corporations have had plenty of scope to maximize profit and growth at any cost; they have been free to become the sort of "institutional psychopaths" described by legal scholar Joel Bakan in his 2004 documentary *The Corporation*. At the other extreme, a few idealistic companies set out to prove that humanized values—empathy, respect, fairness, and generosity—are ingredients for building sustainable businesses. In the middle is a quickly growing group of companies that have realized, to a greater or lesser extent, that it makes solid economic sense to make common cause with the common good while also seeking to maximize growth and profits.

As we have illustrated throughout this book, the business case for humanizing companies has been solidifying. Now, as the world struggles with the global economic crisis, we believe that case is moving from optional to imperative. This may seem counterintuitive at a time when so many businesspeople see anything more than hard-nosed survival tactics as a luxury. The *Economist*, in its publication *The World in 2009*, espoused precisely this view, predicting what amounts to a "dehumanizing" of corporations:

> For the past decade the prevailing wind in boardrooms has been gentle. Emotional intelligence and innovation have been what counted, and what leaders professed to value. But those ideas are all but finished. No one will talk of EQ ("emotional intelligence quotient") any more. It will be EVA ("economic value added") instead.[2]

We would counter that, while businesses must look after themselves, they do not operate in a vacuum. They depend on the goodwill of all stakeholders, including society. As Francis Fukuyama noted, attitudes toward business are changing. Consumers and politicians are questioning whether free-wheeling free-market capitalism really serves the common good and, if it does not, whether society can permit it to continue. With governments bailing out banks and finance houses, many commentators have observed that we're seeing "capitalism on the way up and socialism on the way down" or "the privatization of profits and the socialization of losses"—meaning that businesses are getting the benefits in good times, and society (i.e., taxpayers) is bearing the losses in bad times. The general public has lost patience with corporations that treat people badly, damage the environment without concern or consequence, and line the pockets of their senior executives while taxpayers are losing their jobs and homes.

The net effect of all this is likely to be a sea change in the public attitude toward business, an attitude, we believe, that will persist for the foreseeable future. The new U.S. administration won the 2008 presidential election with promises of change, including more attention paid to environmental and social issues. As President Barack Obama said in his inaugural speech:

> Nor is the question before us whether the market is a force for good or ill. Its power to generate wealth and expand freedom is unmatched, but this crisis has reminded us that without a watchful eye, the market can spin out of control—that a nation cannot prosper long when it favors only the prosperous.[3]

As the world hauls itself through the economic crisis and prepares for a new start, corporations will need to decide: Is their future best served by being lean, mean, and hard-nosed? Or is it worth investing resources in building a strong corporate brand based on more humanized principles? It is a Darwinian dilemma: Which use of resources will best adapt the company to the future?

In all likelihood, companies of both sorts will survive and thrive: the lean-and-mean and the humanized. However, we believe that as economies reconfigure, it will be those corporations that have taken the humanization of business into their brand DNA that will have the greatest influence with policy makers and the best chance of engaging talent, consumers, and investors alike.

WHY STRONG CORPORATE BRANDS WILL WIN

Some older ideas about brands still apply, of course. There will always be a need for product and service brands that engage consumers. And there will always be companies whose corporate entities are less well known than the brands in their portfolios. The simple truth, however, is that in this wired, intrusive, hyperconnected world, consumers are not the only stakeholders, and products and services are not a sufficient embodiment of the brand. Today, everything about a company and its brands communicates something, sooner or later. Official news of a product launch or a reduction of an organization's carbon footprint will duly make its way into the public domain through the official channels. But behind-the-scenes, off-the-record information will also spread through electronic media. And that will become permanently available to anyone who is interested: consumers, journalists, fans and foes, lawyers, legislators, competitors—anyone. Companies must assume they are always but a mouse-click away from information getting out, that they are open to public scrutiny at any time.

For old-style corporate mindsets, this new reality is a recipe for paranoia. How can a company get on with its business if it always has to be on its best behavior? A natural instinct might be to protect itself under a blanket of disclaimers and other legal paraphernalia.

For the Conscious Corporation, in contrast, the new landscape presents a golden opportunity. These organizations can use the reality of "everything communicates" as a prism through which to align their actions and their brand values. They can be confident about tapping into new communication channels to connect their corporate brand with stakeholders.

But what does this sort of branding require and, above all, what is the return on investment? The answer is familiar enough for those in product branding, which is mostly peripheral to the operations of the company: Branding a product takes a marketing department, creative executions (TV commercials, print ads, brochures, etc.), and media exposure, with the eventual benefit of better sales and margins if all goes well. With corporate branding, the process cannot be peripheral because the brand *is* the company; it is not about the design and functionality of a product line, it is about the attitudes and behavior of the entire organization.

Investing in a strong corporate brand takes more resources than just a marketing budget. It takes investments of time and attention and care to embed the corporate brand into the company culture so that it becomes truly "the way things are done here." The ROI of investing in a strong corporate brand may be less immediately obvious and measurable than with a product brand, but the benefits accrue across a much wider range of activities.

A strong corporate brand provides instant recognition and, hence, a fast track to communicating and building on the overarching brand essence; the branding makes it easy for stakeholders to transfer the brand values onto new products and activities. By the same token, a strong corporate brand becomes a highly visible platform from which to communicate (and get credit for) good works. In an ever more cluttered media environment, strong corporate brands are better positioned to break through and stand out.

Strengthening the corporate brand can also make for efficiencies of scale in distribution and marketing. Using the corporate brand as the "guarantor" of products in its portfolio, a company can cut down on the number of stand-alone brands needing stand-alone support.

Within the organization, a strong corporate brand has a powerful effect on what companies often like to call their most valuable asset: their people. It engages and motivates. When the company consistently articulates shared values and demonstrates them in action, it gives employees a common sense of purpose and meaning. This applies to all activities in the company and is especially useful in providing strategic focus for developing and positioning products.

And finally, a strong corporate brand, by definition, combines awareness and appeal in the public domain with a strong sense of the company's distinctive culture and purpose. It is this combination that earns the brand attention from stakeholders and gives it the authority to communicate and be taken seriously. These are essential attributes of a strong corporate reputation.

APPLYING THE FOUR CORNERSTONES TO BUILDING THE CORPORATE BRAND

Making money is essential. Whether it is called "making a profit" or "creating shareholder value," it comes down to the same thing. And the need to do it is beyond dispute. Even not-for-profit organizations have to make money; they just retain any profit within the organization rather than distributing it to the owners and top executives. The core premise of this book is that the Conscious Corporation will be much more than an efficient machine with no purpose other than generating profits. It will be skilled at galvanizing stakeholders by connecting with what really matters to them.

In Chapter Three, we laid out these cornerstones on which the Conscious Corporation builds its brand:

- *Has a purpose beyond profit:* Consistently making a profit must be the goal of any self-supporting organization, but if it is the company's sole reason for being and employees' sole reason for working there, it is threadbare. Strong corporate brands motivate employees, create engagement, and foster goodwill by having a clear purpose that is aligned with the greater good.

Like great sports coaches, these companies understand that the prospect of winning in and of itself is not always the best motivator of people over time.

- *Maintains a people-focused culture:* People prefer to be treated decently, with respect and honesty. Sounds too obvious to be worth spelling out, doesn't it? Then how come so many companies fail to do it? The Conscious Corporation makes a point of treating people well—customers, staff, suppliers, investors, and local communities. It doesn't do it in a calculated way, solely to gain advantage. It does it because it is the right thing to do, and because once one begins to think of business in a more humanized light, it comes naturally.

- *Champions sustainability:* What was idealism a decade ago is now seen as self-preservation and common sense. People are expressing increasing concern about issues such as global warming, environmental destruction, workers' rights, and threats to energy and water supplies. *Sustainability* is a handy portmanteau word for the aspiration to live and consume more moderately and responsibly, with an eye to the future. The Conscious Corporation understands the brand opportunity inherent in taking a lead on sustainability, and it figures out ways to make environmental responsibility a smart business strategy.

- *Respects consumers' power:* The relationship between companies and consumers has changed profoundly. On the supply side, there are more product categories and brands competing for consumers' attention and money. On the demand side, consumers have become more skeptical, more powerful, more difficult, and more fickle. The new consumers expect to communicate how and when they like, to be given access to corporate information, and to be taken seriously when they talk back. Big Business has become their business, and they take that responsibility to heart.

USING BRAND MOMENTUM TO IDENTIFY
THE LEADING BRANDS OF TOMORROW

In today's dynamic markets, perceptions and behavior change fast. Pervasive, "always on" news and hyperconnectivity tend to magnify and accelerate even small movements. As a consequence, these movements very often translate into disproportionately significant changes in the fortunes of brands, be they corporate brands, product brands, media brands, or, indeed, personal brands (any public figure).

For many years, Euro RSCG Worldwide has been tracking changes in consumers' perceptions of brands and corporations. The agency calls its tool "Brand Momentum," borrowing a term from physics.[4] Of course, brands are ideas, not objects, but in their own way they have a sort of momentum in the marketplace. We see significant changes in a brand's momentum when a large number of consumers (mass) perceive a brand to have gained or lost ground (velocity). The agency's measurements involve calculating the simple net gain/loss score[5] and then the more telling momentum factor.[6]

The momentum of a brand matters because it translates into changes in consumers' behavior: whether and how they consider, buy, and recommend the brand. In tracking the momentum of hundreds of brands across major markets, Euro RSCG has found a strong correlation between leadership in Brand Momentum and the four cornerstones of the Conscious Corporation. Why is that?

Most categories are populated by plenty of corporations and brands that satisfy the basic requirements of competence, product performance, and affordability; the scope for differentiation versus competitors in these areas is limited. By contrast, there is plenty of scope to command more attention through the four cornerstones. Achieving and communicating outstanding performance in at least one of these areas gives people more reasons to pay attention to the brand. In no way are cornerstone behaviors a substitute for the basic requirements of profitability and performance; rather, they are proving to be a more effective way of delivering these business fundamentals.

TOP MOMENTUM BRANDS: BEST PRACTICES

In the following pages we focus on a half dozen of the corporations and brands that have scored particularly well in Euro RSCG's Brand Momentum tracking: Google, Target, eBay, Tesco, Whole Foods, and Toyota. While each succeeds in all cornerstone behaviors, there is often one core area of emphasis in which it is truly leading its category, and business in general.

All companies included here were selected on the basis of their achievements in Euro RSCG's rankings up to late 2008. During that fateful year, the crisis claimed several venerable names in finance (AIG, Lehman Brothers, Merrill Lynch, Washington Mutual). Since then most industries have been hit by falling sales, and our selection of companies has not been untouched by the crisis.

There is no way to know for sure how these high-momentum brands—or, indeed, any company or brand—will fare through to the end of the crisis. What we do know is that these companies have decided that their future success depends in part on the health of the communities in which they operate and the viability of the natural environment that supports us all. It is our firm belief that the decisions they have been making to grow their businesses in a conscious and humanized way will hold them in good stead.

Google: Connecting the World with Information

As one would expect, Google has been a Brand Momentum leader for the past four years. It stays firmly on the world's radar because it is outstanding at its core service (Internet search) and at developing innovative and relevant services such as Web-based applications (e.g., Gmail, Google Calendar) and advertising. However, Google also performs outstandingly on all four cornerstones, as we have noted elsewhere in this book.

Purpose beyond profit

Google's guiding principle of "Don't be evil" is one of the most widely known corporate mottoes. It is not sophisticated, but it is clear and simple and has a ring of authenticity. As the company website explains:

> The Google Code of Conduct is one of the ways we put "Don't be evil" into practice. It's built around the recognition that everything we do in connection with our work at Google will be, and should be, measured against the highest possible standards of ethical business conduct. We set the bar that high for practical as well as aspirational reasons: We hire great people who work hard to build great products, and it's essential that we build an environment of trust—among ourselves and with our users. That trust and mutual respect underlie our success, and we need to earn it every day.[7]

People-focused culture

The code of conduct cited above is clear about the value of people. Google puts that into practice in ways that have become corporate legend. As one example, all employees are treated to free, wholesome gourmet food provided in its famed cafeterias.[8] And, as noted in Chapter Six, all Google engineers are encouraged to spend around a fifth of their time on projects of personal interest. According to Google vice president for search products and user experience Marissa Mayer, half of the product launches at Google can be traced to ideas hatched during this 20 percent of work time.[9]

In both 2007 and 2008, Google topped *Fortune*'s list of "Best Companies to Work For." As one employee commented in an article on The Great Places To Work Institute's website:

> I have been in the high tech industry for 15 years and have worked at 8 different companies, large and small. Google is by far the most dynamic and meaningful company I've worked at. The company founders are candid and accessible. Management processes are transparent. Promotions are determined by peer reviews. Engineering decisions are made by engineers. This is a company that is trying to make a difference in the world in all ways, including fixing global warming (giving $5,000 rebates to employees if [they] buy a hybrid car, lining the rooftops with solar panels, giving employees bikes to ride around campus). The "Don't be evil" mantra is more than skin deep; it is the core of the culture.[10]

Championing sustainability

As a major user of electricity, Google is working on its direct environmental impact as well as investing in other environmentally friendly technologies, such as plug-in cars. The company's California headquarters boasts one of the world's biggest solar power arrays.[11] Beyond worrying about its own ecological footprint, the company is also seeking to help consumers reduce theirs. In cooperation with GE, Google is working on a tool called Google PowerMeter, which will allow consumers to monitor their electricity consumption in near real-time via a secure iGoogle Gadget. The meter will help people calculate such things as how much energy is consumed by leaving their televisions plugged in all day or how much they could save by turning an air-conditioner up one degree.

Respecting consumers' power
When Google entered the search category in 1998, it was a new-comer in a market segment that already had several dominant play-ers. It quickly achieved preeminence by paying close attention to what its users wanted, needed, and actually did. In all its work, Google is mindful of the people who make up its user base.

Target Corporation: Giving People More for Less

Target is the number-two discount retailer in the United States, behind Wal-Mart. With around 1,699 Target and SuperTarget stores in forty-nine states, it has carved out a distinctive niche by offering more upscale, fashion-forward merchandise than rivals Wal-Mart and Kmart, all while operating under a promise of "Expect More. Pay Less."

Purpose beyond profit
"Ethical" is the bull's-eye for Target. Think tank Ethisphere Institute named it among the world's most ethical companies three years run-ning (2007–2009).[12] Target's values are very much about community. Founder George D. Dayton started the company tradition of giving 5 percent of pretax profits to community outreach in three areas: edu-cation, especially early-childhood reading and resources for teachers and classrooms; programs, exhibits, and performances that make artis-tic and cultural experiences more visible and accessible to families; and the provision of basic needs to families in crisis. All in all, with a com-bination of direct contributions, support, and volunteer time, Target gives more than $3 million a week to the communities it serves. It also makes a point of involving staff in community projects: In 2008, more than 70,000 employees, retirees, family, and friends donated in excess of 315,000 volunteer hours to charities across the United States.[13]

People-focused culture
Target promises a working environment that is "fast, fun, and friendly." The company prides itself on its diversity; as of the begin-ning of 2009, 59 percent of "team members" were female and 42 per-cent were minorities.[14] *Black Collegian* magazine ranked Target sixth among its "Top 100 Employers" in 2008, while *BusinessWeek* ranked it twentieth among its "Top 50 Best Internships." In 2007 Universum Communications listed Target among its top ten "Ideal Employers."

Championing sustainability

As a "big box" retailer moving hundreds of millions of physical items, Target has plenty of opportunities to work toward greater sustainability. It has been a member of the U.S. Green Building Council (USGBC) since 1997 and is one of thirty-two companies participating in the USGBC pilot Portfolio Program to explore retailers' sustainable design needs and advance the use of Leadership in Energy and Environmental Design (LEED) standards. At the time of writing, three Target stores had been certified under the LEED for New Construction guideline. Recycling and reusing are also big agenda items: 70 percent of materials previously destined for landfills are now reused, recycled, or rethought.

Respecting consumers' power

Target's brand promise ("Expect More. Pay Less.") does more than differentiate the company from its competitors; it clearly defines its strategy for creating a better customer experience. Customers are considered and treated as "guests." The company continuously strives to see things from guests' perspective and then sets out to find ways to surprise and delight them during store visits.

One way in which Target delights guests is through its focus on design. Good design provides an opportunity to meet shoppers' needs while making them feel good and enjoy life's simple pleasures. The company's first design partnership was with architect Michael Graves in 1998. The following year, the retailer offered a redesigned Graves teapot for $35, priced $100 less than the original version. The stores have since featured collections by Philippe Starck, Cynthia Rowley, Isaac Mizrahi, and others.

In 2005, Target was honored with the Consumer 360 Award, cosponsored by three VNU business publications: *Progressive Grocer*, *Convenience Store News*, and *Brandweek*. The award honors the retailer in the consumer packaged goods industry that has demonstrated the best understanding of the consumer in its year-round merchandising activities.

eBay, Inc.: Creating Commerce and Community

Since its beginnings as a hobby on Pierre Omidyar's home computer in 1995, eBay has grown to become the world's largest online marketplace and has made it possible for anyone to sell virtually anything online. With a presence in thirty-nine markets and approximately 84 million active users worldwide, it has cocreated the face of Internet commerce. In 2007, the value of sold items on eBay's trading platforms reached nearly $60 billion; this means eBay users worldwide trade in excess of $1,900 worth of goods on the site every *second*.[15]

Purpose beyond profit
eBay has always been a humanized enterprise, but it hasn't made a big thing of being led by a higher purpose. As a successful business and an icon in its field, eBay has "done the right thing" by putting its influence and some of its money toward supporting larger causes. In Chapter Four, we discussed the virtual auction house's values-based "social ventures": MicroPlace, WorldofGood.com, and eBay Giving Works/eBay for Charity. Through these initiatives, eBay empowers consumers to shop in a way that reflects their personal and social values. And, in so doing, it offers support to indigent communities and nonprofits around the globe.

People-focused culture
In 2009, *Fortune* rated eBay one of the "100 Best Companies to Work For" for the second year in a row. Employees at corporate headquarters in San Jose, California, enjoy on-site perks such as golf lessons, bike repair, and a dentist, plus prayer and meditation rooms. The company also provides four-week paid sabbaticals after every five years of employment.

Championing sustainability
At its roots, eBay is all about recycling, enabling sellers to unload things they no longer need and buyers to find them. Though the business model is not driven by the ideal of sustainability, in practical terms it has facilitated the reuse of an estimated $100 billion in goods since 1998.[16] It has extended the useful life of products that might otherwise have ended up in landfills, and it has reduced the need for the raw materials to manufacture new items.

Beyond what it does naturally for sustainability, eBay has looked for ways to reduce waste and improve its environmental impact. Refurbishing data-center technology in 2007 resulted in a 25 percent improvement in energy efficiency. Its new building on the North

Campus in San Jose was built to the LEED Gold standard for new construction. In 2008, eBay installed 3,248 roof-mounted solar panels, which will take up to 18 percent of campus energy demand off the grid completely.

eBay further aims to reduce its carbon footprint by investing in five high-quality offset projects around the world: a wind project in China, a small run-of-the-river hydroelectric project in the Brazilian Amazon, a conservation forestry project in Madagascar, an agricultural methane–capture project in Wisconsin, and a landfill gas–capture project in Mexico.

Respecting consumers' power

As with many Internet-only businesses, it is the interactions between and among eBay's customers that are the essence of its product. eBay's success has been built on paying close attention to consumers' suggestions and feedback, explicit and implicit (i.e., how they use the site). As noted earlier, the company recently gave a boost to buyers on the site by no longer allowing sellers to rate them. It is eBay's way of protecting consumers from malicious "tit for tat" negative ratings from sellers.

Tesco PLC: "Every Little Helps"

Since becoming a limited company in 1932, U.K.–based Tesco has grown into the world's third-largest grocery retailer, operating just fewer than 4,000 supermarkets and convenience stores and employing some 440,000 people. It is the largest private-sector employer, the largest food retailer, and the largest seller of gasoline in the United Kingdom. Its website, Tesco.com, is the largest online supermarket in the world.[17]

Purpose beyond profit

Like everything about the company, Tesco's stated purpose is simple and pragmatic: "to create value for customers to earn their lifetime loyalty." The company focuses on running its business responsibly, which it defines as follows:

> Responding to customer trends such as healthy eating, organics, and fair-trade; treating our suppliers fairly so they can deliver for customers; managing our environmental impacts to help reduce costs and inconvenience; treating our staff as we like to be treated

so they do a great job for customers; and helping our staff and customers to support the local organizations and causes they care about.[18]

In 2008 Tesco was among the first group of companies to be awarded a CommunityMark by Business in the Community. This new national standard in the United Kingdom recognizes business excellence in community investment.

People-focused culture

Tesco is clear that its success depends on people: the people who shop at its stores and the people who work in them. Its core aim with employees is to offer a great place to work, which translates into "treating people how we like to be treated." To every employee it pledges four things: "to be treated with respect," "a manager who helps," "an interesting job," and "an opportunity to get on."[19] In February 2009, Tesco announced that more than 52,000 of its employees would be sharing in a £126 million payout from the company's Save As You Earn investment program. While the global economy was tanking, Tesco employees who participated in the savings plan reaped returns of between 45 and 88 percent over three to five years.[20]

Championing sustainability

In January 2008, Tesco opened a store in Manchester, England, with a carbon footprint reduced 70 percent compared with an equivalent store built in 2006. Using 2006 as its benchmark, Tesco aims to halve carbon emissions from all new and existing stores by 2020, and to halve the CO_2 created per case of goods delivered worldwide by 2012. The company's energy use per square foot in its U.K. facilities is now half what it was in 2000, thanks in part to a nearly £60 million investment in energy-saving and low-carbon technologies in 2008.[21]

The retailer has undertaken a broad range of initiatives to address and raise awareness of sustainability issues under its Greener Living banner: reducing "food miles" (the distance food is transported from the time it is produced until it reaches the consumer) by buying local products in season; offering home insulation services; and promoting products that save energy, reduce waste, and are more easily recycled.

Respecting consumers' power

Tesco's approach to customers reads like a condensed *Customer Service 101* manual. The brief checklist for the experiences customers should be able to take away is as follows: "aisles are clean," "I can get what I want," "prices are good," "I don't queue" (stand in line), and "staff are great." The thoughts aren't revolutionary and the words aren't stirring, but they have clearly worked. In 2007, a challenging year for many retailers, Tesco saw sales increase 11.1 percent, to £51.8 billion.

Whole Foods Market: A Leader in Conscious Commerce

Founded in Austin, Texas, in 1980, Whole Foods Market has been a pioneer in selling natural and organic products. As a consequence of being free of pesticides, preservatives, sweeteners, and cruelty, its products are also largely free of the bitter taste of guilt. We have covered Whole Foods in previous chapters, but we think it worth recapping what has led to the brand's success and impressive momentum. Despite the economic downturn, Whole Foods saw sales increase 24 percent in 2008, to $8 billion.[22]

Purpose beyond profit

The name says it all, and the company motto spells out its holistic purpose: "Whole Foods. Whole People. Whole Planet." Dig deeper and the company's statement of purpose is "success in customer satisfaction and wellness, employee excellence and happiness, enhanced shareholder value, community support, and environmental improvement."[23]

People-focused culture

Whole Foods has been ranked as one of *Fortune*'s "100 Best Companies to Work For" for twelve consecutive years. *Fast Company* described the distinctive company culture as "democratic capitalism." As we noted earlier, cash compensation for executives is capped at a multiple of nineteen times the average annual wage of hourly workers, and the entire company is organized into teams, rather than as a hierarchy. Sensitive data on store sales, team sales, profit margins, and even salaries are available to every employee across the company.[24]

Championing sustainability

Whole Foods was the first major retailer to offset 100 percent of its energy use with wind energy credits. It received the U.S. Environmental Protection Agency's Green Power Leadership Award in 2004 and 2005 and Partner of the Year award in 2006 and 2007, and continues to be a member of the Green Power Leadership Club.[25]

In addition to its support of organic and locally grown food, Whole Foods has built an environmentally friendly showcase supermarket in Missouri. Using innovative merchandising displays, refrigeration systems, installation, and sustainable technologies, the store will cut greenhouse gas emissions by around 22.5 million pounds and reduce energy usage by as much as 30 percent a year.[26] The company is also acting to scrap plastic shopping bags in favor of paper and reusable cotton.

Respecting consumers' power

CEO John Mackey uses his blog and the company's blog, Whole Story, to keep customers and others up to date on developments at the company; the blogs also serve as a medium through which to respond directly and proactively to the company's various stakeholders. His actions over the years have shown he has a clear understanding that the strength of Whole Foods rests on the trust it has engendered among the eco- and health-conscious consumers who make up its base. Criticisms from customers and eco-bloggers have spurred the company to make numerous changes, including creating the Animal Compassion Foundation, focused on improving the conditions under which farm animals are raised; instituting stricter guidelines for suppliers in response to cruelty claims; and increasing its offerings of locally produced goods. In 2007, Whole Foods launched the Local Producer Loan Program, through which the company will provide up to $10 million in low-interest loans to small, local producers.

Toyota Motor Corporation: Finding New Ways Forward

Toyota has achieved global distinction three times. It was the centerpiece of a five-year Massachusetts Institute of Technology study of the 1980s automobile industry that resulted in a celebrated book, *The Machine That Changed the World: The Story of Lean Production*.[27] Then it launched the hybrid-drive Prius car in Japan in 1997 and in North

America, Europe, and other markets in 2000; the Prius has become the first eco-minded car model to achieve mainstream success and is now an icon of environmentally friendlier car design. Finally, and not unrelated to the first two distinctions, in 2008 Toyota ended General Motors's seventy-seven-year reign as the world's top-selling car company. Although both companies were hit by the global economic crisis, Toyota's sales fell less sharply.[28]

Purpose beyond profit

As befits a Japanese engineering company founded more than seventy years ago, Toyota has a sophisticated philosophy: The Toyota Way. It is based on fourteen management principles, which can be summarized as having a philosophical sense of purpose, thinking long-term, having a process for solving problems, adding value to the organization by developing its people, and recognizing that continuously solving root problems drives organizational learning.[29] Seeking to be a "vehicle for change," the automaker supports programs focused on education and on environmental and safety initiatives "that help strengthen the communities where we live and work—for today and for the future."[30]

People-focused culture

Toyota revolutionized car-manufacturing quality by giving all production-line workers responsibility for spotting defects and granting them the power to halt production to correct those faults.[31] Toyota embodies the distinctive Japanese focus on continuous organizational learning to achieve ever-improving quality. Because it sees employees as knowledge workers, it takes care to cross-pollinate the knowledge and experience of all workers at every level.

Championing sustainability

If any car company has environmental credibility, it is Toyota. The hybrid-drive system used in the Prius has been the most widely adopted alternative to gasoline and diesel engines, making it the darling of green chic. The company "is committed to developing hybrid systems as the core technology for eco-cars, combining different power sources in ways that maximize the strengths of each."[32] To prove the point, a Highlander SUV with a hybrid fuel-cell system showed its capabilities in 2007 by traveling 2,300 miles from Fairbanks, Alaska, to Vancouver, Canada, emitting nothing but water vapor along the way.[33]

Respecting consumers' power

Gathering customer feedback is ingrained in Toyota's thinking. Part of its original success can be credited to its practice of going directly to existing customers when planning new products—treating them as part of the Toyota family.[34] Further, Toyota's approach of building quality into every car resonates strongly with consumers. In major markets outside Japan, Toyota (along with other Japanese brands) is credited with having raised the bar on durability, quality, and reliability.

THE TIME IS RIGHT FOR THE HUMANIZED CORPORATION

> There are times when the structure of the world as we know it just collapses in front of us. The curtain drops, and we step back and lose our breath and go, "Oh my God, is this the world I'm living in?" Tremendous global economic challenges. All of a sudden, the economic powerhouse of the world is not standing supreme anymore. Oh my God, metastasizing threats to our security without possibly the strength to deal with them. That "New Frontier" that John F. Kennedy talked about years ago—guess what? It is really here now.
>
> —Alex Castellanos, political media strategist and partner, National Media Inc.[35]

While the humanization of the corporate world might have been welcomed at earlier points in history, it is even more deeply needed today. In an environment marked by constant change and diminishing certainty, people are looking to organizations that offer stability and a sense of mindfulness about the common good.

The Conscious Corporation Offers Sense Amid Confusion

Over the past two decades or so, we have experienced bewildering changes in all aspects of life. Some changes have been sought by consumers or made in response to consumer preferences. However, most have been beyond the control or the will of individuals. Among other examples:

- The global population has grown from around 5.3 billion in 1990 to 6 billion in 1999 and 6.8 billion in 2009.[36] The global economy has also swelled as more countries have joined—most notably Brazil, Russia, India, and China.

- Technology has connected virtually everyone through the Internet and mobile devices. It has sped up life, too, and made just about everything imaginable available remotely at all times of the day and night.
- There are increasing numbers of product categories from which to choose—digital cameras, mobile devices, energy suppliers, TV channels, social networking sites—and growing numbers of brands and products within those categories.
- There has been growing concern about complicated "big issues": terrorism and security, energy and water supplies, climate change, food safety, and social breakdown.

The sheer volume and pace and complexity of all these changes has been heady for some and hard to follow for many, even when things were running smoothly. And now, in the wake of the global financial crisis that began in earnest in 2008, things have been running far from smoothly. It feels as if change has accelerated and veered off track. It all seems out of control.

This bewildering environment, which has many people frozen in fear, may be great for hard-nosed businesses that like to move fast and hard, to swat or snap up competitors and drive down costs; it is an ideal environment for profit-driven predators. It is also an environment that poses opportunities for businesses that have a purpose beyond profit. It is an environment that cries out for humanized companies inclined to work with stakeholders, whether customers or employees, shareholders or NGOs, to grow in a way that benefits everyone. We believe the latter type of company will ultimately offer greater value—to itself and its shareholders, and to all those who are affected by its existence.

The Conscious Corporation Fosters Community

As noted earlier, the past three decades have also seen a steady decline in social interaction. In their working lives people have become busier and more mobile—more likely to change employers, more likely to relocate for work, and more likely to commute some distance each day for work. In their travel, workers can shut out the world with personal

MP3 players and video players, sound-blocking headsets, and other devices. During leisure time, consumer electronics and the Internet deliver a virtually infinite menu of information and entertainment into the insulated, isolated comfort and safety of the home. In shopping, the personal touch of smaller traditional stores and market stalls has been superseded by the bigger range and lower costs of big-box retailers.

A study conducted jointly by sociologists at Duke University and the University of Arizona compared data from 1985 and 2004 and found that the mean number of people with whom Americans can discuss matters important to them had dropped by nearly one-third, from 2.94 people in 1985 to 2.08 in 2004. The percentage of people who talk *only* with family members about important matters increased from about 57 percent to about 80 percent, while the number of people who depend totally on their spouses has increased from about 5 percent to about 9 percent.[37] Membership in social clubs and leisure organizations has seen a steep decline. As Robert Putnam commented in his national bestseller, *Bowling Alone*, "Somehow in the last several decades of the twentieth century…community groups…across America began to fade."[38]

All in all this decline in social interaction has generated a widespread sense of disconnect and a desire to belong to some larger group. After all, human beings are social animals. In recent decades, consumers have found some sense of community "secondhand" by tuning in to friendship-based TV shows (*Cheers, Friends, Seinfeld, Sex and the City, Desperate Housewives*). More recently, social media such as MySpace, Facebook, and Twitter have provided more dynamic, interactive ways of connecting.

It would be unreasonable to expect companies to fix this social disconnect on their own. But as our top Brand Momentum examples show, companies can certainly be part of the solution, by humanizing themselves and fostering interaction among their stakeholders.

The Conscious Corporation Inspires and Provides Role Models

Over the past decade and more, business has become part of popular culture as consumers have taken a more active interest in brands and the people behind them. Business figures such as Jeff Bezos, Richard Branson, Bill Gates, Steve Jobs, Tom Peters, Donald Trump, and Jack Welch have become familiar personalities.

Part of this can be explained by the increased public appetite for celebrities of any sort; a business leader who is willing to be interviewed and say interesting things can easily become a media fixture. But more important, consumers yearn for figures who have qualities they admire and to which they aspire. They want role models that embody archetypal qualities and have a story to tell. Warren Buffett is not just a successful investor running a popular investment company; he is the grandfatherly billionaire "Sage of Omaha" who lives simply and dispenses wry, folksy wisdom. Ben and Jerry are not just a couple of bearded ice-cream entrepreneurs; they are a pair of loveable eccentrics who made hippie values work within the context of a successful business.

Unlike with sports heroes and media heroes and politicians, consumers have everyday interactions with brands and companies. These dealings offer more "touch points," so people can monitor how the brand is performing in real time. Hero brands are not in the game purely for their own glory; they stand or fall by their ability to do the right thing consistently and reliably.

CONCLUSION: A DECISIVE MOMENT FOR CORPORATIONS

The economic crisis that began for real in 2008 and earlier corporate scandals have triggered a massive loss of trust in the free-market system, in the integrity of business leaders, and in the competence of decision-makers. They have revealed shocking cases of high-level selfishness, greed, and utter incompetence. In late January 2009, President Obama berated financial executives' bonus awards as "the height of irresponsibility" and "shameful."[39] In France, millions took to the streets to protest that the government under President Nicolas Sarkozy had done too much to bail out fat cats and banks, and not enough to protect jobs and help workers make ends meet.[40]

In light of the crisis, the burning question for the ordinary consumer is this: Which people and which organizations can I trust to act competently and with an eye to the long-term common good? In this environment businesses will no longer be able to count on paid lobbying, "spray on" branding, media blitzes, and PR spin to further their interests. From now on, it is businesses and leaders who truly "walk the talk" that will wield influence, that consumers and their elected representatives will trust to shape the future.

Throughout this book we have described the sorts of behavior that build trust. We have looked at some of the corporate brands that have demonstrated how humanized, enlightened self-interest creates success on many levels. These are the sort of corporate brands that earn the loyalty of people as consumers and their support as shareholders and voters.

Consumers are feeling individually powerless in the face of the complex problems facing the world in so many areas, notably the economy, energy, the environment, national and personal security, healthcare, education, and social cohesion. As our showcased corporate brands have illustrated, people respond enthusiastically to companies that demonstrate real leadership on bigger issues. They trust and admire corporate brands that address the twin pulls of selfishness and altruism, and help consumers feel that what is good for them is also good for the world. These are the companies that will lead us into a more optimal version of the future.

APPENDIX

I. FINDINGS FROM EURO RSCG WORLDWIDE'S THE FUTURE OF THE CORPORATE BRAND

About the study: The Future of the Corporate Brand was fielded by Market Probe International in December 2007 and completed in 2008. The online survey was conducted in three markets: the United States (*n* = 700), France (*n* = 450) and the United Kingdom (*n* = 700). The study explores evolving consumer expectations and demands, and their potential impact on the future of the corporate brand.

Percentages indicate how many respondents agreed or strongly agreed with each statement.

MORE POWER, MORE RESPONSIBILITY

Over the past five years, companies and corporations have become more profitable.

Global:	79%
U.S.:	80%
France:	79%
U.K.:	80%

Over the past five years, companies and corporations have become more philanthropic.

Global:	24%
U.S.:	29%
France:	8%
U.K.:	29%

Over the past five years, companies and corporations have raised their standards.

Global: 47%
U.S.:   39%
France: 58%
U.K.:   48%

Over the past five years, companies and corporations have become more accountable.

Global: 46%
U.S.:   44%
France: 33%
U.K.:   57%

Over the past five years, companies and corporations have become better positioned to create positive social change.

Global: 59%
U.S.:   62%
France: 48%
U.K.:   63%

Businesses bear as much responsibility as governments for driving positive social change.

Global: 74%
U.S.:   72%
France: 80%
U.K.:   71%

Corporations have become a more important part of our culture.

Global: 56%
U.S.:   54%
France: 63%
U.K.:   53%

CONSUMERS DEMAND SOCIALLY CONSCIOUS CORPORATE BEHAVIOR

Within the last few months, I have actively looked for information on the reputation or ethics of a company.

Global: 42%
U.S.:   37%
France: 53%
U.K.:   38%

I have become more interested in corporations' conduct and brand image over the past few years.

Global: 57%
U.S.:   64%
France: 51%
U.K.:   53%

Over the last year, nonbranded blogs or forums made me change my mind about a product or service I had intended to buy.

Global: 27%
U.S.:   20%
France: 40%
U.K.:   26%

As a consumer, I have a responsibility to censure unethical companies by avoiding their products.

Global: 76%
U.S.:   80%
France: 81%
U.K.:   69%

I have made a purchase decision based on a company's conduct.

Global: 63%
U.S.:   65%
France: 69%
U.K.:   58%

Corporate reputation on social and environmental responsibility is a key driver of confidence.

Global: 80%
U.S.:   80%
France: 86%
U.K.:   76%

Ethical conduct is a key factor for good business.

Global: 85%
U.S.:   91%
France: 91%
U.K.:   76%

The most successful and profitable businesses in the future will be those that practice sustainability.

Global: 73%
U.S.:   69%
France: 79%
U.K.:   73%

It is important that companies stand for something other than profitability.

Global: 85%
U.S.:   86%
France: 89%
U.K.:   81%

The most important duty of a CEO is to generate profits for shareholders.

Global: 35%
U.S.:   37%
France: 33%
U.K.:   33%

When a company is allocating funds for philanthropic purposes, which of the following should receive priority?

	Global Total %	U.S. Total %	France Total %	U.K. Total %
Environment	65	60	70	66
Health	61	67	50	62
Education	44	55	24	46
Social issues	39	37	46	35
Infrastructure in less-developed regions	23	14	29	27
Culture/art	11	11	15	9
Sports	9	6	11	11

CORPORATIONS ARE FALLING SHORT OF EXPECTATIONS

I find I admire business and business leaders more these days.

Global:	22%
U.S.:	18%
France:	20%
U.K.:	27%

How are companies doing in terms of bringing about positive social change?

	Global Total %	U.S. Total %	France Total %	U.K. Total %
Not doing enough	42	40	57	35
Exceeding my expectations	13	15	9	13

How are companies doing in terms of working ethically with governments for the good of society?

	Global Total %	U.S. Total %	France Total %	U.K. Total %
Not doing enough	48	46	60	41
Exceeding my expectations	11	14	7	11

How are companies doing in terms of encouraging mutually beneficial trade with developing countries?

	Global Total %	U.S. Total %	France Total %	U.K. Total %
Not doing enough	38	25	63	36
Exceeding my expectations	15	19	10	15

How are companies doing in terms of making environmental impact a core factor in corporate decisions?

	Global Total %	U.S. Total %	France Total %	U.K. Total %
Not doing enough	50	47	68	42
Exceeding my expectations	12	15	8	11

How are companies doing in terms of paying fair value for the use of natural resources?

	Global Total %	U.S. Total %	France Total %	U.K. Total %
Not doing enough	48	42	63	43
Exceeding my expectations	10	14	7	8

How are companies doing in terms of respecting the rights and needs of employees?

	Global Total %	U.S. Total %	France Total %	U.K. Total %
Not doing enough	49	48	68	39
Exceeding my expectations	14	17	8	14

Big corporations do not share enough profit with all employees.

Global:	60%
U.S.:	59%
France:	75%
U.K.:	52%

COMMUNICATING WITH THE EMPOWERED CONSUMER

Public opinion should drive a company's conduct and overall strategy.

Global:	61%
U.S.:	56%
France:	66%
U.K.:	63%

Businesses need to open a dialogue with their consumers.

Global:	82%
U.S.:	80%
France:	92%
U.K.:	78%

Businesses must inform and educate their consumers.

Global: 79%
U.S.:   78%
France: 91%
U.K.:   72%

Businesses must be completely open and transparent.

Global: 74%
U.S.:   65%
France: 82%
U.K.:   80%

It is a positive thing for a business to publicize its corporate social responsibility works, charitable contributions, etc.

Global: 73%
U.S.:   73%
France: 76%
U.K.:   70%

II. FINDINGS FROM EURO RSCG WORLDWIDE'S THE FUTURE OF SHOPPING

About the study: The Future of Shopping was fielded by Market Probe International in January 2008. The online survey was conducted in four markets: the United States ($n = 700$), France ($n = 700$), the United Kingdom ($n = 700$), and China ($n = 700$). The study explores the future of the retail category, with an emphasis on how evolving consumer demands and behaviors are changing the shopping experience.

Percentages indicate how many respondents agreed or strongly agreed with each statement.

THE INTERNET IS CHANGING THE WAY PEOPLE SHOP

Even if I don't make a purchase online, the Internet is a very important part of my shopping.

Global:	81%
U.S.:	85%
France:	78%
U.K.:	80%
China:	83%

For major purchase decisions, my first step is usually the Internet.

Global:	76%
U.S.:	78%
France:	74%
U.K.:	77%
China:	74%

The Internet has had little to no impact on my shopping.

Global:	15%
U.S.:	9%
France:	22%
U.K.:	10%
China:	22%

I do lots of [consumer] research online.

Global:	63%
U.S.:	71%
France:	45%
U.K.:	68%
China:	69%

I read consumer product feedback and reviews online before making a purchase.

Global:	79%
U.S.:	81%
France:	70%
U.K.:	73%
China:	91%

I search for customer reviews online while making purchase decisions.

Global:	86%
U.S.:	88%
France:	86%
U.K.:	81%
China:	88%

I write online product or retailer reviews.

Global:	51%
U.S.:	51%
France:	56%
U.K.:	34%
China:	60%

I request or download coupons or coupon codes online.

Global:	75%
U.S.:	88%
France:	63%

U.K.:   75%
China: 73%

I subscribe to a retailer's e-newsletter.

Global: 79%
U.S.:   80%
France: 81%
U.K.:   77%
China: 78%

I would like to be part of an online community of customers who share opinions and information about companies and brands.

Global: 60%
U.S.:   51%
France: 51%
U.K.:   57%
China: 84%

I participate in online auctions.

Global: 69%
U.S.:   69%
France: 60%
U.K.:   80%
China: 67%

CONSCIENTIOUS CONSUMPTION

I purchase environmentally friendly products.

	Global Total %	U.S. Total %	France Total %	U.K. Total %	China Total %
Do it now	79	80	78	78	79
Do it now and am likely to do it more in the future	51	48	56	43	57

I buy energy-efficient (e.g., compact fluorescent, LED) light bulbs.

	Global Total %	U.S. Total %	France Total %	U.K. Total %	China Total %
Do it now	82	77	83	83	86
Do it now and am likely to do it more in the future	60	56	52	52	67

I bring reusable bags to the grocery store.

	Global Total %	U.S. Total %	France Total %	U.K. Total %	China Total %
Do it now	70	45	93	78	63
Do it now and am likely to do it more in the future	53	32	78	58	45

I avoid shopping at stores that don't treat their employees fairly.

Global:	58%
U.S.:	59%
France:	59%
U.K.:	37%
China:	78%

I buy or refuse to buy products based on a company's expressed values or political/social activities.

Global:	50%
U.S.:	56%
France:	47%
U.K.:	40%
China:	60%

I avoid buying products from a particular country or region.

Global:	46%
U.S.:	47%
France:	50%
U.K.:	40%
China:	47%

I am willing to pay a bit more for a product if a portion of the proceeds goes to a good cause.

Global:	50%
U.S.:	53%
France:	50%
U.K.:	28%
China:	70%

NOTES

PREFACE

1. ProCon.org, http://www.procon.org/viewbackgroundresource.asp?resourceID= 001465.
2. Richard L. Grossman and Frank T. Adams, *Taking Care of Business: Citizenship and the Charter of Incorporation* (New York: CIPA/The Apex Press, 1993), http:// www.ratical.org/corporations/TCoB.html.
3. Touro Law Center, *Santa Clara County v. Southern Pacific Railroad Company*, http://www.tourolaw.edu/patch/Santa/.
4. "A Short History of Corporations," *New Internationalist*, July 2002, http://www. newint.org/features/2002/07/01/history-of-corporations/.
5. Eigen's Political & Historical Quotations, http://www.politicalquotes.org.
6. Sarah Anderson and John Cavanagh, Institute for Policy Studies, "Top 200: The Rise of Corporate Global Power," http://www.corpwatch.org/article.php?id=377.
7. The Corporation.com 2.0, http://www.thecorporation.com/index.cfm?page_id=2.
8. Muhammad Yunus, "How to Succeed in 2007," *Business 2.0*, CNNMoney.com, 2006, http://money.cnn.com/popups/2006/biz2/howtosucceed/16.html.
9. "Regulatory Risk: Trends and Strategies for the CRO," Economist Intelligence Unit, July 2005, http://graphics.eiu.com/files/ad_pdfs/eiu_CRO_RISK_WP.pdf.

CHAPTER ONE

1. Henry H. Klein, *Dynastic America and Those Who Own It* (New York: Henry H. Klein, 1921), p. 171.
2. The Population Institute, "Population News," October 16, 2006, http://www. populationinstitute.org/newsroom/population-news/?id=42.
3. Sarah Anderson and John Cavanagh, "Top 200: The Rise of Corporate Global Power," Institute for Policy Studies, December 4, 2000, http://www.corpwatch. org/article.php?id=377.
4. Ibid.
5. The Gallup Organization, "Americans' Confidence in Congress at All-Time Low," June 21, 2007, http://www.gallup.com/poll/27946/Americans-Confidence-Congress-AllTime-Low.aspx.
6. Mark Dolliver, "Corporate Reputation Hits a New Low," *Adweek*, April 28, 2009, http://www.adweek.com/aw/content_display/data-center/research/e3i0dac803 b1646d6af9cc89a12ad823619.

7. Andrew Edgecliffe-Johnson, "No Consensus on Restoring Trust in Business," *Financial Times*, February 1, 2009, http://www.ft.com/indepth/davos (accessed May 12, 2009).

8. Bill & Melinda Gates Foundation, "Foundation Fact Sheet," http://www.gatesfoundation.org/about/Pages/foundation-fact-sheet.aspx (accessed May 12, 2009).

9. Donald G. McNeil, Jr., "Gates Foundation's Influence Criticized," *New York Times*, February 16, 2008, http://www.nytimes.com/2008/02/16/science/16malaria.html?_r=1.

10. Barbara Thiede, "Tsunami Relief Marks Shift in Corporate Efforts," *Charlotte Business Journal*, February 11, 2005, http://charlotte.bizjournals.com/charlotte/stories/2005/02/14/focus3.html.

11. "The Home Depot CEO Bob Nardelli to Chair Business Roundtable's Partnership for Disaster Response Task Force," news release, May 30, 2006, http://www.csrwire.com/News/5676.html.

12. Cone Inc., "2005 Cone Katrina Survey Fact Sheet," http://www.coneinc.com/stuff/contentmgr/files/0/4a66e29480192d592bf21dcdc22f3191/files/2005_cone_disaster_response_survey_fact_sheet.pdf.

13. Mindy Fetterman, "Corporate Muscle Is Brought to Bear on National Disaster Planning," *USA Today*, October 12, 2006, http://www.usatoday.com/money/companies/management/2006-10-11-disaster-planning_x.htm.

14. Euro RSCG Worldwide's Prosumer Pulse® 2004–05 study was conducted among more than 21,000 consumers in ten markets: China, France, Germany, India, Japan, Mexico, Russia, Spain, the United Kingdom, and the United States.

15. Pinny Cohen, "Case Study: JetBlue, from Meltdown to Recovery," Life of an Intranet Entrepreneur (blog), March 1, 2007, http://www.pinnycohen.com/2007/03/01/marketing-wisdom/case-study-jetblue-from-meltdown-to-recovery/.

16. Luke 12:48.

17. Forty-seven percent of total respondents to Euro RSCG Worldwide's Future of the Corporate Brand study agreed that corporations have raised their standards over the past five years. Forty-six percent agreed corporations have become more accountable.

18. Mary Weisnewski, "Bypass the Brain and Go Straight to the Heart: Connecting with Emotion Builds a Brand and Keeps It Vital," BrandChannel.com, http://www.brandchannel.com/papers_review.asp?sp_id=1232.

19. Mark Schapiro, "Interview with George Soros, Chairman, Soros Fund Management," State of the World Forum, September 6, 2000, http://www.simulconference.com/clients/sowf/interviews/interview3.html.

20. Charles Dickens, *A Christmas Carol*, Literature.org, http://www.literature.org/authors/dickens-charles/christmas-carol/chapter-01.html.

21. *The Simpsons*, "The Old Man and the Lisa" (season 8, episode no. 21), first broadcast April 20, 1997 by FOX. Directed by Mark Kirkland and written by John Swartzwelder.

22. "Rethinking the Social Responsibility of Business: A Reason Debate Featuring Milton Friedman, Whole Foods' John Mackey, and Cypress Semiconductor's T. J. Rodgers," *Reason*, October 1, 2005, http://www.reason.com/news/show/32239.html.

23. FamousQuotes.com, http://www.famousquotes.com/show/1032524/.

24. "NASDAQ's William McGinty Delivers Keynote Address at Intangible Asset Finance Society's Fall Conference," Business Wire, September 28, 2007, http://www.businesswire.com/portal/site/home/permalink/?ndmViewId=news_view&newsId=20070928005512&newsLang=en.

25. "A Matter of Choice—The Future of the Company," *Economist*, December 22, 2001, U.S. edition.

CHAPTER TWO

1. Lilei Chow, "Net Boost for Consumers," *New Straits Times* (Malaysia), June 8, 2008, Local, 22.

2. Euro RSCG Worldwide, Prosumer Pulse® 2004–2005.

3. "Complete Consumer Generated Content Study Reveals Opportunities for Travel Marketers," PR Newswire, April 30, 2007, http://www.competeinc.com/news_events/pressReleases/182/.

4. Ibid.

5. TNS Global, "New Future in Store: How Will Shopping Change Between Now and 2015?" May 2008, http://www.tnsglobal.com/news/key-insight-reports.

6. VMS, video ID 070700516, http://www.vmsinfo.com/ (accessed January 7, 2009).

7. Barry Silverstein, "LendingTree Branching Out," brandchannel.com, December 15, 2008, http://brandchannel.com/features_profile.asp?pr_id=417.

8. Ibid.

9. Martin Nieri, "Digital Direct: It's a Fine Line and We Must Be Careful Not to Overstep It," *Revolution UK*, March 14, 2008, http://www.revolutionmagazine.com/news/793653/Digital-direct-Its-fine-line-careful-not-overstep/.

10. "'A Person Like Me' Now Most Credible Spokesperson for Companies; Trust in Employees Significantly Higher Than in CEOs," *Edelman News*, January 23, 2006, http://www.edelman.com/news/showone.asp?id=102.

11. Dave Sifry, "The State of the Live Web, April 2007," Sifry's Alerts (blog), April 5, 2007, http://www.sifry.com/alerts/archives/000493.html.

12. Euro RSCG Worldwide, The Future of Shopping, 2008.

13. "Green Living, U.S.," Mintel International, January 2009, 72.

14. Euro RSCG Worldwide, The Future of Shopping, 2008.

15. Euro RSCG Worldwide, Value Study, January 2009. Fifty-three percent of the U.S. sample agreed: "I get a sense of satisfaction from reducing my purchases"; 30 percent agreed: "My life would be better if I owned fewer things"; 46 percent agreed: "I won't go back to my old shopping patterns even when the economy rebounds."

16. "Going Green 2," *The Yankelovich Perspective*, September 2008, http://gateway.yankelovich.com/live/2008/live_oct_monitor_kickoff.pdf.

17. The Futures Company, "The Upside of the Downturn," *Yankelovich MONITOR Minute*, October 27, 2008, http://www.yankelovich.com/images/minute08/2008_October_27/2008_MonitorMinute_October27.pdf.

18. The Simple Living Network, "Bumper Stickers," http://www.simpleliving.net/main/category.asp?catid=16 (accessed May 15, 2009).

19. Euro RSCG Worldwide, The Future of the Corporate Brand, 2008.

20. Ibid.

21. Thomas L. Friedman, "Marching with a Mouse," *New York Times*, March 16, 2007, section A, 23, http://select.nytimes.com/2007/03/16/opinion/16friedman. html?_r=1&scp=1&sq=marching%20with%20a%20mouse&st=cse.
22. Ibid.
23. Ibid.
24. Ibid.
25. Euro RSCG Worldwide, The Future of the Corporate Brand, 2008.
26. Ibid.
27. Ibid.
28. Michel Pireu, "The Eyes Have It," *Business Day* (South Africa), November 22, 2004, 16.
29. "Jeff Bezos on Word-of-Mouth Power," in "Special Report: The Best Global Brands," *BusinessWeek*, August 2, 2004, http://www.businessweek.com/magazine/content/04_31/b3894101.htm.

CHAPTER THREE

1. "Amory Lovins," GoGreenOnline, http://gogreenonline.com/index.php?option= com_content&view=article&id=137:amory-lovins&catid=930:original-green-heroes&Itemid=91.
2. Interview with Polly LaBarre by Euro RSCG Worldwide, 2007.
3. Lynn B. Upshaw, *Building Brand Identity: A Strategy for Success in a Hostile Marketplace* (Hoboken, N.J.: John Wiley and Sons, 1995), 110.
4. Google, "Our Philosophy," http://www.google.com/corporate/tenthings.html (accessed May 16, 2009).
5. "comScore Releases January 2009 U.S. Search Engine Rankings," press release, February 18, 2009, http://www.comscore.com/press/release.asp?press=2729.
6. Scott Bedbury, "Nine Ways to Fix a Broken Brand," *Fast Company*, January 2002, 72, http://www.fastcompany.com/magazine/55/brokenbrand.html?page=0%2C0.
7. Sarah Skidmore, "Nike Reports 12 Percent Jump in Q4 Net Income," The Associated Press, June 28, 2008.
8. Kyle Nagel, "Nike Still Winning the Shoe Wars: But Adidas Is Courting College Athletics to Make Up Some Ground," *Dayton Daily News*, August 4, 2007, Sports, B3.
9. Kimberly Palmer, "Retailers Move to Organics 2.0," *U.S. News & World Report*, June 4, 2007, 56.
10. "High Growth Forecasted for the Natural and Organic Food and Beverage Trends: Current and Future Patterns in Production, Marketing, Retailing, and Consumer Usage, 2nd Edition," Market Wire, October 8, 2008, http://www.redorbit.com/news/business/1583706/high_growth_forecasted_for_the_natural_and_organic_food_and/.
11. Organic Trade Association, *Organic Trade Association's 2007 Manufacturer Survey*, Executive Summary, http://www.ota.com/pics/documents/2007ExecutiveSummary.pdf (accessed January 10, 2009).
12. The term *C-suite* refers to the "chief officers" of a business organization, e.g., chief executive officer (CEO), chief financial officer (CFO), chief operating officer (COO).
13. "Our Mission Statement," http://www.benjerry.com/our_company/our_mission/ (accessed May 18, 2009).

14. "Brewing a Better World," http://www.greenmountaincoffee.com/ContentPage. aspx?Name=Brewing+A+Better+World (accessed February 1, 2009).
15. "Tasting Notes," http://www.greenmountaincoffee.com/Coffee/K-Cup-Fair-Trade-Organic-Heifer-Hope-Blend (accessed May 18, 2009).
16. Euro RSCG Worldwide's "Politics and Brand Marketing: Momentum Matters" panel discussion, held in New York City on November 14, 2008.
17. "Cheatsheet," http://www.innocentdrinks.co.uk/press/cheatsheet/ (accessed February 17, 2009).
18. "Our Story: The Untold Truth," http://www.innocentdrinks.co.uk/us/? Page=our_story (accessed February 17, 2009).
19. "Sharing the Profits," http://www.innocentdrinks.co.uk/us/ethics/sharing/ (accessed February 17, 2009).
20. "Join the Family," http://family.innocentdrinks.co.uk/ (accessed February 17, 2009).
21. "The Innocent AGM," http://www.innocentdrinks.co.uk/AGM/ (accessed February 17, 2009).
22. Jacob Gordon, "The Tree Hugger Interview: Yvon Chouinard, Founder of Patagonia," Treehugger.com, February 7, 2008, http://www.treehugger.com/ files/2008/02/the_th_interview_yvon_chouinard.php.
23. The Official Website of Mark Twain, http://www.cmgww.com/historic/twain/ about/quotes2.htm (accessed February 19, 2009).
24. David Phillips, "Employees & Executives Alike Feel the Hunger at Whole Foods," BNET, January 27, 2009, http://blogs.bnet.com/secdocuments/?p=235 (accessed May 18, 2009).
25. Stephen Taub, "The Top 25 Moneymakers: The New Tycoons," *Alpha*, April 2007, http://www.iimagazine.com/Article.aspx?ArticleID=1328498&Position ID=25424.
26. "Whole Foods Market Announces Changes in Salary Cap and CEO Compensation," November 6, 2006, http://www.wholefoodsmarket.com/ company/archives/pr_06-11-02.php.
27. David Phillips, "Employees & Executives Alike Feel the Hunger at Whole Foods," BNET, January 27, 2009, http://blogs.bnet.com/secdocuments/?p=235.
28. Sharon Begley, "The Battle for Planet Earth," *Newsweek*, April 24, 2000, Science & Technology, 50.
29. Jim Hanas, "A World Gone Green," *Advertising Age*, June 8, 2007, Special Report: Eco-Marketing, S-1.
30. Mike Verespej, "Get Green Before It Gets You, Speaker Says," *Plastics News*, November 24, 2008, http://plasticsnews.com/headlines2.html?id=08112400401 &q=get+green+before+it+gets+you.
31. *Invest and Deliver Every Day: GE 2007 Annual Report*, http://www.ge.com/ ar2007/ltr_performance.jsp (accessed May 18, 2009).
32. "GE's Ecomagination Revenues to Rise 21%, Cross $17 Billion," Business Wire, October 21, 2008, http://ge.ecomagination.com/site/news/press/2008 revenuesrise.html.
33. Interview with Jake Siewert, vice president, business development and public strategy for Alcoa, by Euro RSCG Worldwide, 2007.
34. Marks & Spencer, *Your M & S: How We Do Business Report 2008*, http:// corporate.marksandspencer.com/documents/publications/2008/2008_hwdb_ report.pdf (accessed May 18, 2009).

35. Julia Finch, "Recycled Coathangers and Cheerier Chickens Feature in M & S Environmental Pledge," *The Guardian* (London), June 7, 2007, Financial Pages, 28.
36. Marks & Spencer, *Your M & S: How We Do Business Report 2008*, http://corporate.marksandspencer.com/documents/publications/2008/2008_hwdb_report.pdf (accessed May 18, 2009).
37. "Energy Initiative: Remarks by Rupert Murdoch, Chairman and Chief Executive Officer, News Corporation" (presented at Hudson Theater, New York City, May 9, 2007), http://www.newscorp.com/energy/full_speech.html.
38. "Wal-Mart Sustainability Fact Sheet, December 2008," http://walmartstores.com/FactsNews/FactSheets/#Sustainability (accessed February 17, 2009).
39. "Wal-Mart Launches 5-Year Plan to Reduce Packaging," http://walmartstores.com/FactsNews/NewsRoom/5951.aspx (accessed February 17, 2009).
40. "Wal-Mart Takes Lead on Environmental Sustainability," http://walmartstores.com/download/2392.pdf (accessed February 17, 2009).
41. "Stonyfield Farm's Blog Culture," *BusinessWeek*, May 5, 2005, http://www.businessweek.com/magazine/content/05_18/b3931005_mz001.htm.
42. Jean Halliday, "Toyota Turns a Niche into Anti-Waste Zealotry," *Advertising Age*, June 11, 2007, Special Report: Eco-Marketing, S-4.
43. Wal-Mart, "Jewelry Products," http://walmartstores.com/Sustainability/8454.aspx.
44. Phone interview by Andrew Benett with Alex Castellanos, political media strategist and partner, National Media Inc., January 9, 2009.
45. Euro RSCG Worldwide, The Future of the Corporate Brand, 2008.
46. Kenneth Hein, "Frontiers of Marketing: They Feel Your Pain," Brandweek.com, June 16, 2008, http://www.brandweek.com/bw/superbrands/article_empathetic.html.
47. Peter Valdes-Dapena, "Laid Off? Hyundai Will Take Your Car Back," CNN Money, January 5, 2009, http://money.cnn.com/2009/01/05/autos/hyundai_assurance/index.htm.
48. Phone interview by Greg Welch with Steve Knox, CEO, Procter & Gamble Tremor division, January 8, 2009.
49. Ibid.
50. Ibid.
51. Deborah Yao, "Comcast Startles Customers with Cyberteam Help," *USA Today*, October 22, 2008, http://www.usatoday.com/tech/products/2008-10-22-538002369_x.htm.

CHAPTER FOUR

1. Ansi Vallens, "The Importance of Reputation," *Risk Management*, April 2008, 55, no. 4: 36.
2. Mary Williams Walsh, "At A. I. G., the Brand Is Tarnished," *New York Times*, March 23, 2009, http://www.nytimes.com/2009/03/23/business/23aig.html.
3. Telephone interview by Greg Welch with Peter Sieyes, global digital and relationship marketing director, Diageo, November 7, 2008.
4. Ibid.
5. Interview by Euro RSCG Worldwide with Elizabeth Spiers, founder of Dealbreaker.com, 2007.
6. Vallens, "The Importance of Reputation."

7. Bruce Haynes at Euro RSCG Worldwide's "Politics and Brand Marketing: Momentum Matters" panel discussion, held in New York City on November 14, 2008.

8. Telephone interview by Greg Welch with Patrick Doyle, president of, Domino's USA, December 4, 2008.

9. "Double Investment in Research and Development," GE ecomagination statement, http://ge.ecomagination.com/site/vision.html#subsection1 (accessed May 21, 2009).

10. Telephone interview by Greg Welch with Beth Comstock, chief marketing officer and senior vice president, GE, January 8, 2009.

11. "GE Launches 'Healthymagination'; Will Commit $6 Billion to Enable Better Health Focusing on Cost, Access and Quality," press release, May 7, 2009, http://www.genewscenter.com/content/Detail.asp?ReleaseID=6760&NewsAreaID=2.

12. Telephone interview by Greg Welch with Beth Comstock, chief marketing officer and senior vice president, GE, January 8, 2009.

13. Joel Makower, "'Ecomagination': Inside GE's Power Play," May 11, 2005, http://www.greenbiz.com/blog/2005/05/11/ecomagination-inside-ge's-power-play.

14. Peppercom, "Survey Results Remove the Gray from Green," March 17, 2008, http://www.peppercom.com/whatwedo/greenenvironmentalpr.

15. Robin Givhan, "Lord of the Fries; Morgan Spurlock Got His Fill of Ailments Making 'Super Size Me,' But He's Been Fortified by Its Impact," *Washington Post*, May 2, 2004, Sunday Arts, 1.

16. Telephone interview by Greg Welch with Mike Minasi, president of marketing, Safeway Inc., December 16, 2008.

17. Jerry Wolffe, "Grocery Chain Stops Selling Cigarettes," *Oakland Press*, January 15, 2009, http://www.theoaklandpress.com/articles/2009/01/15/business/doc496f1957998be549988819.txt.

18. Ibid.

19. Greta Guest, "Hiller's Markets End Cigarette Sales," *Detroit Free Press*, January 15, 2009.

20. Wolffe, "Grocery Chain Stops Selling Cigarettes."

21. Tina Reed, "Hiller's Markets Decides to Butt Out Cigarette Sales at Its Stores, Including Ann Arbor Location," *Ann Arbor News*, January 14, 2009, http://www.mlive.com/news/ann-arbor/index.ssf/2009/01/hillers_markets_decides_to_but.html.

22. Marks & Spencer, *Your M & S: How We Do Business Report 2008*, http://corporate.marksandspencer.com/documents/publications/2008/2008_hwdb_report.pdf (accessed February 19, 2009).

23. Interview by Euro RSCG Worldwide with Margaret Carlson, chief political columnist, Bloomberg News, and Washington editor, *The Week*, 2007.

24. Liz Jones, "You Couldn't Make Blake Up—He's Handsome, Rich and Helps Children in the Third World," *Daily Mail* (London), December 15, 2008, 45.

25. Ibid.

26. eBay, "eBay Inc. Global Citizenship: Social Ventures," http://pages.ebay.com/aboutebay/socialventures.html (accessed February 19, 2009).

27. "MicroPlace Marks Anniversary with Special Visit from Muhammad Yunus," press release, November 13, 2008, http://www.microplace.com/press_room/show/microplace_marks_anniversary_with_special_visit_from_muhammad_yunus.

28. WorldofGood.com, "Trustology," http://content.worldofgood.ebay.com/ns/AboutTrustology.html (accessed February 19, 2009).
29. eBay Inc. Global Citizenship: Social Ventures, http://pages.ebay.com/aboutebay/socialventures.html (accessed February 19, 2009).
30. Lush, "A Lush Life We Believe…," http://www.lush.co.uk/index.php?option=com_content&view=article&id=6289&Itemid=66 (accessed February 19, 2009).

CHAPTER FIVE

1. Dale Buss, "Agenda 2008," *Chief Executive*, December 2007, http://www.chiefexecutive.net/ME2/dirmod.asp?sid=&nm=&type=Publishing&mod=Publications%3A%3AArticle&mid=8F3A7027421841978F18BE895F87F791&tier=4&id=C2F3AE61F6DF4EF9A1A4C6876D2E6283.
2. "Who's in Charge Here?: A Semiotic Take on the Future of Leadership," Euro RSCG Worldwide, December 2008.
3. David D. Kirkpatrick, "Case Re-elected to AOL Board; Margin Is Called Underwhelming," *New York Times*, May 17, 2003, sec. C, 1.
4. Jennifer Reingold, "CEO Departures Break Record," CNNMoney.com, January 15, 2009, http://money.cnn.com/2009/01/15/magazines/fortune/management/CEO_fired.fortune/index.htm.
5. "Quotes: CEO," CEOGO, http://www.ceogo.com/pages/ceocommunications/quotes_ceo.jsp (accessed May 23, 2009).
6. Adam Lashinsky, "The Genius Behind Steve: Could Operations Whiz Tim Cook Run the Company Someday?" *Fortune*, November 10, 2008, http://money.cnn.com/2008/11/09/technology/cook_apple.fortune/index.htm (accessed May 23, 2009).
7. Joe Nocera, "Talking Business: Running G.E., Comfortable in His Skin," *New York Times*, June 9, 2007, C1.
8. Raymond Gilmartin, Frances Hesselbein, Frederick Smith, Lionel Tiger, Cynthia Tragge-Lakra, Abraham Zaleznik, "All in a Day's Work," *Harvard Business Review*, December 2001, 54.
9. Sundance Catalog, "A Place. An Idea. Celebrating and Enriching the Human Experience,"http://www.sundancecatalog.com/About_Us/about+us.html (accessed March 3, 2009).
10. "CEO Quotes," ReputationRX.com, http://www.reputationrx.com/Default.aspx/CEOREPUTATION/CEOQUOTES (accessed May 22, 2009).
11. Ibid.
12. James S. Kunen, "Enron's Vision (and Values) Thing," *New York Times*, January 19, 2002, sec A, 19.
13. Bill Breen, "How EDS Got Its Groove Back," *Fast Company*, December 19, 2007.
14. Telephone interview by Greg Welch with James M. Kilts, partner, Centerview Partners, and former CEO of Gillette, January 15, 2009.
15. Jeffrey M. O'Brien, "Zappos Knows How to Kick It," *Fortune*, February 2, 2009, http://money.cnn.com/2009/01/15/news/companies/Zappos_best_companies_obrien.fortune/.
16. Brian Morrissey, "Q & A: Zappos CEO Tony Hsieh," *Adweek*, December 22, 2008, http://www.adweek.com/aw/content_display/news/strategy/e3id78469d81136853904418d754416855e?pn=2#.
17. Helen Coster, "A Step Ahead," *Forbes*, June 2, 2008, http://www.forbes.com/global/2008/0602/064.html.

18. Del Galloway, "In Today's Absence of Trust and Truth, PR Is Paramount," *PR Week*, March 15, 2004, OP-ED, 6.
19. Curtis C. Verschoor, "Tyco: An Ethical Metamorphosis," *Strategic Finance*, April 2006, http://www.imanet.org/pdf/4ethics.pdf (accessed March 3, 2009).
20. Telephone interview by Greg Welch with Jack Krol, chairman of the board, Tyco, January 6, 2009.
21. Ibid.
22. SWOT: strategic-planning method involving analysis of strengths, weaknesses, opportunities, and threats.
23. Tyco Corporate Responsibility, http://www.tyco.com/TycoWeb/pages/Our+Commitment/Governance/Governance+Changes.html (accessed March 3, 2009).
24. CNET Networks Business Research, BNET CEO Report Card, June 2007, http://www.bnet.com/2436-13058_23-173261.html?tag=content;col1.
25. Jeremy Mero, "Inside the 'Cranium' of a Human Game Boy: An Interview with Richard Tait, Cofounder, CEO, Cranium," *Fortune*, March 16, 2007, http://money.cnn.com/magazines/fortune/fortune_archive/2007/03/19/8402337/index.htm.
26. Chris Kent, "Is It Time for the CEO to Twitter? One Tweet Ahead of the Crowd, Zappos.com CEO Tony Hsieh Has Taken the Next Step in Front Line Communication," *Speechwriter's Newsletter*, August 2008, Executive Communications, 2.
27. Twitter.com, @zappos, http://twitter.com/zappos, February and March 2009.
28. David Wilkie, managing director, World 50, interviewed in person by Greg Welch on December 12, 2008 and by e-mail on January 9, 2009.
29. Ibid.
30. Ibid.
31. Ibid.
32. Marketing 50 Gauge Questionnaire, December 2008.

CHAPTER SIX

1. Andy Parsley, "Employee Engagement: The What, Why and How," Management-Issues, http://www.management-issues.com/display_page.asp?section=opinion&id=2830.
2. Telephone interview by Greg Welch with Jack Krol, chairman of the board, Tyco, January 6, 2009.
3. Eugene Scott, "Pupils Blend Profit, Social Ethics," *Arizona Republic*, February 14, 2007, Ahwatukee Republic, 11.
4. "Four Out of Five College Students and Recent Grads Prefer Jobs at Green Companies," press release, Experience, Inc., August 4, 2008, http://www.experience.com/corp/press_release?id=press_release_1217864768328&channel_id=about_us&page_id=home&tab=cn1.
5. Brittany Hite, "Employers Rethink How They Give Feedback," *Wall Street Journal*, October 13, 2008, http://online.wsj.com/article/SB122385967800027549.html.
6. Ibid.
7. Ibid.
8. Eric Lesser and Ray Rivera, "Closing the Generational Divide: Shifting Workforce Demographics and the Learning Function," IBM Institute for Business

Value Executive Brief, 2006, http://www.astd.org/NR/rdonlyres/68C2653A-8A55-4008-9E2F-B39CD33256F7/0/ASTD_IBM_Changing_Worker_Demographics_Study.pdf.

9. "Generation Y Goes to Work," *Economist*, December 30, 2008, http://www.economist.com/business/displaystory.cfm?STORY_ID=12863573.

10. "Southwest Airlines Fact Sheet," http://www.southwest.com/about_swa/press/factsheet.html#Fun percent20Facts (accessed March 9, 2009).

11. James K. Dittmar, et al., "Trust and Engagement," *Leadership Excellence*, November 2007, http://www.sixdisciplines.com/CMS/uploads/LeadersSeek Excellence.pdf.

12. Amy Lyman, "Great Workplaces Push 'People Power,'" *Motivation Strategies*, http://www.motivationstrategies.com/Great_Workplaces_Push_People_Power.722.0.html (accessed May 24, 2009).

13. Ibid.

14. "How Investing in Intangibles—Like Employee Satisfaction—Translates into Financial Returns," *Knowledge@Wharton*, January 9, 2008, http://knowledge.wharton.upenn.edu/article.cfm?articleid=1873.

15. Hay Group, "Employee Engagement," http://www.haygroup.com/ww/services/index.aspx?ID=117 (accessed May 24, 2009).

16. Dittmar, et al., "Trust and Engagement."

17. Maria Halkias, "Pioneering Retailer in Storage Niche Leaves Rivals in Dust," *Seattle Times*, January 31, 2007, http://seattletimes.nwsource.com/html/businesstechnology/2003548721_containerstore310.html?syndication=rss.

18. Jennifer Taylor Arnold, "Customers as Employees: Your Best Job Candidates Might Be Right in Front of You," *HR Magazine*, April 1, 2007, 76.

19. Ibid.

20. Telephone interview by Alexa Knight of Euro RSCG New York with Aaron Magness, director of business development, Zappos.com, February 2, 2009.

21. Ibid.

22. Mark Borden, "The Fast Company 50," *Fast Company*, February 11, 2009, http://www.fastcompany.com/fast50_09/profile/list/zappos.

23. Telephone interview by Alexa Knight of Euro RSCG New York with Aaron Magness, director of business development, Zappos.com, February 2, 2009.

24. Ibid.

25. Mark Potts, "Steve Jobs' Quiet Odyssey Doesn't Include Publicity," *Washington Post*, October 18, 1987, Financial, H3.

26. Andrew Tilin, "What Is a Millennial?" BNET.com, May 16, 2008, http://www.bnet.com/2403-13059_23-201716.html.

27. Chuck Salter, "Google: The Faces and Voices of the World's Most Innovative Company," *Fast Company*, February 14, 2008, http://www.fastcompany.com/magazine/123/google.html.

28. Chuck Salter, "Anne Driscoll—Human Resource Manager," *Fast Company*, February 19, 2008, http://www.fastcompany.com/fast50_08/google_anne-driscoll.html.

29. The Container Store, "Learn About Us," http://www.containerstore.com/learn/index.jhtml#people (accessed March 9, 2009).

30. Innocent Drinks, "Your Career," http://www.innocentdrinks.co.uk/careers/your_career/development/ (accessed March 9, 2009).

31. Joe Robinson, "How We Live: Bring Back the 40-Hour Workweek—and Let Us Take a Long Vacation," *Los Angeles Times*, January 1, 2006, Current, M1.
32. Jessica Stillman, "Americans Suffering 'Vacation Starvation,'" BNET1 (blog), July 9, 2008, http://blogs.bnet.com/bnet1/?p=485.
33. Expedia, *2008 International Vacation Deprivation Survey Results*, http://www.expedia.com/daily/promos/vacations/vacation_deprivation/default.asp (accessed March 9, 2009).
34. Robinson, "How We Live: Bring Back the 40-Hour Workweek—and Let Us Take a Long Vacation."
35. "Your Career," http://www.innocentdrinks.co.uk/careers/your_career/life/ (accessed March 9, 2009).
36. Jeffrey M. O'Brien, "Zappos Knows How to Kick It," *Fortune*, January 22, 2009, 54.
37. "REI's Culture & Values," http://www.rei.com/jobs/culture.html (accessed March 9, 2009).
38. "100 Best Companies to Work For: 2009," *Fortune*, http://money.cnn.com/magazines/fortune/bestcompanies/2009/snapshots/1.html.
39. Telephone interview by Alexa Knight of Euro RSCG New York with Aaron Magness, director of business development, Zappos.com, February 2, 2009.
40. Ibid.
41. Amanda Griscom Little, "The Whole Foods Shebang—An Interview with John Mackey, Founder of Whole Foods," *Grist*, December 17, 2004, http://www.grist.org/article/little-mackey/.
42. William F. Baker and Michael O'Malley, *Leading with Kindness: How Good People Consistently Get Superior Results* (New York: AMACOM, 2008), x–xi.
43. "Key Findings: An Interview with Julie Gebauer on Towers Perrin's Just Released Global Workforce Study" in *Towers Perrin 2007–2008 Global Workforce Study* (Towers Perrin, 2008).
44. O'Brien, "Zappos Knows How to Kick It," 54.

CHAPTER SEVEN

1. Tonya Garcia, "New Edelman Trust Barometer Finds Trust in US Companies at a Low," *PRWeek*, January 27, 2009, http://www.prweekus.com/New-Edelman-Trust-Barometer-finds-trust-in-U.S.-companies-at-a-low/article/126407/.
2. Mark Glaser, "Sue Different: Apple Threatens Insider Sites After Leaks," Knight Digital Media Center, January 25, 2005, http://www.ojr.org/ojr/stories/050125glaser/.
3. "Employees More Credible Than Media, Corporate Communications and the Internet," study published by Edelman, February 27, 2009, http://edelmanchange.blogspot.com/2009/02/employees-more-credible-than-media.html.
4. E-mail submission to the authors from Graham Massey and Steven Fuller, April 13, 2009.
5. JobVent.com, http://www.jobvent.com/.
6. Telephone interview by Alexa Knight of Euro RSCG New York with Aaron Magness, director of business development, Zappos.com, February 2, 2009.
7. Ibid.
8. "About Us," The Ritz-Carlton Hotel Company, http://corporate.ritzcarlton.com/en/About/GoldStandards.htm (accessed March 12, 2009).

9. Gethuman database, http://www.gethuman.com/ (accessed March 11, 2009).
10. "Morgan Stanley Conference—March 1, 2004," ifoAppleStore, www.ifoapplestore.com/stores/analyst_conf.html (accessed March 12, 2009).
11. "Retail Store Hiring," ifoAppleStore, http://www.ifoapplestore.com/the_stores.html (accessed March 12, 2009).
12. Ibid.
13. Alex Frankel, "Magic Shop," *Fast Company*, December 19, 2007, 45.
14. Ibid.
15. Robert Evatt, "Apple Store a Click Away," *Tulsa World*, March 24, 2007, Package, E1.
16. "Microsoft Appoints David Porter as Corporate Vice President of Retail Sales," press release, Microsoft.com, February 12, 2009, http://www.microsoft.com/presspass/press/2009/feb09/02-12CVPRetailStoresPR.mspx.
17. "Smugmug, Inc.," Freebase, www.freebase.com/view/en/smugmug (accessed March 12, 2009).
18. "Smugmug," Epinions.com, www.epinions.com/content_189483748996 (accessed March 12, 2009).
19. "Blogging in the Workplace: Building a Safe Culture," *Personnel Today*, April 3, 2007, http://www.personneltoday.com/articles/2007/04/03/39967/blogging-in-the-workplace-building-a-safe-culture.html.
20. Anushree Chandran, "Employees Becoming Central to Brand Creation, Evangelization," Livemint.com, August 6, 2008, http://www.livemint.com/2008/08/06231422/Employees-becoming-central-to.html.
21. Ibid.
22. "Awards & Achievements," IBM, http://researchweb.watson.ibm.com/resources/awards.shtml (accessed March 10, 2009).
23. "History of the OSI," OpenSource.org, http://www.opensource.ac.uk/mirrors/www.opensource.org/docs/history.html (accessed March 12, 2009).
24. *Understanding Our Company, An IBM Prospectus 2004*, www.ibm.com/annualreport/2004/prospectus/mgmt_c_flash.shtml (accessed March 12, 2009).
25. Matthew P. Gonring, "Customer Loyalty and Employee Engagement: An Alignment for Value," *Journal of Business Strategy*, 29, no. 4 (2008), www.eiu.com/report_dl.asp?mode=fi&fi=1723571357.PDF&rf=0.
26. Telephone interview by Alexa Knight of Euro RSCG New York with Aaron Magness, director of business development, Zappos.com, February 2, 2009.
27. Ibid.
28. "The Shadowland/Lightroom Development Story," PhotoshopNews.com (not affiliated with Adobe Systems Inc.), http://photoshopnews.com/2006/01/09/the-shadowlandlightroom-development-story, January 9, 2006.
29. "Announcing Adobe Lightroom," PhotoshopNews.com (not affiliated with Adobe Systems Inc.), http://photoshopnews.com/2006/01/09/announcing-adobe-lightroom, January 9, 2006.
30. "100 Best Companies to Work For," CNNMoney.com, January 21, 2009, http://money.cnn.com/magazines/fortune/bestcompanies/2009/.
31. Brendan I. Koerner, "Geeks in Toyland," *Wired*, February 2006, http://www.wired.com/wired/archive/14.02/lego.html.
32. "Ask the NXTperts," http://mindstorms.lego.com/askthenxtperts/default.aspx (accessed March 12, 2009).
33. "Give Back Getaway," http://corporate.ritzcarlton.com/en/About/Community.htm (accessed March 12, 2009).

34. "The Feelgood Factor," *Economist* (U.S.), January 19, 2008.
35. "TNT Moves Biscuits to Flooded Bihar India," Movingtheworld.org, http://www.movingtheworld.org/emergency_response_in_india (accessed May 25, 2009).
36. TNT, "Blogs," www.movingtheworld.org/blog (accessed March 12, 2009).
37. Euro RSCG Worldwide, The Future of the Corporate Brand, 2008.
38. Telephone interview by Alexa Knight of Euro RSCG New York with Brigitta Witt, vice president for environmental affairs, Global Hyatt Corporation, February 24, 2009.
39. E-mail interview by Andrew Benett with John Wallis, chief marketing officer, Global Hyatt Corporation, February 24, 2009.
40. Telephone interview by Alexa Knight of Euro RSCG New York with Brigitta Witt, vice president for environmental affairs, Global Hyatt Corporation, February 24, 2009.
41. Ibid.
42. Ibid.
43. Ibid.
44. Ibid.
45. E-mail interview by Andrew Benett with John Wallis, chief marketing officer, Global Hyatt Corporation, February 24, 2009.
46. Larry Weber, *Marketing to the Social Web: How Digital Customer Communities Build Your Business* (Hoboken, N.J.: John Wiley & Sons, Inc., 2009), 112.
47. Liz Bigham, "Experiential Marketing: New Consumer Research," JACK360.com, June 14, 2005, http://360.jackmorton.com/articles/article061405_2.php.
48. Leander Kahney, "Mac Loyalists: Don't Tread on Us," *Wired*, December 2, 2002, http://www.wired.com/gadgets/mac/news/2002/12/56575.
49. "Theory of a Dead Man and The Trews Announced as Vancouver Headliners for the Nike+ Human Race—The World's Largest One Day Running Event," Nike Canada Ltd, press release, August 13, 2008, http://www.marketwire.com/press-release/Nike-Canada-Ltd-889259.html.

CHAPTER EIGHT

1. From http://www.cyburbia.org/forums/showthread.php?t=25844 (accessed February 15, 2009).
2. Scott Adams, "Dilbert," http://www.witiger.com/ecommerce/dilbertObjectives.gif (accessed May 26, 2009).
3. Ben & Jerry's, "Our Mission Statement," http://www.benandjerrys.com/our_company/our_mission/ (accessed February 15, 2009).
4. Telephone interview by Greg Welch with Steve Knox, CEO, Procter & Gamble Tremor division, January 8, 2009.
5. Whole Foods Market, "Our Core Values," http://www.wholefoodsmarket.com/company/corevalues.php (accessed February 13, 2009).
6. Google, "Our Philosophy," http://www.google.com/corporate/tenthings.html (accessed February 15, 2009).
7. Ibid.
8. "Starbucks Chairman Warns of 'The Commoditization of the Starbucks Experience,'" Starbucks Gossip, February 23, 2007, http://starbucksgossip.typepad.com/_/2007/02/starbucks_chair_2.html.

CHAPTER NINE

1. James Manyika, "Google's View on the Future of Business: An Interview with CEO Eric Schmidt," *McKinsey Quarterly*, September 2008, http://www.mckinseyquarterly.com/Googles_view_on_the_future_of_business_An_interview_with_CEO_Eric_Schmidt_2229.

2. "Bill Gates Releases Mosquitoes into Audience," msnbc.com, February 4, 2009, http://www.msnbc.msn.com/id/29022220/.

3. *The Greater Good™: Social and Environmental Progress Report, 2008 & Before*, Burt's Bees, http://catalog.digicatalog.com/showmag.php?mid=wqqsph&spid=-3#/page4/ (accessed February 21, 2009).

4. Burt's Bees, "Our Mission & Vision," www.burtsbees.com/webapp/wcs/stores/servlet/ContentView?storeId=10001&langId=-1&catalogId=10051&contentPageId=22 (accessed February 21, 2009).

5. Telephone interview by Greg Welch with John Replogle, president and CEO, Burt's Bees, January 30, 2009.

6. Ibid.

CHAPTER TEN

1. Francis Fukuyama, "The Fall of America, Inc.," *Newsweek*, October 13, 2008, http://www.newsweek.com/id/162401/page/1.

2. Lucy Kellaway, "The World in 2009: The Year of the CFO," *Economist*, November 19, 2008, http://www.economist.com/theworldin/displaystory.cfm?story_id=12494665.

3. "Barack Obama's Inaugural Address," BBC News, January 20, 2009, http://news.bbc.co.uk/1/hi/world/americas/obama_inauguration/7840646.stm.

4. In physics, the momentum of an object is the product of its mass times its velocity, where velocity is the rate of change of position.

5. Figures derived by subtracting the percentage of respondents rating a brand as having "lost ground" from those rating it as having "gained ground."

6. Figures derived by dividing the net momentum percentage by the percentage of respondents who perceive no change or don't know.

7. Google, "Investor Relations: Google Code of Conduct," http://investor.google.com/conduct.html (accessed March 14, 2009).

8. Tony DiRomualdo, "Is Google's Cafeteria a Competitive Weapon?" *WTN News*, August 30, 2005, http://wistechnology.com/articles/2190/.

9. Marissa Mayer, "MS&E 472 Course: Entrepreneurial Thought Leaders Seminar Series," Stanford University, video, May 17, 2006, http://stanford-online.stanford.edu/courses/msande472/060517-msande472-300.asx (accessed May 28, 2009).

10. The Great Place To Work Institute, "Google: Take Two," www.greatplacetowork.com/best/100best2008-google.php (accessed March 14, 2009).

11. Bob Keefe, "Meet Google's Chief Sustainability Officer (What a Cool Job!)," DivineCaroline, http://www.divinecaroline.com/article/22277/44799 (accessed March 14, 2009).

12. "2008 World's Most Ethical Companies," *Ethisphere*, June 3, 2008, http://ethisphere.com/wme2008/.

13. "Target Team Members Volunteer," Target.com, April 15, 2009, http://sites.target.com/site/en/company/page.jsp?contentId=WCMP04-032391 (accessed May 27, 2009).

14. "Our Commitment to Our Team," *2008 Corporate Responsibility Report*, Target Corporation, http://sites.target.com/site/en/company/page.jsp?content Id=WCMP04-034164 (accessed May 27, 2009).

15. "eBay Inc. Awarded the National Medal of Technology and Innovation for Advancing Global Entrepreneurship," *Business Wire*, September 29, 2008, http://investor.ebay.com/releasedetail.cfm?releaseid=337160.

16. eBay, "eBay Inc., Global Citizenship: Social Ventures," http://pages.ebay.com/aboutebay/socialventures.html (accessed March 14, 2009).

17. Tesco, *Annual Review and Summary Financial Statement 2008*, http://www.tescoreports.com/areview08/index.html (accessed March 14, 2009).

18. Tesco, "Our Approach," http://www.tescoplc.com/plc/corporate_responsibility/approach (accessed March 14, 2009).

19. Tesco, "Our Values," http://www.tescoplc.com/plc/about_us/values (accessed March 14, 2009).

20. Tesco, "Tesco Staff Share in £126 Million Payout from Save As You Earn Share Scheme," February 9, 2009, http://www.tescoplc.com/plc/media/pr/pr2009/2009-02-09.

21. *Corporate Responsibility Report 2009*, Tesco.com, http://www.investis.com/plc/cr09/crr09.pdf (accessed May 28, 2009).

22. "Letter to Stakeholders," *Annual Stakeholders' Report 2008*, Whole Foods Market, http://www.wholefoodsmarket.com/company/pdfs/ar08_letter.pdf (accessed May 28, 2009).

23. Whole Foods Market, "Watching Your Wallet, Waistline & Wellness with the Whole Deal at Whole Foods Market," January 7, 2008, http://www.wholefoodsmarket.com/pressroom/2009/01/09/watching-your-wallet-waistline-wellness-with-the-whole-deal%E2%84%A2-at-whole-foods-market.

24. Charles Fishman, "Whole Foods Is All Teams," *Fast Company*, December 18, 2007, http://www.fastcompany.com/magazine/02/team1.html.

25. U.S. Environmental Protection Agency, "Partner Profile," http://www.epa.gov/greenpower/partners/partners/wholefoodsmarket.htm (accessed March 14, 2009).

26. "Hussmann Helps Whole Foods Build 'Green' Showcase Supermarket," U.S. Newswire, November 18, 2008, http://media.prnewswire.com/en/jsp/search.jsp?searchtype=full&option=headlines&criteriadisplay=show&resourceid=3868113.

27. James P. Womack, Daniel T. Jones, and Daniel Roos, *The Machine That Changed the World: The Story of Lean Production*, (New York: Free Press, 2007).

28. "GM Loses Top Sales Spot to Toyota," BBC News, January 21, 2009, http://news.bbc.co.uk/1/hi/business/7842716.stm.

29. Jeffrey K. Liker, *The Toyota Way: 14 Management Principles from the World's Greatest Manufacturer* (New York: McGraw-Hill, 2004), 37–41.

30. Toyota, "Doing Good Work Where We Work," http://www.toyota.com/about/our_commitment/philanthropy (accessed March 14, 2009).

31. Womack et al., *The Machine That Changed the World: The Story of Lean Production*, 56.

32. Toyota, "Towards the Ultimate Eco-car," http://www.toyota.eu/04_environment/03_towards_ultimate/index.aspx (accessed March 14, 2009).

33. Sam Abuelsamid, "LA 2007: Toyota Fuel Cell Highlander Runs 2300 Miles from Fairbanks to Vancouver," November 14, 2007, http://www.autobloggreen.com/2007/11/14/la-2007-toyota-fuel-cell-highlander-runs-2300-miles-from-fairba.

34. Womack et al., *The Machine That Changed the World: The Story of Lean Production*, 68.
35. Euro RSCG Worldwide's "Politics and Brand Marketing: Momentum Matters" panel discussion, held in New York City on November 14, 2008.
36. U.S. Census Bureau, International Data Base, http://www.census.gov/ipc/www/idb/worldpop.html (accessed March 14, 2009).
37. Duke University, "Americans Have Fewer Friends Outside the Family, Duke Study Shows," June 23, 2006, http://www.dukenews.duke.edu/2006/06/socialisolation.html.
38. Robert D. Putnam, *Bowling Alone: The Collapse and Revival of American Community* (New York: Simon and Schuster, 2001), 16.
39. Sheryl Gay Stolberg and Stephen Labaton, "Obama Calls Wall Street Bonuses 'Shameful,'" *New York Times*, January 29, 2009, http://www.nytimes.com/2009/01/30/business/30obama.html?_r=1.
40. Angelique Chrisafis, "A Million on Strike as France Feels Pinch," *Guardian*, January 30, 2009, International Pages, 27.

INDEX